Brand Up

Brand Up 2.0: Propel Your Early Career Success

Stacey Ross Cohen

With Allison Kluger and Kudzi Chikumbu

Brand Up

Brand Up 2.0: Propel Your Early Career Success

Stacey Ross Cohen

Brand Up

Brand Up 2.0: Propel Your Early Career Success

SECTION A: DISCOVERY

PART I – DO YOU KNOW WHO YOU ARE?

CONTENTS

SECTION B: DEVELOPMENT

SECTION C: DELIVERY

PART V – AMPLIFYING YOUR CAREER THROUGH SOCIAL MEDIA

Kudzi Chikumbu

PART VI – NETWORKING FOR SUCCESS

TESTIMONIALS

"We all need to be aware of how we are presenting ourselves to the world, and young adults must be intentional about building a positive digital footprint. Whether seeking to become an influencer, score a dream job, or start a business, this book will get you started on your journey to success. Packed with tips, tricks, and strategies, Brand Up 2.0 is a must-read for any young professional who wants to get ahead in today's competitive world. ."

– Courtney Spritzer, CEO of Socialfly

"With the rise of technology and the gig economy, it's more important than ever to prepare for the future. That's where Brand Up 2.0 comes in. The book provides early-career professionals with skills to achieve career success, including goal-setting, building a strong online presence, interviewing, networking, entrepreneurship, and so much more."

– Harry Moseley, Former Global Chief Information Officer of Zoom Video Communications

"Stacey Ross Cohen returns with a follow-up to her highly engaging and successful book. Brand Up 2.0 is an essential resource and pivotal entry point for early-career professionals and anyone looking to highlight their strengths and gifts. In a world where a robust digital presence is paramount, she delivers practical tools and insights. Brand Up 2.0 empowers readers to elevate their personal brand, ensuring they shine brightly in the eyes of current and potential employers. A must-read for anyone looking to make a lasting impression in their career journey!"

– Sean Gaillard, Author of *The Pepper Effect: Tap into the Magic of Creativity, Collaboration, and Innovation*, School Leader, Podcaster, and Leadership Coach

"Brand Up 2.0 is an absolute game-changer in today's competitive job market. Stacey Ross Cohen emphasizes the significance of personal branding and outlines a comprehensive yet achievable 360 strategy to help you stand out and secure the right opportunities. If you're looking to pave the way for long-term career success, Brand Up 2.0 is a must-read. Highly recommended!"
– Cassandra Thompson, Founder of One Hello and Workplace Connection Speaker, Trainer, and Coach

"Drawing on her unparalleled experience and insights, Stacey Ross Cohen doesn't just dispense advice; she provides early-career professionals with a tangible roadmap to success. Brand Up 2.0 is an essential companion, equipping individuals with the tools to flourish in an era defined by constant change and limitless opportunities. Dive into this must-read manifesto to navigate your future with purpose and confidence."

– Craig Vezina, PhD, Co-Founder and CEO of The Spaceship Academy

"Brand Up 2.0 is a game-changer. It shows early-career professionals how to create a brand that will make them stand out and get noticed by employers, clients, strategic partners, and more. It also provides the tools to level up essential life skills such as networking, goal-setting, and interviewing."

– Julie Cottineau, Founder and CEO of BrandTwist

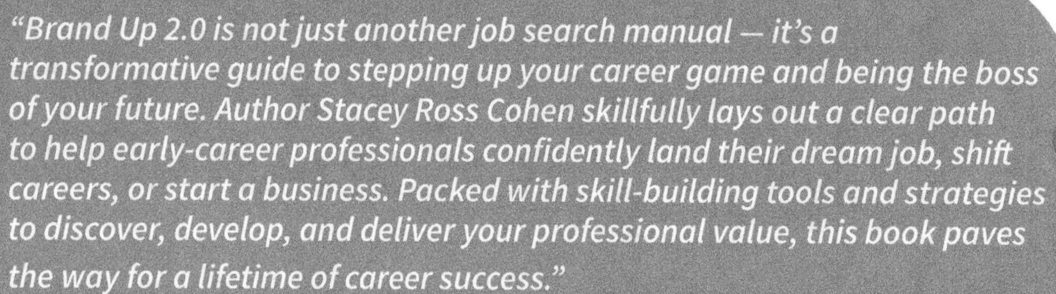

"Brand Up 2.0 is not just another job search manual — it's a transformative guide to stepping up your career game and being the boss of your future. Author Stacey Ross Cohen skillfully lays out a clear path to help early-career professionals confidently land their dream job, shift careers, or start a business. Packed with skill-building tools and strategies to discover, develop, and deliver your professional value, this book paves the way for a lifetime of career success."

– Dorie Clark, Wall Street Journal Bestselling Author of The Long Game and Executive Education Faculty Member at Columbia Business School

"Brand Up 2.0 is the ultimate playbook for Gen Z future trailblazers ready to fast-track their careers. Packed with cutting-edge strategies, essential tools, and insider tips, this guide helps you unleash your hidden talents, master critical skills, and crush your career goals with confidence."

– Aliza Licht, Founder of Leave Your Mark and Author of On Brand

"Brand Up 2.0 is a master class in career acceleration! Bursting with practical tips and Stacey Ross Cohen's contagious enthusiasm, it's a must-read for anyone looking to make their mark in the professional world. Read this book! Then watch your career soar to new heights."

– Dave Kerpen, CEO of Apprentice and *NY Times* Bestselling Author of *Get Over Yourself*

"As an HR executive committed to changing the status quo, I know the impact of a strong digital presence. Brand Up 2.0 is a must-read for young professionals. It's packed with practical advice and real-world strategies to help you elevate your career, build a personal brand, and confidently navigate the evolving landscape. Trust me, this is a must-read for anyone looking to make their mark!"

– Jessica D. Winder, Founder of Hidden Gem Career Coaching

"Whether you're working on getting a job, moving into the world of trade or entrepreneurship, or chasing your greatest aspirations, Brand Up 2.0 is a great guide to help build your personal brand and get an edge over your competition."

– David Meltzer, Co-Founder of Sports 1 Marketing, Bestselling Author, and Top Business Coach

A POST HILL PRESS BOOK

ISBN: 979-8-88845-759-7

Brand Up
Brand Up 2.0 :
Propel Your Early Career Success
© 2024 by Stacey Ross Cohen with Allison Kluger and Kudzi Chikumbu
All Rights Reserved

Cover design by Cecile Rothschild

Post Hill Press
New York • Nashville
posthillpress.com

Published in the United States of America
1 2 3 4 5 6 7 8 9 10

ACKNOWLEDGMENTS

'm forever grateful for the support of many on my journey writing *Brand Up 2.0*, I never dreamed this book would be birthed so soon after *Brand Up: The Ultimate Playbook for College and Career Success*, which continues to empower teens and unlock their potential. The joy of giving back feeds my soul: I've donated countless books to underserved youth, led lively sessions at high schools, and launched a teen ambassador program. Its global impact has exceeded my expectations, reaching Ukrainian refugees in Poland and so much more. You all have made me and my book — now a movement that has become my life's calling — infinitely better.

Above all, I want to thank my husband, Bruce, and two daughters, Kelsey and Amanda. They are my biggest fans, always rooting for me and offering love and encouragement at every step. I couldn't love you more!

A heartfelt thanks to David Bernstein, Aleigha Koss, and the Post Hill Press team for bringing this book to life. Your partnership, support, and belief in me mean everything and then some.

I'm incredibly grateful to collaborate with my colleagues and contributing authors Allison Kluger and Kudzi Chikumbu. Few people have the personal branding, reputation management, and social media insight of these two trailblazers. There's a unique backstory, too: Kudzi was Allison's student at the Stanford Graduate School of Business, where she is a highly acclaimed professor. I had the privilege of seeing this firsthand as a guest in her class and interviewing her for several *Huffington Post* articles. These chapters make the perfect addition, infusing the book with their brilliance and providing readers with valuable real-world examples.

Thanks to my dear friend and creative genius Cecile Rothschild, who has been an important part of the *Brand Up* dream team, creating stunning visuals that captivate and inspire. And Kevin Zawacki, my editor extraordinaire, thank you for your above-and-beyond effort through every twist and turn of this book's journey. It's a true privilege to work alongside such super talents as Cecile and Kevin, whose partnership has been priceless.

I also thank the HR professionals, recruiters, psychologists, CEOs, entrepreneurs, and early-career professionals with stellar brands who supported me by generously sharing their wisdom and knowledge.

I want to shout out to my work family at Co-Communications — especially Jess, my business partner (the Thelma to my Louise), who always has my back and knows me so well she can finish my sentences.

And the many others who have been a big part of my getting here: Joanie Banks, Jason Shaffer, Alan Katzman, Abby Elyssa, David Lewis, Diane Silver, Randi Childs, Sandy Wollman, Craig Vezina, Shannon Malkin Daniels, Jeanne Stafford, and Wendi Silverman.

I want to thank my mother, Faith, for always having faith in my entrepreneurial spirit, even when I was just 14 and starting my first business. She has been one of my biggest supporters and inspirations — and is the wind beneath my wings and "can-do" attitude.

Finally, I want to acknowledge my readers. I wrote this book to help you unleash your inner champions. Regardless of your path in life, you will learn how to share your unique talents and perspectives with the world. I can't wait to see what you achieve!

THANK YOU ALL FROM THE BOTTOM OF MY HEART.

INTRODUCTION/ PROLOGUE

Making Your Mark

Brand Up 2.0: Propel Your Early Career Success equips young professionals with the skills and attitude they need to build a positive personal brand and launch a successful career. Personal brands and career success now go hand in hand. In a digital world, how you show up and present online determines whether you land that interview, earn that raise, or get your business off the ground.

To those just starting their careers, it may seem that personal brands "just happen" — that they're a byproduct of professional accomplishments. In truth, it's the other way around: accomplishments follow a solid personal brand. Young professionals must identify, refine, and advertise their skills and abilities from *day one* — or risk being overlooked by recruiters, managers, mentors, and others. Here's why:

Job recruitment is no longer based solely on your résumé. Companies of all sizes are looking beyond the résumé to a potential new hire's online presence. Your LinkedIn profile, old tweets, past blogs, and other elements of your digital footprint are all on the table. How well or poorly your personal brand shows up online can help you nab that coveted job — or lose it.

Modern entrepreneurship necessitates digital savvy. A handful of new trends — like the gig economy and remote work — mean entrepreneurship is on the rise. But more entrepreneurs also mean more competition. For those starting their own businesses, finding customers and investors requires an unforgettable personal brand.

This book highlights the importance of a strong personal brand for young professionals and provides a precise blueprint for building one. Integral to the conversation is the need to hone real-world skills like networking, interviewing, and communications.

Brand Up 2.0: Propel Your Early Career Success draws on my 25-plus years of experience building personal brands for CEOs, business owners, entrepreneurs — and, yes, young professionals. I'm a storyteller at heart who is adept at crafting narratives and has a talent for launching brands into the spotlight. I cherish my gift of leveraging each client's unique voice to make an outsized impact in job interviews, boardrooms, and everywhere in between. As a twin, forging a unique identity wasn't a choice; it was a necessity. The longing to distinguish myself resonates deeply with me. My experience as a twin sharpened my ability to stand out in the face of constant comparisons, insensitive remarks, and name mix-ups. Growing up, the best compliment I ever received was, "Stacey, you are so unique!"

I'm incredibly fortunate to have collaborated on this playbook with close business colleagues and contributing authors Allison Kluger and Kudzi Chikumbu, giants in personal branding, reputation management, and social media. I also tap into the wisdom of entrepreneurs, HR executives, hiring managers, recruiters, CEOs, and young professionals who successfully built stellar brands. Throughout the book, you'll find concrete, actionable tactics complemented by a list of "Brandamentals," or key takeaways.

I call this process **Personal Branding in 3D** because it's made up of three core "Ds": Discovery, Development, and Delivery. Here's a bit more about each of these phases and what to expect ahead:

1. **Discovery:** This first phase is all about self-reflection: Who am I? And how do others see me? I'll walk you through the Me Squared™ process to map your strengths, passions, goals, and values. I also share popular and helpful personality tests, which can further crystallize what makes you, **YOU.** The purpose of all this is to develop a clear, compelling Uniquely Me statement. This is the personal branding message you'll send out into the world.

2. **Development:** This phase is about packaging your story and creating a shiny digital portfolio to showcase your talents and accomplishments. Interview tips, sample cover letters, résumés, and thank-you letters are part of this step. These essentials will give you the confidence to present yourself effectively and stand out in the competitive job market. Emphasis is placed on our era's most influential personal branding platform: LinkedIn.

3. **Delivery:** You have your story and structure — now it's time for delivery. This phase examines how to share your value and expertise with the world loudly and often. We'll discuss social media management, networking best practices, and more.

While this isn't a workbook per se, I've sprinkled exercises in the Discovery and Development phases, which are essential for establishing a solid foundation for career success. Completing these exercises will help you reflect on and effectively present your unique strengths and value in the competitive job market. Through guided introspection and actionable insights, you'll uncover your superpowers and leverage them for a successful professional journey.

With this book by your side, you'll be ready to take on even the biggest challenges in your budding career, stand out in the best way possible, and set yourself up for decades of professional success. Devoting time to build your brand isn't just a vanity project; it's a savvy career move that will allow you to stand out from other candidates. By doing so, you're showing employers what you're bringing to the table and painting a picture that shows your good-fit qualities.

Assess Your Personal Brand and Online Presence (Quiz)

Let's get started. How does your personal brand measure up?
Try answering these 15 questions:

- ☐ Have you identified your "it" factor, or what makes you stand out?
- ☐ What would make an employer choose you out of a large pool of applicants or for a promotion?
- ☐ Do you know what makes you a good investment?
- ☐ Do you have a 30-second elevator pitch about yourself?
- ☐ Do you have a strong online profile/bio?
- ☐ Do you know how others perceive you?
- ☐ Who is your target audience (i.e., the people that you most want to impress)?
- ☐ Do you have a personal and/or business brand domain name?
- ☐ Do you have Google Alert keywords set up to monitor your reputation?
- ☐ Do you have your privacy settings correctly set up in all social networks?
- ☐ Are you using your name consistently on all social media networks?
- ☐ Do you have a content strategy for your blog and social networks?
- ☐ Do you have a maintenance plan to review social media networks?
- ☐ Does your personal brand accurately represent who you are?
- ☐ Do people (other than family and your closest friends) respond favorably to your postings, blogs, and/or website?

If you responded "no" or even "not sure"
to more than three of these, this book is for you.

Why Personal Branding?

Before we get into the benefits of personal branding, let's define it and take a peek at its history.

The Origins of Personal Branding

The phrase "personal branding" was coined in the late '90s by management guru Tom Peters. In 1997, Peters wrote in a *Fast Company* article: "Often, people confuse "personal brand" and "personal branding."

So, let's make the distinction clear:"

Your **personal brand** is the public's perception of you based on the values, strengths, passions, experience, skills, and achievements that you present to the world. A personal brand is more than an online profile or résumé; it is the essence of YOU — the authentic and curated parts of your story that highlight your best self to help you achieve your goals. A personal brand is created through the strategic process of personal branding.

Personal branding is an intentional effort to identify, shape, and communicate your value. It is about differentiating yourself from the competition to achieve career success, personal success, thought leadership, or even celebrity status. Personal branding entails honing your narrative to establish an identity, which is then amplified through social media and other channels.

The Many Benefits of Personal Branding

Personal branding is the marketing of you. In essence, you are the brand manager and must play an active role in making the most of what you offer. And it's not just about making yourself an attractive hire or business partner for others. Personal branding provides you with several long-term benefits that will span your career:

Self-awareness. Personal branding requires a deep look inside yourself — a valuable experience! You'll better understand (and even discover) your talents, strengths, and passion, giving your life more meaning and direction.

Reputation. A strong, positive personal brand makes you stand out and forms a lasting impression. Consistently sharing your brand through online and offline channels builds recognition and prestige.

Uniqueness. You can distinguish yourself from the competition by recognizing and developing your unique talents. Standing out from the crowd in a positive way is a surefire way to have a winning career.

Confidence. Self-esteem soars from knowing your strengths and the unique value you bring to the world. This confidence puts you at ease in social and professional situations. Introducing yourself and sharing your story becomes second nature.

Clarity. Clarity makes it easier to identify goals and provides direction in your career. It helps you focus your efforts and make informed decisions about your career path.

Credibility. Building a solid track record of success begins with delivering on your brand promise. In addition, having others speak on your behalf (e.g., job references, testimonials) will reinforce your credibility.

Professional advancement. Personal branding yields increased career opportunities, including higher salaries, promotions, rewarding partnerships, new clients, and business opportunities.

Portability. Personal brands are portable. You can take your brand with you wherever life takes you.

AUTHENTICALLY YOU

BE REAL.
BE YOU.
BE HUMAN.
BE RELATABLE.
BE VULNERABLE.

Personal branding is about expressing your authentic self and celebrating your individuality. It's about digging deep within yourself to identify the blend of strengths and attributes that make you unique. It's not about changing who you are, compromising your values, or playing a role, but being **true to yourself**.

It's about knowing your innate strengths and then broadcasting those skills and that progress to the world. As you build your personal brand, authenticity should be your guiding principle — no exceptions. While developing your brand can boost your career, remember that its impact is limited if it stays invisible to others.

WORD OF CAUTION:

Avoid tailoring your brand too much to the audience. Make your brand about you first.

Be the Brand Boss of You

At the beginning of my presentations, I often conduct a poll: "Who believes they have a personal brand?" Typically, only about 30 percent respond affirmatively. However, it's essential to recognize that everyone has a brand, whether positive, negative, or neutral.

Whether you choose to embrace it or not, personal branding is like your shadow: it's always there, made up of your skills, achievements, interests, and reputation, following you and living in the minds of those around you. People will always form an opinion of you, so you might as well take an active role in shaping that opinion, especially in a digital world where news travels fast — and poorly thought-out social media posts travel even faster.

Indeed, those who ignore their personal brands often end up with negative ones. Those who nurture and monitor their personal brands come across as more adept and charismatic.

First, you need to get inside the target market's mindset and answer the question: "What's in it for me?" Effective brand marketing talks about benefits — the value that a product or service brings to the end-user (the customer) — rather than features. Let's use a yogurt company as an example. Rather than highlighting features like the yogurt having 10 mg of protein, it's far more advantageous to emphasize the yogurt's *benefits*: consumers will be healthier and reduce digestive issues. Similarly, you should advertise not just the bullet points on your résumé but *what they can provide for employers, partners, or investors.*

This approach helps you stand out in a sea of résumés. With a strong enough personal brand, you don't even *need* a résumé — or, in extreme cases, a last name! Think of Beyoncé, Adele, Oprah, or Usher.

Google has indeed become the new résumé. The shift toward digital validation is undeniable. In fact, did you know there are approximately 6.3 million Google searches per minute ("Data Never Sleeps" Report, Domo, 2023)? When someone searches for you (and they will), you want to greet them with positive, appealing, honest, and consistent accounts of yourself. It's not about bragging — it's about what you have to offer and how you want to present that to the world. If you're not cultivating and monitoring your brand, those results could include embarrassing, problematic, or incorrect content.

There's no need to be super polished or to formally present your brand. A little fun, even humor, and a sparkling personality is okay. Just make sure you're running everything through the **PURE Test**. Is it **P**ositive, **U**nbiased, **R**espectful, and **E**thical? Then, add one more filter for good measure: The Grandma Test. *What would your grandmother say if she saw this post, photo, or comment?* And, of course, you can always ask a peer for feedback on that new headshot or LinkedIn article.

Also, be sure to pay attention to your important work offline. Personal branding isn't just about leaving your mark in the digital world. Spend time thinking about and engaging with your aspirations, your community, your causes, and the people physically around you.

Personal brands aren't just vital to starting careers — they often get a business off the ground. Young entrepreneurs seeking funding should know that investors value the person behind the product or service. Investors want to put their money behind someone they can trust to make that business successful, which takes us right back to the personal brand. Every investor's due diligence includes researching the entrepreneur they are considering working with. And know this: if you're starting a business at age 25, an inappropriate comment or photo from a decade ago can come back to hurt you.

Personal Branding Myth-Busting

Let's pause here and take a moment to debunk some myths about personal branding.

False: Those who practice personal branding are narcissists and braggarts.

True: Personal branding is not about *me, me, me.* It's mainly about the value you bring to others.

False: Personal branding is a fad.

True: Personal branding is here to stay — the internet has cemented its importance.

False: Personal branding is just for celebrities and those who want to become famous.

True: Personal branding is for everyone: the college-bound, career seekers, CEOs, and everyone in between.

False: Personal branding is all about having a big presence on social media with many followers.

True: While social media can amplify your brand, a solid social media presence alone does not equal a strong personal brand.

False: Personal brands are short-lived.

True: Personal branding is a lifelong effort that's constantly evolving and requires regular maintenance.

> *Candidates can bring their résumé, experience, and personality to life on social media. Employers and recruiters are increasingly turning to social media as a talent source versus traditional job boards and career fairs. Perception is reality, so ensure that you are in control of your digital footprint. Ensure you are crafting a narrative to attract potential employers and use LinkedIn, Facebook, Instagram, or TikTok to show your industry expertise. Not utilizing social media to elevate your professional brand leaves you at a disadvantage. There's no time like now to get started.*
>
> **– Debbie Douglas, Director of Recruiting-Talent Acquisition at Paramount**

Putting Your Best Digital Foot Forward

We all have a digital footprint: a bundle of information (social media profiles, photos, blog posts, news articles, etc.) that shows up when we Google ourselves — or, more likely, when someone else Googles us. And that footprint is often reflective of your personal brand.

A positive footprint — curated, professional, compelling — can unlock job interviews, promotions, and more. Alternatively, the wrong footprint — inappropriate, juvenile — can hinder opportunities.

But the term "digital footprint" is a bit misleading. Footprints fade away. Digital footprints, however, can last forever. They are visible to anyone, anywhere. For this reason, managing your online reputation is an absolute necessity. If you don't control your online presence, someone else most certainly will.

On a similar note, always assume what you post online is public. A dedicated searcher can find you on even the most "private" social networks.

BRANDAMENTALS

Commit these top takeaways to memory:

1 The term "personal branding" may be relatively new, but the general idea is age-old. A professional's reputation has always been their most valuable currency.

2 The internet has made personal branding a necessity. If you neglect your online presence, someone else will write your story.

3 Personal branding isn't immodest. It's about collaboration — showing others how you can help them achieve their goals.

4 Personal branding isn't just for executives and celebrities. It's just as important for young professionals, no matter their field.

SECTION A: DISCOVERY

PART I — DO YOU KNOW WHO YOU ARE?

A fundamental step in developing one's brand is to figure out who you really are (strengths, values, passions, achievements), how you differ from the competition, and who you want to reach.

Your unique skills and experiences are selling points in the job market. By deeply understanding them, you can tailor applications, perform confidently in interviews, and align your career with your strengths. We will begin by taking inventory of both your hard (technical) and soft (interpersonal) skills.

Getting to Know Yourself

The unsung hero of success? **Self-awareness**. There's a glut of research that reveals that those with a high level of self-awareness — who have a firm grasp of their passions, strengths, weaknesses, and values — are at an advantage and achieve greater academic and career success. In fact, self-awareness has been cited as the most critical capability for leaders to develop, according to the authors of "How to Become a Better Leader" (*MIT Sloan Management Review*, 2012), who conducted more than 2,000 in-depth interviews with executives worldwide.

It won't come as a surprise, then, that self-awareness is also the foundation of personal branding. So, what does it entail, exactly? I asked leading expert Dr. Tasha Eurich, organizational psychologist, author of *Insight: The Surprising Truth About How Others See Us, How We See Ourselves, and Why the Answers Matter More Than We Think*, and the creator of a TED Talk on this same topic. In our conversation, Dr. Eurich explained that self-awareness actually has two distinct parts. There is *internal self-awareness*, which is all about understanding yourself — your passions, values, aspirations, strengths, and weaknesses. Then there's *external self-awareness*, which is about understanding how others see you.

Dr. Eurich also has a wake-up call: we're not as self-aware as we think. She and her fellow researchers conducted a study that revealed 95 percent of people *believe* themselves to be self-aware, while in reality as few as 10 percent of us truly are. Why is this? Because external self-awareness is actually pretty hard to come by. Says Dr. Eurich: "It is more difficult to achieve than an internal perspective. We need to take the time to understand the point of view of others, which can give us a much more objective view of ourselves."

What can we do to improve our external self-awareness? Consider how different people (e.g., colleagues, managers, mentors) might view your actions, behaviors, and how you present yourself. Of course, other people will have different points of view, depending on how well they know you and in what circumstances you interact with them. Take the time to understand their unique perspectives and incorporate the best traits others see in you while avoiding negative characteristics and behaviors.

Sounds daunting? Don't be deterred: Dr. Eurich believes self-awareness is an "infinitely learnable skill." And your efforts will pay off. "There is strong scientific evidence that people who know themselves and how others see them are happier," Dr. Eurich explains. "Self-aware people are better performers at work, more confident communicators, and achieve greater success academically and career-wise."

Clearly, the famed Greek philosopher Socrates was onto something when he said, "To know thyself is the beginning of wisdom."

How does this translate to career success? By identifying your strengths, interests, skills, and values, you'll know which job opportunities are worth pursuing and which ones you can confidently bypass. Regular, objective reflection is key to increasing self-awareness. And there is broad agreement among experts that journaling and mindfulness are best practices for this. (More on that in the next section.)

We are ready to embark on the Discovery phase of **Building Your Personal Brand in 3D: Discovery, Development, and Delivery**. The first essential task is to uncover your "wow" factor — what stands out about you and deserves to be the centerpiece of your personal branding efforts. And remember: **Personal branding is not a matter of *me, me, me* — it's about your value to others.** Reflect deeply and ask yourself: Who am I? How did I get here? What do I have to give? What do I want to do, and how do I succeed?

Also included is a list of career assessment tests that can further hone what makes you *you*. Now, let's get started.

Personal branding answers the million-dollar question: Why would someone choose YOU?

Why should YOU be selected for that promotion?
Why should YOU get hired for that job?
Why should someone invest in YOUR business idea?

Finding Your Perfect Adjectives

Building a personal brand entails telling a story. All your content — your blogs, social media posts, emails, and more — add to your professional *story*. Stories are among the most powerful tools humans have at their disposal. They enlighten us, compel us, and enrapture us — and have for centuries. And, of course, to be a good storyteller, you must be good with words.

Adjectives are not just words but the building blocks of your brand. They breathe life into your story, describing your character and the environment you operate in. They communicate who you are and why you're unique.

So, how do you go about identifying your perfect adjectives? Below are seven qualities that recruiters, investors, and others commonly look for. Each attribute is accompanied by 20–25 powerful adjectives that you can highlight when applying for a job, seeking a promotion, courting investors, and more. Circle three to four adjectives in each category that best represent you.

Leadership. A leader is on the front lines and helps others achieve goals. Even young professionals can be leaders, showing creativity and innovation, managing small teams, and mentoring less-experienced colleagues. You can use leadership adjectives to demonstrate your ability to guide others to success.

Leadership Adjectives

Assertive	Determined	Enterprising	Dynamic	Courageous
Influential	Bold	Solution-oriented	Problem-solver	Accomplished
Reliable	Competent	Responsible	Goal-oriented	Impactful
Resilient	Passionate	Inspiring	Confident	Accountable
Proactive	Decisive	Enthusiastic	Persistent	

Creativity. The ability to think outside the box is valuable across the board, whether you're an engineer, artist, or marketer. Employers are always seeking candidates who can think of novel solutions to problems.

Creativity Adjectives

Cutting-edge	Leading-edge	Inventive	Forward-looking	Innovative
Inspired	Imaginative	Creative	Artistic	Unique
Forward-thinking	Ground-breaking	Ingenious	Exclusive	Revolutionary
Advanced	Breakthrough	Progressive	Original	Visionary

Team Player. Individual accomplishments are important, but businesses and organizations are most successful when teams come together to meet and exceed goals. The cliché is true: we're greater than the sum of our parts. The adjectives below will help you showcase your teamwork credentials to everyone you interact with.

Team Player Adjectives

Amiable	Amicable	Tolerant	Collective	Combined
United	Joint	Associated	Shared	Integrated
Respectful	Diplomatic	Cooperative	Supportive	Harmonious
Cheerful	Congenial	Receptive	Welcoming	Courteous
Collaborative	Communicative	Connected	Team-minded	

Work Ethic. Hard work and perseverance are key ingredients to success. The late Colin Powell, former Secretary of State, once said: "A dream does not become a reality through magic; it takes sweat, determination, and hard work." Perhaps more than any other characteristic, decision-makers in the workforce are looking for people with relentless drive and deep commitment.

Work Ethic Adjectives

Diligent	Grit	Tenacious	Self-starter	Ambitious
Determined	Self-motivated	Organized	Methodical	Detail-oriented
Enthusiastic	Dedicated	Passionate	Enterprising	Driven
Persistent	Energetic	Systematic	Committed	Motivated
Prepared	Disciplined	Focused		

Critical Thinking. To truly be an asset in the workforce, young professionals must demonstrate critical thinking, an ability to analyze information and come away with novel insights and answers. Your critical thinking ability is essential to highlight if you work in fields such as engineering, political science, or business.

Critical Thinking Adjectives

Inquiring	Precise	Methodical	Investigative	Curious
Questioning	Inquisitive	Analytical	Problem-solving	Progressive
Challenging	Persistent	Diligent	Meticulous	Inventive
Intellectual	Logical	Discerning	Detail-oriented	Knowledgeable
Perceptive	Thorough	Insightful		

Open-Minded. Innovation and breakthroughs often occur when professionals are willing to challenge assumptions or admit they may be wrong. Keeping an open mind to diverse ideas and perspectives is important, as it often leads to the solution you need. Successful businesses place a high value on employees who are nimble and adaptable.

Open-Minded Adjectives

Agile	Capable	Perceptive	Nimble	Versatile
Resourceful	Dynamic	Responsive	Flexible	Positive
Broad-minded	Adaptable	Tolerant	Accepting	Multifaceted
Quick-thinking	Flexible	Unbiased	Receptive	Comprehensive
Energetic	Prompt	Diverse		

Socially Conscious. Over the past couple of decades, there's been a big shift in the corporate world. Companies today prioritize both their profits and the social impact they make. Many organizations and investors seek individuals with a sense of purpose and concern for others.

Socially Conscious Adjectives

Empathetic	Generous	Contributing	Caring	Philanthropic
Charitable	Considerate	Responsive	Perceptive	Compassionate
Altruistic	Supportive	Humanitarian	Understanding	Engaging
Sympathetic	Sensitive	Feeling	Accommodating	Cooperative

Many companies, organizations, and investors share the traits they seek in an individual, so always do your due diligence before developing your résumé, cover letter, or other correspondence. While no magic word will land you that job, having the right adjectives and telling the right story can go a long way. The bottom line is to make every word count and demonstrate your traits with tangible examples in your application and every interaction.

Me Squared™: Self-Audit

Okay: Now that you know how important the right story can be and have some excellent adjectives in your pocket, let's put all that to use, answering the big question: Why Choose You? We will employ the Me Squared process, my proprietary method for mapping core values and generating a "Uniquely Me" statement to capture your professional identity and career aspirations.

Exercise:

Here is the Me Squared quadrant and accompanying directions for each quadrant:

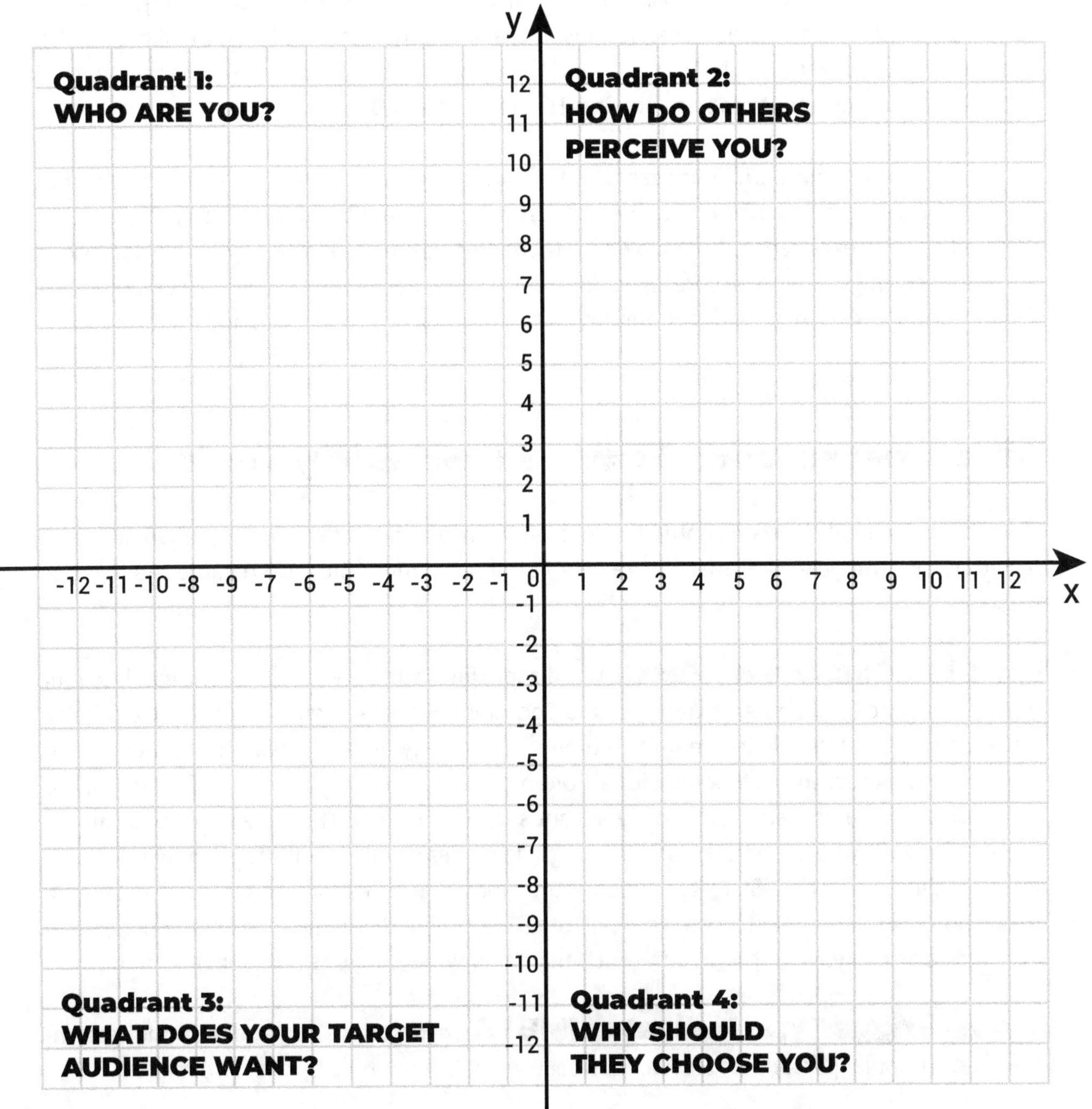

Quadrant 1: WHO ARE YOU?

Review the previous section, "Understanding Your Perfect Adjectives." Generate 10 adjectives or phrases that describe your core strengths and then place them in Quadrant 1. These can be soft skills (e.g., adaptable, enthusiastic) and hard skills (e.g., artificial intelligence, video production). Both soft and hard skills are essential to your career success. Make sure you put an asterisk by your superpower — your number-one trait.

Here's an example of this exercise: Meet Michael, a 25-year-old with a computer science degree and an entry-level web developer job. He's keen to either earn a promotion at his current company or secure a more senior position at another company. Michael listed five adjectives for his soft skills: analytical, driven, creative, positive, and enterprising. He listed three hard skills: database management, Google Analytics, and UX design. Michael's superpower is "analytical," and he is passionate about problem-solving. He places this in Quadrant 1.

A final note about this quadrant: In this quadrant, reflect on what you have to offer potential employers. It is essential to identify strengths relevant to your desired positions and highlight specific experiences that showcase them. Recognize areas where you may lack skills or experience and strategize accordingly. Consider your career goals and seek opportunities for skill development, such as certifications, volunteer work, or internships, to address any gaps.

Dive Deeper with These Personality Tests

To supplement the Me Squared process, you can take one of the many personality tests developed over the years that are widely available online. Some of the most reliable and rigorous tests are:

The DISC Personality Test (www.discprofile.com) categorizes individuals into four types: Dominance, Influence, Steadiness, and Conscientiousness. Identifying these traits helps individuals understand their strengths, communication styles, and areas for improvement. The DISC model recognizes that individuals often display a combination of the four traits; it is common to have a primary trait and significant secondary traits. This self-awareness can enhance teamwork, improve relationships, and guide career development by aligning roles with natural inclinations. The DiSC test includes approximately 80 questions and takes 15 to 20 minutes. Upon completion, you'll receive a personalized profile detailing your unique behavioral style, strategies for engaging with different personality types, and preferred environment.

Myers-Briggs Type Indicator (MBTI) (myersbriggs.org and mbtionline.com) is the most popular personality test worldwide, used in 26 countries by over two million individuals — from students and employees to soldiers and even potential marriage partners. The test consists of 90-plus "forced choice" questions, which provide insight into the subject's perception, decision-making, leadership skills, and other attributes. The questionnaire segments subjects into 16 distinct personality types, using combinations of the following designations: Introvert (I) vs. Extrovert (E); Intuitive (N) vs. Sensory (S); Thinking (T) vs. Feeling (F); and Perceiving (P) vs. Judging (J). For example, if you're an "ENFP" (extroverted, intuitive, feeling, and perceiving) type, here is how you are described on the website: "Enthusiastic innovators, always seeing new possibilities in the world around them. Their world is full of possible projects or interests they want to pursue. Imaginative, high-spirited, and ingenious, they can often do almost anything that interests them. They are confident, spontaneous, and flexible and often rely on their ability to improvise. They value home, family, friendships, creativity, and learning." The results of each test provide a list of specific occupations compatible with one's profile.

CliftonStrengths Assessment (formerly called the Clifton StrengthsFinder) **www.gallup.com/cliftonstrengths** is a popular web-based personality assessment that measures natural aptitudes in interpersonal skills, leadership abilities, and creative potential in 34 different areas. It is based on the research of psychologist Don Clifton and was developed by Gallup, Inc. The CliftonStrengths assessment takes approximately 30 minutes and presents 177 items/questions (20 seconds to respond to each item). Each item consists of potential self-descriptors, such as "I read instructions carefully" versus "I like to jump right into things." The in-depth report highlights your top five strengths, which can help you advance your goals, address challenges, and develop your strengths.

Enneagram (enneagraminstitute.com) is based on an ancient body of wisdom that identifies nine core personality types (the Reformer, the Helper, the Achiever, the Individualist, the Investigator, the Loyalist, the Enthusiast, the Challenger, and the Peacemaker) and how each sees and interacts with the world. The Enneagram system believes that each of us has a dominant personality type inside of us that drives how we think, behave, learn, see the world, and evolve. The test is about recognizing our core drivers and the impact of our experiences, motivations, attitudes, and fears.

16 Personalities (16personalities.com) is one of the most popular personality quizzes online, with over 26 million tests taken. It takes fewer than 12 minutes to complete. Based on MBTI, the 60-question, free-of-charge personality test assesses who you really are by asking you to indicate how much you agree with statements like "You cannot stand chaos." Like the classic MBTI, your answers determine where you fall on four spectrums: extroverted/introverted, sensing/intuitive, thinking/feeling, and judging/perceiving. At the end, it provides your personality type. Many reviews on the test describe it as fun, engaging, and accurate.

If you opted to take a personality test, be sure to integrate these findings with the ones you have reflected on in the previous section. Are the results in sync?

Quadrant 2: HOW DO OTHERS PERCEIVE YOU?

Face it: We all have personal blind spots. We don't always accurately see how the outside world reads us. The true measure of your brand comes from self-reflection combined with feedback from those who know you best. Just as we conduct a focus group in traditional marketing to understand consumer perceptions of a brand, you need to determine how others view you. It is prudent to seek feedback to continually fill that gap. If you don't, you're limiting your potential, career, and success.

It's equally important to understand what your audience expects or wants from you, what they need, how they function, and what drives them to take action. The impression we give is often made before walking in the door. Google can be our best friend or our worst enemy when it comes to personal branding. It has become our new reference check — those vetting you often start there when searching for information about you.

So, what is the best way to get feedback? Here are three ideas from Dr. Eurich:

1 **Select a few "loving critics" who can provide honest feedback.** These critics can be close coworkers, a trusted mentor, and even family or friends.

2 **Give them guidance.** Ask your "loving critics" to repeat the Quadrant 1 exercise and list your strengths and soft and hard skills. Also ask them to highlight your superpower.

3 **Establish a habit of "The Daily Check-in."** Each day, start taking stock of the ups and downs: What went well and what didn't? What can I do to improve tomorrow? Dr. Eurich notes that by reflecting on your day, you'll better understand yourself and how you relate to others.

Next, using the feedback from your "loving critics," fill out Quadrant 2 (see page 37). Does your self-assessment dovetail with their feedback? Highlight similar adjectives.

Let's return to Michael for another example. His critics are two close peers at his company and a friend from a previous internship. He asks them: What are my five strengths? And what is my superpower among those five strengths?

The following list contains his critics' responses — and Michael notes he has a "super-power" match with "analytical."

Quadrant 3: WHAT DOES YOUR TARGET AUDIENCE WANT?

One phrase you'll frequently hear during job searches and interview processes is "best fit" — that is, the candidate whose skills, experience, and education are the right match for a company. Specific qualities in high demand include leadership skills, determination, curiosity, adaptability, communications savvy, and a devotion to public service.

There are two steps to completing Quadrant 3:

1. Identify your target audience. In short: Who are you trying to impress? For purposes of this exercise, let's stick with hiring managers. You can expect better results when you identify your target audience and center your messaging on their wants and needs. Feel free to repeat this exercise with a different target audience (e.g., investors).

2. What is your target audience looking for? As mentioned previously, hiring managers seek applicants who are a good fit for their organization. But let's get more specific. Every company is unique — why not sleuth and see if you can get some intelligence on your dream company? After all, you are so much more than your résumé. In order to present your best self, you need to get into the recruiter's mindset and consider how to best present yourself. Jot down your findings about your dream company's good fit values on paper.

It's time to fill in Quadrant 3 (see page 37). Pick five or so attributes that your desired recruiters and companies value most.

Quadrant 4: WHY SHOULD THEY CHOOSE YOU?

In the professional world, you need to be able to answer this question from hiring managers: "What is it that makes you unique, and how will you contribute to our company?" Start by gathering intelligence on your competition and what they offer — and then identify your points of difference. Next, consider speaking to a few existing staff or company alumni who can highlight your dream company's characteristics. Why should they select you over other applicants for that coveted role? What distinctive benefits do you bring to your audience?

As mentioned, this process is similar to positioning a consumer product. Great companies create value propositions for their products. They define how the product differs in ways that their target audience values. Of course, value propositions go beyond just products — **your personal value proposition is at the heart of your career strategy.**

For Quadrant 4, please review all the previous quadrants and mull over the two to three things that answer the question "Why Choose Me?" Then, write them down (see page 37). In his Quadrant 4, Michael listed the following "Why Choose Me?" adjectives: driven, analytical, and leader.

Bravo! You've finished the more difficult part of personal branding. Last but not least, let's develop your Uniquely Me statement.

Uniquely Me Statement

Your Uniquely Me statement is your elevator pitch: a concise, compelling blurb that sums up who you are and why people should pay attention. It's similar to a tagline or slogan, and like any good marketing phrase, it should appear often. Your Uniquely Me statement should show up in your LinkedIn bio, cover letters, interviews, and elsewhere.

These statements often begin with active, first-person language like "I am," "I help," or "I work with." To start developing yours, review your four quadrants, particularly your unique promise in Quadrant 4. Then, see how you might distill all this information into one or two sentences, with no more than 25 words total. Here are a couple of Uniquely Me examples for inspiration:

Marketing professional: "I use a mix of creativity and analytics to create successful marketing campaigns."

Software developer: "I'm a team player who uses technical skills, hard work, and curiosity to motivate others and build great products."

For every assertion you make in your Uniquely Me statement, have evidence ready to back it up. This strengthens your statement and instills confidence in your abilities and achievements. The marketing professional mentioned above can give an example of leveraging data science in a campaign. And the software developer should be able to provide an example of how he inspired past teammates.

Now, let's go back to Michael and see what his Me Squared statement is: "My curious, creative, and analytical nature drives me to generate new ideas to solve complex business challenges." Michael has ample proof of this: in his current role, he had an outside-the-box idea for fixing a bug in his company's software that saved significant time and money.

Ready to give your statement a go?

____

____

____

____

Your Uniquely Me statement should be equal parts informative and compelling. Before you finalize your statement, ensure it checks these boxes:

☐ Does it highlight my strengths?

☐ Is it concise?

☐ Is it memorable?

☐ Is it personal and authentic?

Well done! With your Uniquely Me statement complete, our personal branding journey is off to a successful start! And take note: this statement is a living, breathing entity. It evolves as you continue to advance in your career. Update it whenever it feels stale. This will enable you to write strong résumés and cover letters and effectively prepare for interviews. This concept will be covered in depth in the Interviewing section.

Clarifying Your Career Aspirations

Before we dive into job search strategies in the next chapter, let's explore your career aspirations. It's essential to clarify what you want before applying for jobs. Are you seeking full-time, part-time, or freelance positions? Do you prefer office-based work, or is remote work more appealing? Consider the type of company culture and industry you're interested in. These questions will guide your job search and enhance its effectiveness. Reflect on the type of company that is a good fit — a corporation, start-up, or nonprofit. Imagine yourself in specific roles, your daily routine, and the particular skills and responsibilities you will use in those roles. What does your ideal workday look like?

Answer the following questions to streamline your search process and increase its effectiveness.

Expertise: What skills, experience, and knowledge can you bring to a position? What do you offer that sets you apart from other candidates? Provide examples of your unique qualifications.

Geography: In what location do you envision your ideal role? How far are you willing to commute for your job?

Role/Industry Fit: What specific job roles align with your skills, experiences, and interests? What sectors are you most passionate about?

Company Culture: What company culture aligns best with your values and working style?

Long-Term Vision: Where do you see yourself in five years, 10 years, and beyond?

Job Role Alignment: Identify specific roles that align with your skills, experiences, and interests.

Company Culture: What type of company culture aligns with your values? Consider factors like company size and work environment.

Growth Priorities: What opportunities for growth and advancement do you prioritize?

Compensation Package: What salary, benefits, and *work-life balance factors* are non-negotiable to you?

Work Style Preferences: How do you prioritize remote, hybrid, and on-site work options in your job search?

Definition of Success: What does success mean to you? What motivates you?

Your answers to these questions will shed light on your goals and allow you to make informed decisions throughout your job search journey. This information will help you focus your job search plan and create a list of top employers to target.

What will tomorrow's job board look like?

We're all familiar with the saying, "If you keep doing the same thing, you'll get the same result." In reality, this often leads to stagnation. My motto? Embracing innovation and change is the new key to staying ahead.

In a world where innovation reigns supreme, "Jobs We Don't Have Yet" takes center stage. New roles and career paths emerge that were once unimaginable. These positions will encompass artificial intelligence engineering, space tourism advising, virtual reality therapy, tidewater architecture, smart home design, and quantum computing consulting.

This mindset challenges us to remain adaptable and continuously refine our skills. It serves as a stark reminder that the future of work is unpredictable — so let's welcome the challenges and seize the opportunities of the ever-changing workforce.

Ultimately, the average person is likely to experience multiple career changes; it's estimated that most people will hold 12 different jobs throughout their careers. This underscores the importance of flexibility and lifelong learning in one's professional journey.

Career Shifters

Career shifters bring diverse experiences and fresh perspectives, making them valuable assets to employers. For those making a transition, it is important to identify transferable skills and craft a narrative highlighting their unique journey. For instance, a former teacher transitioning to corporate training can emphasize their expertise in curriculum development, public speaking, and mentoring to appeal to potential employers.

Let's see what a career transitioner and consultant have to say on this topic:

Embracing change as a constant will allow you to seize new opportunities and continuously reinvent yourself in a dynamic job market. By taking a proactive approach and conducting regular self-assessments, you'll make informed decisions that strengthen career resilience and enhance job satisfaction.

BRANDAMENTALS

Remember these key points:

1 **Self-awareness is critical.**
Truly understanding your strengths is the foundation of any personal brand.

2 **Audit the most important person — YOU.** Self-awareness is earned. You must spend time mapping your skills and passions. This map will come in handy down the road, whether writing a cover letter or content for LinkedIn.

3 **Know who your audience is.** Personal brands are just as much about other people as you. What can you do for them? Find out who *them* is: Recruiters? Investors? Mentors?

4 **Nail your slogan.** Your Uniquely Me statement is your bio and your business card all in one, so make sure to get it right — and repeat it often.

PART II – YOUR PERSONAL ROADMAP FOR CAREER SUCCESS

Take a breath — you earned it. In the last chapter, you defined yourself in preparation for your job search and reflected on your career aspirations. That's no easy task. But there's still more to uncover. Now we'll embark on the journey of discovery *outside* ourselves. How? By crafting a stellar job search strategy. You will pore over industry trends, identify potential employers, and more.

> *I liken the job search to college admissions: You have your reach and safe schools. Like admission officers, employers often favor candidates who haven't had everything handed to them. They value those with humble beginnings, perhaps starting at a cash register or cleaning golf clubs. This journey can form the backbone of a compelling résumé for a recent college graduate; internships don't always mark the starting point. It's not essential to bring a specific skill from a previous job; you can acquire it, such as through certification. Analyze numerous job descriptions to understand the requirements for your desired role. For those in the job market for a few years, a matured LinkedIn profile and résumé with regularly updated accomplishments, achievements, and results will serve as the foundation of their professional narrative.*
>
> **– Naomi Koller, Naomi Koller Careers**

Your Job Search Strategy

No job search strategy in place? That's like trying to bake a cake without a recipe!

It's easy to feel stuck when searching for a job — there's so much to do and so many potential avenues to explore. But an actionable job search plan can get you *un*stuck. Rather than tossing an endless stream of résumés into the void, limit the number of applications you send and make each one count. By applying to fewer jobs, you can customize each application and increase your chances of success.

It's important to remember that career paths resemble choose-your-own-adventure novels, not straightforward roadmaps. In my journey, my undergraduate degree in human development didn't align with my career trajectory. I began my career in HR at a large advertising agency but quickly found myself drawn to marketing. I moved to a marketing position at CBS, where I pursued an MBA in marketing at night. More zigzags followed: I briefly worked in marketing at a bank (even earning Series 7 and 53 certifications) before founding my PR/marketing agency.

The lesson? Embrace the detours; they lead to positive destinations. If you're content with your current employer but not your position, check out internal job openings. Companies generally give preference to internal candidates (though it's important to still bring your A-game to the interview).

For those in transition, it's essential to carefully assess your financial situation and consider taking on freelance projects. Transitions often come with irregular income and unexpected challenges, making preparation essential.

Approach your job search as if it were a job, investing your time and passion and setting clear, achievable goals (see Managing Time and Setting Goals, page 65). Set aside time daily, ideally during peak productivity hours. Experts suggest allocating at least 15 hours per week for employed job seekers and double for the unemployed. Consider dedicating Tuesday mornings to following up on applications from the previous week while reserving Wednesdays for networking activities.

To formalize the structure, use my "**REACH**" method: Research, Establish Tracking System, Apply and Shine, Connect, and Hone Results. Let's get started!

> *Confidence is key, and the best way to possess and exude confidence is through knowledge. Research the role and investigate the industry, major players, products/services, and news. Understand the function your new role would play in the company. Why is there an opening? What pain points do the hiring managers have because of the opening? How can you make their lives easier if they hire you? As the big interview day approaches, dedicate time to practice, practice, and practice some more. Armed with confidence and well-informed research, deliver your stories to wow the hiring panel. Show your personality, let your passion shine through, and remember: you're not just a résumé on a screen — you're a talented, unique individual with something incredible to offer.*
>
> **– Matthew Warzel, President of MJW Careers**

RESEARCH

The first part of a successful job hunt is investigation.

Industry/Market Research

Identify industries relevant to your skills, interests, and aspirations. Then, research trends, challenges, and opportunities within those industries. How are politics, culture, and technology shaping the field? Is demand growing or shrinking? Research and identify the skills most valued by employers in your industry so you can create a résumé that aligns with their needs.

Determine Target Job Roles

Thoroughly read job descriptions in your desired industries to understand responsibilities and qualifications. Talk to professionals with experience in your target role, and based on this information, determine what positions align with your goals and skills. Job titles are not universal. Similar roles may have different names depending on the industry, geographic location, company size, or culture. For instance, if your target role is "software engineer," corresponding job titles may include "developer," "programmer," "software developer," or "software architect."

Action Step: Compile a list of five to eight desired job titles and functions. For instance, if you're interested in finance, specify roles like financial analyst, investment banker, or financial consultant and industries such as banking, investment firms, or financial consulting.

Identify Target Companies

Prioritizing "good fit" companies is key. Start by pinpointing companies actively hiring for roles aligned with your career goals and personal preferences, like location and culture. *The 2-Hour Job Search* is a great resource and recommended read. Author Steve Dalton, whom I had the privilege of interviewing, shows how to compile a list of 40 companies, including small to mid-sized organizations. (It's worth noting that while smaller firms and start-ups may lack the prestige of Fortune 500 companies, they often offer unique opportunities.)

Study those companies' missions, cultures, and recent developments. Read websites, annual reports, and news articles, and browse LinkedIn, Glassdoor, and Indeed. If possible (and strongly encouraged), connect with individuals at your target companies.

> **Action Step:** Create a wish list of 25–30 companies you want to work for. Consider their size, industry, location, benefits, remote-work policies, culture, and open job postings.

> **Action Step:** Research and reach out to potential contacts within your target companies to gather insights. You can also network with people who work in your target industry more broadly.

> **Action Step:** Identify relevant networking opportunities, such as professional associations, alumni networks, and online communities.

Know Your Worth

Gather salary information for relevant roles and locations. Many job seekers struggle with salary negotiations, but advocating for fair compensation is essential. When asked about expected salary in interviews, confidently communicate your worth and offer a range. (See Supercharge Your Earnings on page 63.)

> **Action Step:** Tap into resources like Glassdoor, Payscale, and Levels.fyi, along with industry reports and professional networks. Adjust your salary range for factors like benefits, flexibility, and career growth opportunities.

> **Preparation is key:** *Take the time to understand why the company resonates with you and how you can contribute to its mission and/or values. Confidence in your abilities and enthusiasm for the work leave a lasting impression. Companies, especially hiring partners (and managers), are eager to hear why they are your employer of choice and how they can meet your needs.*

– Grace Meidanis, Consultant, Talent Acquisition Leader

ESTABLISH A TRACKING SYSTEM

Before sending out your first application, create a system to stay organized. Given the volume of applications, follow-ups, and replies, keeping track of everything is only possible with a structured system. By tracking your work, opportunities won't slip through the cracks. A centralized tracking system also allows you to tailor your résumé to specific job opportunities quickly. Use a spreadsheet, calendar, app, or even a pen and paper to track the following:

Company Name: Track all organizations you apply to for easy reference. (If you're working with a headhunter, add their targets to your list, too.)

Company Info: Include location, number of employees, and job description.

Contact: Add the hiring manager and recruiter's name, email, and phone.

Dates: Record the date you submit each application and any interview dates.

Salary/Benefits: Include salary information/range and benefits.

Follow-Up: Log any follow-up communication with respective organizations.

Status: Specify the current situation of each application (e.g., application sent, actively interviewing, offer, negotiation, rejection).

Listing Source: Note where you found each job opportunity, like an online platform or networking event.

APPLY AND SHINE

Now it's time to apply. But before you hit send, let me stress the importance of tailoring your résumé and cover letter to each job you apply for. Generic simply won't cut it! It's not just about hitting "send" — it's about hitting the mark.

Here are five tips to increase the chances that your application will be seen:

Timing is everything. What is the best day and time to submit your application? Knowing this could make all the difference. While every hiring manager and recruiter structures their workweek differently, consensus shows that submitting your application on Monday or Tuesday morning is best. David Lewis, CEO of OperationsInc, has a strong preference for Monday. He says that with a fresh start and fewer distractions, recruiters and hiring managers are more inclined to tackle their inbox. Above all, it's advisable to avoid submitting applications on Fridays, holidays, or after 4 p.m.

ZipRecruiter suggests that the timing of your job application can significantly impact your chances. Marissa Morrison, Vice President of People at ZipRecruiter, which boasts 10 million active listings, advises that "Tuesday is the best day to apply to a job since approximately 25% of new jobs are added to the site then. Research suggests you'll have the best results if your application is submitted between 6 a.m.–10 a.m. in the employer's local time zone."

Apply quickly. Apply soon after the job is posted, since companies may receive hundreds of applications within the initial 24 to 48 hours. Many companies close their application portals after reaching a set number of résumés. Morrison emphasizes that "It's important to be among the first applicants to stand out. Submitting your application early provides you with an edge as it increases the chances of being reviewed before the hiring manager is inundated with applications." To stay informed about job openings, set up alerts to receive notifications about new openings that match your criteria.

Keep following up. Don't underestimate the power of a follow-up. Following up encompasses everything from expressing gratitude after an informational interview to checking in with a hiring manager after applying. While response times vary, it's typical to hear back within one to two weeks after applying, so don't hesitate to ask for updates if you haven't heard back within a reasonable time frame. Reach out via email, phone, or LinkedIn to reinforce your interest. Remember, hiring managers and recruiters juggle countless messages, so a friendly follow-up reminding them of previous interactions can nudge them to respond. Several HR pros I interviewed stressed that insufficient follow-up signals disinterest and can hinder progress.

Apply for positions that don't check every requirement. While you should focus on roles that align with your qualifications, feel free to widen your job search net and apply for positions that don't check every box or for which you may be slightly underqualified. Many employers hire for soft skills and likeability. According to Mike Kerrigan, Director of HR at Interactive Brokers, "Skills are frequently transferable and can apply to a variety of jobs, presenting unexpected opportunities."

Create a tailored and truthful application. Ensure your résumé and accompanying materials are customized and in sync with the original job posting. While inserting keywords is important, be honest: avoid listing skills you haven't mastered.

Have 3–4 references "on call." Identify a few trusted individuals who understand your experience and capabilities to provide positive references. After they agree, send them your updated résumé.

CONNECT

Applying online is the norm, but it's essential to complement this virtual approach with real-world networking. In today's competitive job market, networking and relationship-building have become indispensable tools. In many instances, personal connections and recommendations from trusted contacts open doors and provide mentorship, collaboration, and career advancement opportunities. You can expand your circles through networking events, industry conferences, social media platforms, and alumni networks to forge meaningful connections with professionals who can play pivotal roles in your career journey.

HONE

Refining your approach is critical to job hunting. Seek guidance from mentors, interviewers, and advisors to elevate your skills and tactics. Be receptive to feedback and stay informed about company/industry developments and emerging best practices. And consistently review your results, tweak your strategy, and polish your approach. You got this!

Keep in mind that there are two distinct segments of the job market: the open and the hidden. The open job market includes publicly listed openings on company websites and job boards, whereas the hidden market consists of opportunities not widely advertised and mainly known to industry insiders. Often undisclosed due to budget constraints or discreet hiring needs, you can access these roles through many of the tactics above. Despite being challenging to find, these jobs can be very rewarding.

Check out the job search tools in the Resource section (page 223) to better manage your progress and stay on top of your job search.

Job Search: The Winning Mix

Landing your dream job requires casting a wide net. Consider the following avenues for finding that perfect opportunity:

- **Job boards:** Browse sites like Indeed, LinkedIn, and Glassdoor, many of which enable direct résumé and cover letter submission.

- **Networking:** Tap into personal and professional connections. LinkedIn is the gold standard here. (Refer to chapter Part IV (LinkedIn section) for a deeper dive into this incredible resource.)

- **Recruiting agencies or headhunters:** Seek a recruiter specializing in your field. And remember that headhunters typically work on commission.

- **Career fairs:** Attend job fairs and industry events to interact face-to-face with employees (and potential future coworkers).

- **Referrals:** Many companies offer current employees a finder's fee for referring a new hire. Ask for a referral if you know someone at your target company.

- **Social media platforms:** X (Twitter), Facebook, and other platforms can be networking hubs.

- **Professional associations:** Join industry organizations to access job listings and networking opportunities.

- **Company websites:** Bookmark and regularly check the career pages of desired companies.

- **Career coaches:** While they may come with a hefty price tag, they can provide invaluable guidance.

- **Freelance platforms:** Upwork, Freelancer, and similar tools can help you get gigs fast.

- **Alumni networks:** Educational institutions offer advantages that extend well beyond graduation.

- **Direct company outreach:** Leverage tools like Hunter.io and RocketReach to retrieve emails for cold outreach easily.

AI-Powered Job Tips

AI simplifies job searches, making it easier to craft standout applications and prepare for interviews. Here are tips to make the most of AI in your job hunt:

1 **Create ATS-Friendly Résumés.** Use AI tools to tailor your résumé and cover letter for specific job postings. Input the job description and your résumé to get precise suggestions for optimizing keywords and phrases. This ensures your application passes the ATS (Applicant Tracking System) and lands in front of a human.

2 **Get Personalized Feedback.** AI platforms excel at offering tailored tips for conveying your job fit. These tools meticulously analyze your résumé's content and provide actionable insights to enhance clarity and impact, giving you an edge.

3 **Simulate Real Interviews with ChatGPT.** ChatGPT can be your go-to tool for interview prep. Use prompts like: "Conduct a mock interview for a customer service position, asking one question at a time and waiting for my response" to create a realistic practice session.

4 **Focus on Building Relationships.** Let AI handle your application prep, freeing up time for you to network and build professional relationships. While technology tackles tedious tasks, you can spend your time connecting with key industry players.

5 **Choose the Right Tools.** Researching and selecting AI tools that align with your needs is crucial. Whether perfecting résumés or acing interviews, the right platform can be your secret weapon in achieving job success.

Tapping into AI ensures you're ready and ahead of the game. Use these tips to make your job search smarter and more efficient.

Score Informational Interviews

Informational interviews, also known as exploratory interviews, are essential. They are your backstage pass — a way to see inside the company and meet the people who make it tick. Unlike traditional job interviews, these are simple conversations with professionals about their experiences. By asking the right questions and listening carefully, you can learn about company culture, job expectations, and potential career paths. These interviews can open your eyes to new opportunities, grow your network, and even unlock a job.

If you feel you're imposing by asking someone for an informational interview, remember that people enjoy sharing their wisdom and advice! So, who should you ask? Consider interviewing people both at your level and more senior. To find the right people, network with business colleagues, friends, and family; tap into schools' alumni databases; and attend job and career fairs.

Tips for your informational interviews:

1 **Be prepared.** Show up having done your homework — bring the same level of preparation that you would in a traditional job interview. Beforehand, make sure you learn about the person you are meeting, the company, and the industry at large. Dig into their LinkedIn profile and the company website.

2 **Ask smart questions.** Informational interviews are great opportunities, so get every minute's worth. Ask open-ended questions instead of yes/no questions to elicit rich answers. And be comfortable going off-script when the conversation takes an unexpected but interesting turn.

3 **Take notes.** You don't want any insights to escape. Also, jotting down notes shows the interviewer you care.

4 **Dress sharp.** Once again, treat this as a traditional job interview. Be presentable and leave the torn jeans and scuffed shoes in the closet.

5 **Control your body language.** How you move is just as important as what you say. Be confident, make eye contact, and avoid fidgeting.

6 **Say "thank you."** The interviewer did you a favor by sharing their time and insights, so make sure to show gratitude afterward. Always send a short thank-you email within 24 hours of the chat.

Informational interviews can be a gold mine for your career, providing essential guidance and valuable contacts. If you nail that first impression, who knows: you may just pop into their heads when a job opens!

Experiencing writer's block ahead of the interview? These sample questions work in just about every scenario:

Career-related questions
- How did you get to where you are today?
- What steps do you recommend I take if pursuing a role like yours?
- What are the most rewarding parts of your career? The most challenging?
- What sets successful professionals apart in this field?
- What skills or personality traits are most important for success in this field?
- What kind of growth opportunities are available within the company/industry?
- How would you describe the company culture?
- What is the future outlook for your industry?

Day-to-day-related questions
- What does a typical day or week in your job look like?
- What projects or initiatives are you working on right now?
- Is your schedule flexible or set?
- Does your work require frequent travel?

Training/Education-related questions
- How should people interested in this career best prepare themselves?
- Which entry-level jobs provide the most learning opportunities?
- What experience and skills are most impressive in your field? What is the best way to gain this experience?
- Are there any resources (e.g., networking, websites, associations) that can help in my professional development?

Closing questions
- Are you willing to review my résumé and offer some advice?
- Is there anyone else you recommend I speak with?
- Would you be open to staying in touch?

Informational interviews are particularly essential for career shifters. They offer a unique chance to gain insider knowledge and network with industry professionals. And remember, each conversation moves you closer to your career goals and can potentially open the door to your dream job.

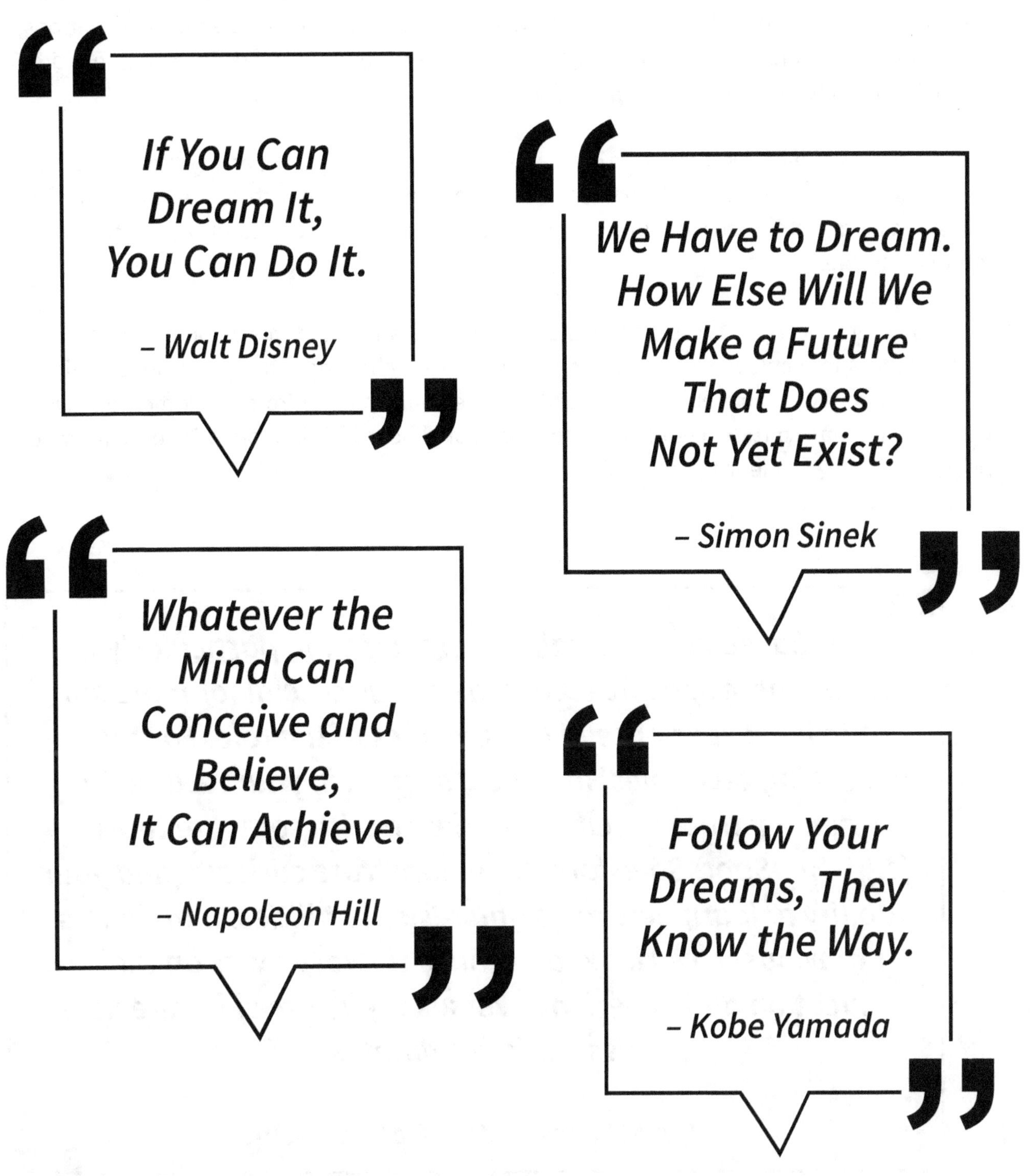

Skill Development Basics

Skills are the engine behind any successful career, so it's crucial to identify the skill sets necessary for your field (this is where those informational interviews come in) and then pursue them. How? Enroll in courses, participate in workshops, join professional associations, subscribe to trade magazines, and engage in internships or volunteer work. Investing your time now will reap valuable rewards down the line.

Right now, remote work skills are in exceptionally high demand. The ability to communicate and problem-solve virtually is valued across all industries. With more organizations transitioning to distributed workforces, proficiency in tools like Slack, Monday.com, and Trello is indispensable.

Continuous learning is essential to stay competitive and adaptable in today's job market. It also signals to employers that you are ready to tackle challenges and seize opportunities. A last word on skills: surround yourself with people you can learn from. Seek mentors, work with coaches, and consider creating your own personal board of directors, with each member bringing unique experience to the table.

Skill-based hiring is gaining momentum, particularly in roles where specific core skills are as crucial (or more so) than just experience in the specifics of the role. For those seeking tech roles, include a section in your résumé to demonstrate specific experience with software tools (e.g., HubSpot, Salesforce). Demonstrate curiosity and your ability to learn new roles and responsibilities. Individuals previously overlooked because the focus was on their education and experience versus their core skills are now desirable candidates.

– David Lewis, CEO of OperationsInc

15 High-Demand Skills to Earn Top Dollar

In the modern world, keeping a job and advancing your career is just as crucial as securing one. High-demand skills are specialized abilities in great demand that open doors to higher-paying positions or boost your earning potential. These skills often require advanced knowledge and experience. Below is a list of 15 high-demand skills that can increase your earning potential and set you apart in the workforce (Indeed, 2024):

1. Artificial Intelligence (AI)
2. Cloud Computing
3. Data Science
4. Machine Learning
5. Blockchain Technology
6. Cybersecurity
7. Digital Marketing
8. Robotics
9. Augmented Reality (AR)
10. Virtual Reality (VR)
11. Internet of Things (IoT)
12. Programming and Coding
13. Design Thinking
14. Natural Language Processing (NLP)
15. 3D Printing

By developing these high-demand skills, you can position yourself as a valuable asset in any industry, opening doors to exciting career opportunities. Embrace continuous learning and stay ahead of the curve to maximize your professional growth and earning potential.

Supercharge Your Earnings: A Salary Conversation FAQ

Talking about money can be awkward, and this discomfort sometimes extends to job interviews when employers ask, **"What are your salary expectations?"** In these scenarios, potential employees do themselves a real disservice by not tackling the issue head-on.

Yes, discussing salary expectations in an interview can be uncomfortable. However, this often-dreaded conversation is not the trap it appears to be. In fact, it's the opposite — it's an opportunity to advocate for your financial future. Let's discuss how in this Salary Conversation FAQ with Dorothy Mashburn, a leading career and salary negotiation coach.

Why Do Employers Ask This?
Employers ask this question for three main reasons:
1. Budget: To ensure they can afford you before moving ahead with the interview process.
2. Market Rate: To assess whether you have an accurate understanding of your market value.
3. Prioritization: To gauge how important salary is to you in your job search.

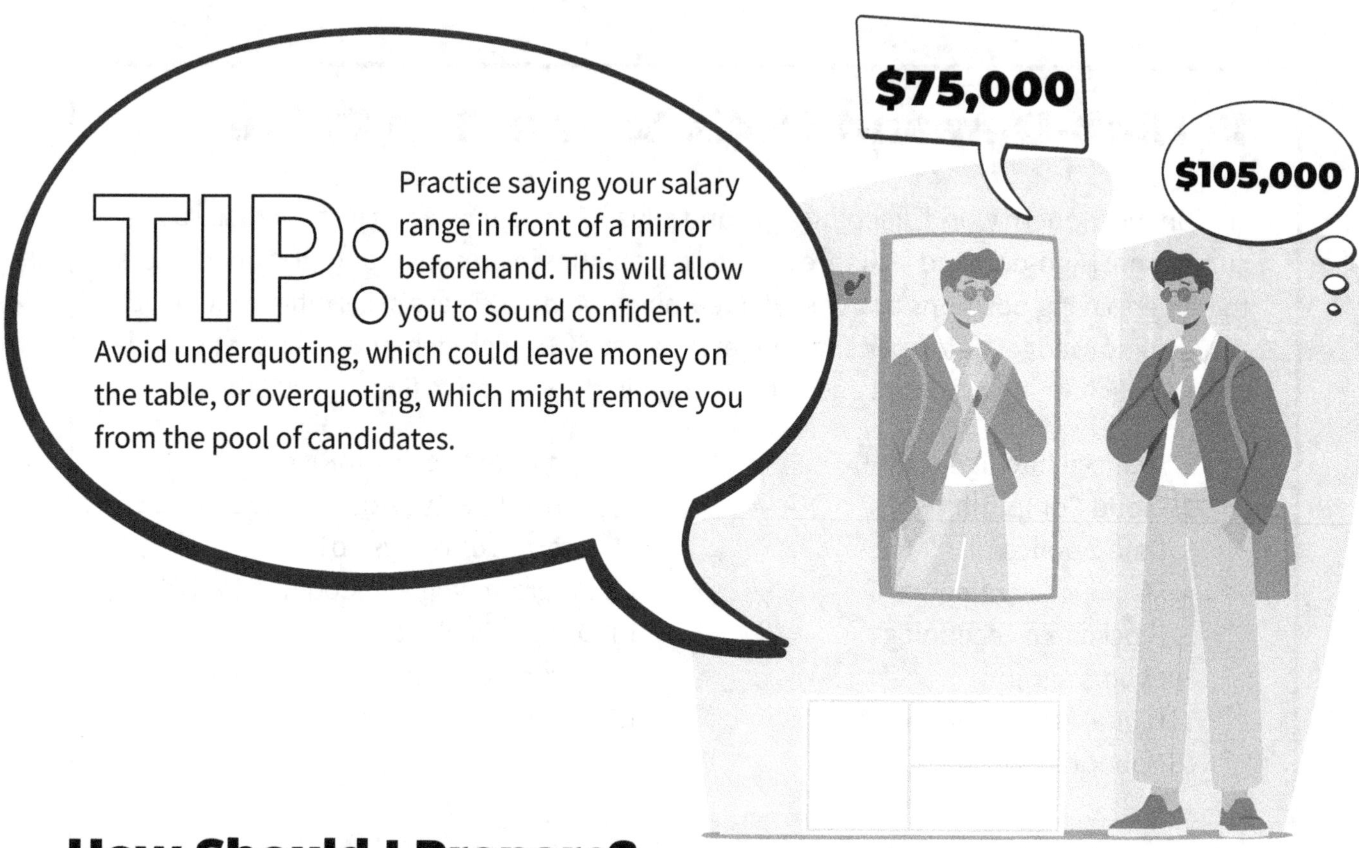

How Should I Prepare?

Always anticipate the salary conversation beforehand, and always do your homework. This is one question where you don't want to wing it. To prepare:

1. Research: Use websites like Glassdoor, Payscale, Blind, H1B Salary Database, and industry-specific sites to understand the average salaries for your role.

2. Network: Talk to people in similar roles to gauge the market rate. Alumni groups are a great resource to use.

3. Consult Mentors: Glean valuable insights from those with experience in your field.

Tip: Customize this boilerplate response: "Based on the market, I would consider a salary between $X and $Y. However, I'm open to discussion and also to considering benefits such as career development opportunities, work-life balance, and other perks."

What If They Ask About My Current Salary?

Some employers might ask, "What is your current salary?" Sharing this information could anchor you to a lower compensation level, and in some jurisdictions, it's illegal or frowned upon to even ask this.

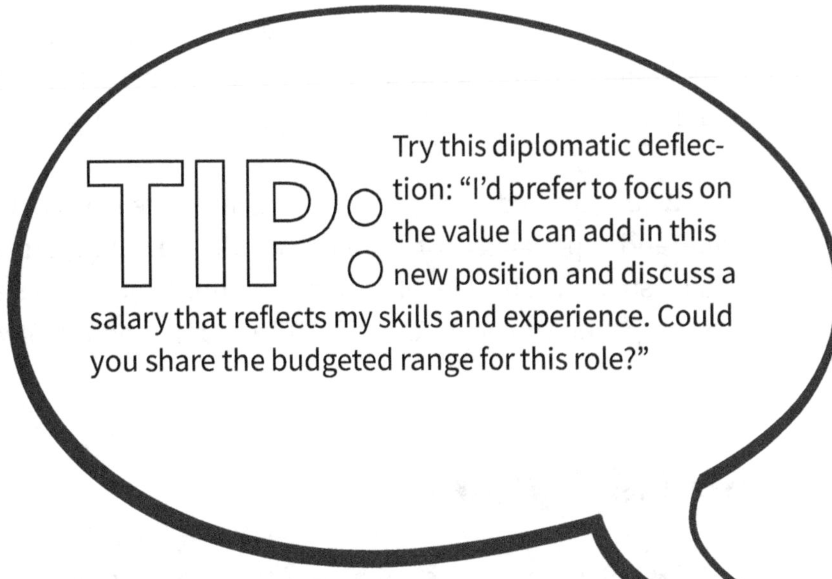

How Should I Answer Salary Questions on Applications?

Sometimes, the salary conversation is preceded by a salary question on the job application. If you encounter this:

1. **Write "Negotiable":** If text is allowed.
2. **Give a Range:** If it requires a numerical value, give a well-researched range. Your desired number should be at the low end of the range.
3. **Don't Lowball:** Never go below the market rate unless there are other significant perks.

What If Recruiters Push Me Toward a Lower Salary?

It's not uncommon for headhunters to push you toward a lower salary. If they do, be polite but firm: "I appreciate the offer, but based on the market rate and the value I bring, I need the salary range to be $X to $Y."

Managing Time and Setting Goals

It's true that all successful people have shared traits. Consider a marathon runner, a valedictorian, and a billionaire: they all know that setting goals is essential for success. If you want to achieve anything meaningful, you can't just sit around and hope for it to happen on its own. You need to manufacture your own opportunities.

A successful job search strategy starts with setting clear, defined goals. Consider your career direction and desired positions. This will help focus your search and tailor applications to match your aspirations, boosting your chances of success.

When you sit down to write your goals, take stock of what's important: your qualifications, skills, and experience. For instance, if you're a young professional, your goals should focus on finding strategic entry-level positions or internships. But setting goals isn't as easy as scribbling a list on paper. You need to be SMART about it, and the SMART approach can help:

SMART goals

SMART (Specific, Measurable, Achievable, Relevant, and Time-bound) is an acronym to guide your goal-setting and ensure its success. Here's how:

Specific. Be crystal clear about what you wish to accomplish. An ambiguous goal — *I want to make more money* — won't get you very far. Goals should answer who, what, when, where, and why. The narrower a goal, the more likely you'll achieve it.

Measurable. Measurable goals are a necessity. They allow you to track your progress and, eventually, declare victory. Setting goal milestones enables you to reevaluate and course-correct as needed.

Achievable. Goals should always be ambitious but not impossible to achieve. Make sure any actions associated with your goal are realistic.

Relevant. Each goal should connect to a bigger strategy. Ask yourself: How will accomplishing this goal contribute toward long-term career success?

Time-bound. A completion date for goals provides motivation and helps you prioritize. *Every* goal should have a deadline.

Now, let's see some SMART goals in action. The following examples are goals for a job seeker just out of college.

GOAL: **I will submit 25 targeted job applications in my desired field by March 31.**
Specific: This goal is straightforward.
Measurable: Progress can be tracked as each application is submitted.
Achievable: Researching a list of 25 opportunities is a realistic goal.
Relevant: Job applications are directly aligned with career aspirations, which makes this goal worthwhile.
Time-bound: March 31 is a clear deadline.

GOAL: **I will schedule six informational interviews by June 1.**
Specific: Once again, the goal is clear and straightforward.
Measurable: Progress can be easily tracked.
Achievable: Lining up six informational interviews is realistic, assuming proper planning and outreach efforts.
Relevant: Informational interviews are beneficial for someone early in their career.
Time-bound: The deadline is June 1.

GOAL: **I will launch an e-commerce site selling sustainable products by June 1 and earn $5,000 in revenue by September 15.**
Specific: This goal clearly defines the business type and a specific revenue target.
Measurable: Progress can be tracked through weekly or monthly sales reports.
Achievable: Existing technology like Shopify allows for the quick and efficient setting up of an e-commerce site.
Relevant: Starting an e-commerce shop is a great way to expand one's résumé.
Time-bound: This goal has two deadlines.

Taking action to achieve your goals

Setting and achieving goals is easier said than done. It's not always easy to determine what we want in life. And when we do, it still takes hard work and tenacity. It's a mental game: you have to *want* it! Consider these three principles to help:

- **Prioritize:** Set aside specific windows for goal-related actions, and don't procrastinate or make excuses.
- **Commit:** There will be hurdles; jump over them. If you need motivation, remind yourself why you set the goal in the first place and how good success will feel.
- **Adapt:** Even the best-laid plans can go awry, but that's okay. Flexibility is critical. Find ways to keep pursuing your goals, even as unexpected things happen with relationships, health, or finances.

As you pursue your goals, always make time to celebrate your wins — even the small ones. Acknowledging your accomplishments is a great way to stay motivated.

10 Commandments of Time Management

Now that we've covered goal basics, let's discuss time management. With proper time management, you can sustain your productivity, meet your deadlines, and have a healthy work-life balance. Allow me to introduce the 10 Commandments of Time Management:

1. You Shall Create a Schedule. Allocate windows each day or week specifically for pursuing your job search goals.

2. You Shall Embrace Technology. Digital tools have the power to significantly streamline the job search process. Leverage apps, browser extensions, automated job alerts, and more.

3. You Shall Not Be Distracted. Create a focused work environment during job search sessions; no texting, scrolling, or unnecessary browser tabs.

4. You Shall Break Tasks into Smaller Steps. Divide larger tasks into manageable chunks. Also, group together similar job search activities, like writing networking emails, to maximize efficiency.

5. You Shall Use Proven Techniques. Experiment with methods like the Pomodoro Technique, a popular time-management method, to enhance focus and productivity. Sort your job search tasks into focused work intervals (e.g., 25 minutes) followed by short breaks.

6. You Shall Refer Back to Your Goals. Revisit them often to ensure you're remaining on target.

7. You Shall Prioritize High-Value Tasks. Focus on activities that yield the greatest impact on your job search success.

8. You Shall Leverage Networking. Networking is essential for career growth; therefore, make it a priority to attend industry events.

9. You Shall Take Breaks. Rest and recharge to maintain productivity and avoid burnout.

10. You Shall Reflect and Adjust. Periodically review your progress and adjust your next steps as necessary.

A common time-waster is applying to ill-fitting jobs. This underscores the importance of crafting your Uniquely Me statement (see page 42), as self-awareness can help weed out opportunities that won't lead anywhere, saving valuable time.

This is not a typo: "To Do" is too passive, so I prefer to call it a "Must Do" list. Ask yourself: *What must I do today to support my purpose and goals? How does this activity help my purpose?* **Clear goals and must-dos are critical to transforming desire into reality and overcoming obstacles, distractions, and burnout.**

A Word About Likeability

The magic of likeability is simple yet profound: people prefer to do business with those they like. This isn't just a social nicety; it's career gold. Likeable people are generally viewed as more approachable, trustworthy, and collaborative, all qualities that enhance professional relationships. Likeability has its rewards. When colleagues and supervisors find someone likable, that person is more likely to be thought of for promotions, leadership roles, and important projects. After all, who doesn't want a leader as pleasant as they are proficient?

Likeability also opens the door to dream jobs in which being a cultural fit is as crucial as having the right skills. In fields like hospitality and health care, teamwork (and likeability) is indispensable.

And let's not forget the cherry on top: friendships. Likeability extends beyond professional advantages and can turn professional contacts into lifelong friends. These relationships often start professionally but can grow to offer support and enrichment beyond the workplace.

In short, likeability isn't just a soft skill — it's a superpower that enhances your career trajectory and enriches your personal life, proving that sometimes, it really is all about who you know and who enjoys knowing you.

Mindset Matters

Let's talk about mindset. Many people don't realize it, but the right mindset is directly linked to achieving your goals.

Your mindset shapes how you feel, think, and act. It is a set of beliefs that profoundly impacts your successes and failures. Mindset also plays an outsized role in how you overcome obstacles.

Don't take my word for it. According to Dr. Carol Dweck, Stanford psychologist and best-selling author of *Mindset: The New Psychology of Success: How We Can Learn to Fulfill Our Potential*, mindset plays a significant role in determining achievement and success. Dweck is re-nowned for her research into human motivation and the theory of fixed mindsets versus growth mindsets.

People with a growth mindset believe they can expand their talents and intelligence through hard work and learning. They have an optimistic, can-do attitude. Alternatively, people with a fixed mindset believe their talents and abilities are set in stone, no matter how much effort they exert. They believe they lack the skills to accomplish certain goals.

So, how can you apply a growth mindset to your career aspirations? The following tactics can help you stay motivated and positive.

• **Acknowledge your abilities.** Write down your existing skills and achievements and how they've fueled your success so far.

• **Embrace challenges.** If you experience a setback, think of it instead as an opportunity for growth.

• **Visualize success.** Regularly imagine yourself working at your dream company in your dream role.

• **Repeat positive affirmations.** Mantras like "I am skilled and experienced" will bolster your confidence.

MINDSET VS. GROWTH MINDSET

The following attitudes characterize a fixed mindset and growth mindset:

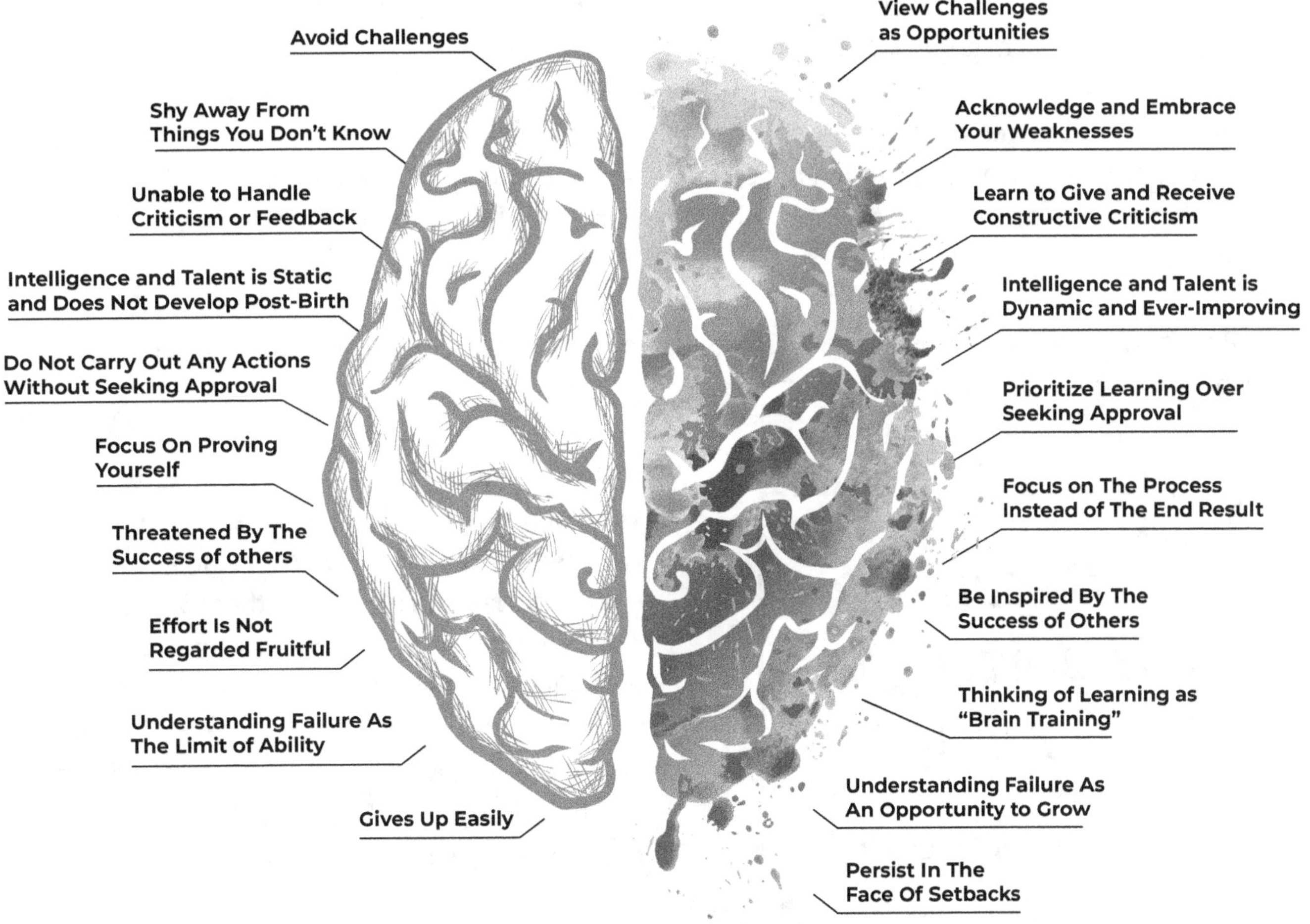

How to unfix a fixed mindset

According to Dweck, you *can change* from a fixed to a growth mindset. Here are some strategies from the *Mindset* book:

• **Focus on learning over achievement.** With a fixed mindset, you focus solely on the outcome and miss out on the learning moments. Instead, learn to enjoy the journey despite setbacks. Experience and personal growth can be more valuable than "winning." Your dream job or promotion you were hoping for falls through. Expect failure; there are lessons to be learned. And remember, each failure is a stepping stone toward success.

• **Pay attention to your words and thoughts.** Be conscious of how you speak to yourself (and others). Replace negative thoughts with more positive ones to build a growth mindset. When a fixed mindset takes hold, incorporate "yet" at the end of the sentence, which signals that you can overcome any struggles. For instance, rather than saying, "I can't learn computer programming," replace it with "I haven't mastered computer programming **yet**." Similarly, imagine you hear about a coveted job position. A candidate with a fixed mindset thinks, "That position is out of my league." Instead, that individual should think, "While the position is challenging and out of my comfort zone, I'm going for it."

• **Take on challenges.** Embrace challenges rather than avoid them. When you face setbacks and criticism and hear that fixed mindset voice, respond with a growth mindset voice. "Maybe I don't have the talent" should be met with "I have no idea how to do it yet, but I'm confident I can learn."

• **Recognize that you have a choice.** Changing your mindset is entirely within your control, as long as you're willing to put the effort in.

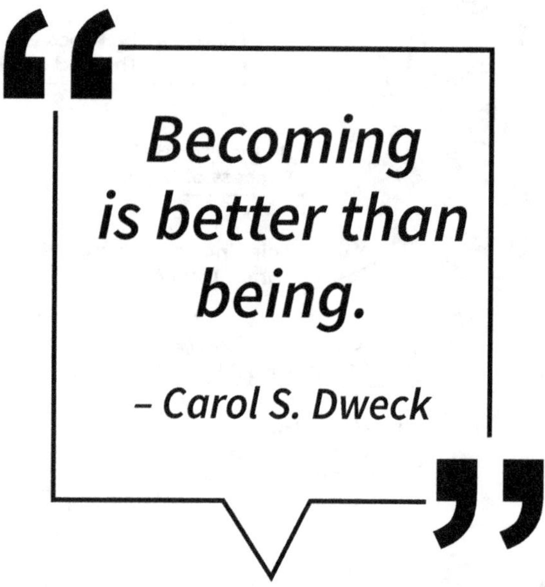

To take a deeper dive into how to shift your mindset and channel positive thinking, I turned to leading mindset coach Natasha Graziano. Natasha developed the MBS Method, a neuroscience-based program that relies on five pillars to develop a mindset that drives success. Natasha hit rock bottom herself eight years ago — divorced and homeless with a newborn baby — and was able to turn her life around using her very own MBS method.

Natasha believes you can rewire your brain and change your thought process by replacing old negative thought patterns with positive ones. "It is not easy to change a negative mindset to a positive one," Natasha explains. "But one of the best tools to help change your thinking is affirmations."

She continues: "The purpose of affirmations is twofold: first, to change your thinking pattern so that you start to see yourself in a more positive light. And second, to train your mind to focus on the positive aspects of any situation instead of the negative ones."

What are affirmations exactly? Affirmations are positive statements that can help you challenge and overcome negative thoughts. For example: "I am strong."

I use affirmations to ace new business opportunities, grow my agency, and empower my team. Affirmations are not magic; they must be accompanied by hard, smart work. But they can still go a long way. Don't just take my word for it. Some of the most successful individuals —

including Arianna Huffington, Oprah Winfrey, and former LinkedIn CEO Jeff Weiner — claim that affirmations have played a significant part in their success.

Now, use thoughts and words from your goal-setting activity (page 65) to write five affirmation statements. For some inspiration, consider these:

- My potential to succeed is limitless.
- I am a success in all that I do.
- My life is a gift, and I'm grateful for everything that I have.
- I'm open to new adventures in my life.
- I am thankful for my family and friends.
- My needs and wants are important.
- I'm worthy of love.
- I act with courage and confidence.

A final and essential word: *mentors*. One of the best ways to invest in yourself is by surrounding yourself with individuals who inspire and teach you. Seek out mentors and seasoned professionals who can offer invaluable insights and support as you navigate your career journey.

I've experienced the transformative impact of mentorship firsthand. Mentors have helped me refine job search strategies, set goals, and ace interviews. They can also introduce you to potential employers or industry contacts, expanding your network.

When seeking mentors, find individuals with a proven track record in your field, particularly if you are navigating career transitions or entering competitive markets. And don't hesitate to inquire about professional development opportunities, strategies for differentiation, and other career-related advice.

BRANDAMENTALS

Remember these key points:

1 **Do your homework.** Whether you're applying for jobs or preparing for an interview, always do your research. Recruiters, hiring managers, and potential mentors can tell when you've done the work — and when you haven't.

2 **Set the right goals.** Career success doesn't "just happen." It's the result of careful planning and hard work. Set goals that are clear, relevant, and ambitious yet attainable.

3 **Cultivate a growth mindset.** Avoid negative thoughts and attitudes like "I won't get the job" or "I can't ace the interview." Instead, replace them with positive attitudes ("I will ace the interview") and positive affirmations.

4 **Seek out a mentor.** You know the adage, "You are the company you keep." If you surround yourself with smart, empathetic, and motivated individuals, you're bound to succeed.

SECTION B:
DEVELOPMENT

PART III – YOUR SUCCESS TOOLKIT

You've just wrapped up the Discovery Stage of your personal brand, the most time-intensive portion. With that complete, you've laid a strong foundation for your brand: you know yourself, your audience, and how to talk about *you*. You have SMART goals and a positive mindset. So, what now?

After Discovery comes Development — building on top of that strong foundation. You'll learn how to tell your story in different ways, to different people, in different mediums. And you'll learn how to do it well.

These days, you can't afford to tell a mundane or boring story. The internet and smartphones have eroded our attention spans. Since 2000, the American attention span has gone from 12 seconds to eight — a 33 percent decrease! Your story needs to be riveting and worthwhile from the very start.

A compelling story begins with compelling messaging: captivating talking points that you can easily adapt for interviews, cover letters, your LinkedIn bio, and beyond. Next comes a compelling portfolio: a website, blog posts, online profiles, and other materials you share with recruiters, mentors, colleagues, and others.

> *The hard part of the job search isn't getting your résumé right. It's getting your résumé seen.*
>
> **– Steve Dalton, Founder and CEO of Contact2Colleague and Bestselling Author of** *The 2-Hour Job Search*

The Art of the Career Narrative

Synthesizing your professional history and accomplishments into a compelling narrative is no easy task, but it is incredibly worthwhile. Mastering the art of the career narrative is a skill you'll use throughout your career. The ability to craft and deploy your own key messages never gets old, from the cover letter for your first job to delivering a keynote at a major conference.

Although my own résumé has words like "CEO" and "marketer," I ultimately consider myself a storyteller. I've been telling clients' stories for nearly 30 years. And one of my biggest learnings from all that storytelling is this: *a successful story makes your audience take action.* When done right, your professional narrative will prompt recruiters to answer the phone, clients to sign on, and employers to prioritize your résumé.

For this reason, every single word of your career narrative should serve a purpose. Each word should add value, not clutter. If your key messaging isn't something your audience can easily remember, ditch it and go back to the drawing board. Make messages short and sweet.

How to Craft a Memorable Message

Your key messages should always have these qualities:

• **Strategic:** Start at a high altitude — your vision, goals, and values. For inspiration, return to your Me Squared statement in Section A.

• **Concise:** Shorter is better. How short? Limit each message to no more than 12 words, and don't craft more than five messages. Avoid jargon at all costs.

• **Consistent:** Whether you deliver your key messages over lunch or in an email, they should always be in sync. People should see the same *you* no matter where they look.

• **Memorable:** Messages need to make a lasting impression. Ensure that messages are easy to recall and repeat.

• **Compelling:** A winning key message makes the reader think, "*Wow.*" Now isn't the time to be modest: if you've doubled sales or launched multiple companies, say so!

• **Positive:** Talk about solutions, not problems. And use the active voice instead of the passive voice to demonstrate confidence.

Know your audience

It doesn't matter how good *you* think your messaging is. If your audience doesn't appreciate it, it's not serving a purpose. You need to know who you're speaking to — their needs, priorities, and vocabulary. The more detailed, the better. If you define your audience too broadly, you'll end up speaking to everybody, which basically means speaking to nobody.

Then, customize your messaging based on that data. You likely have multiple audiences — a recruiter, a manager, a mentor, and so on — which means you'll need different versions of the same core messages. If you define your audience too broadly, the message will likely be impersonal and read as boilerplate.

Building Your Message House

Crafting the right messages is challenging, and so is organizing them. Determining what comes first, last, and in between can be difficult. That's where the messaging house comes in. It's a metaphor to help you assemble the correct sequence of communications.

You start with the roof, which acts as your headline or umbrella statement. And guess what? You've already written yours — it's your Uniquely Me Statement from the earlier Discovery section. The roof is your audience's main takeaway and links all your key messages beneath it.

Next come the pillars, or your key messages. They flesh out your Uniquely Me Statement, providing the who, what, why, where, when, and how. As you write these, keep your goals and your audience's needs top of mind. Also, be intentional and consistent about tone. Depending on your industry, it might be authoritative, technical, strong, trustworthy, or whimsical. Of course, body language matters too when delivering these messages, such as facial expressions, posture, gestures, or eye movement. This comes into play during in person or online interviews.

Last comes the foundation. These are your proof points and supporting statements, which bolster and validate your key messages. You need to back up all your assertions so far with facts, figures, and other evidence. Here's an example of how your pillars and foundation should work together:

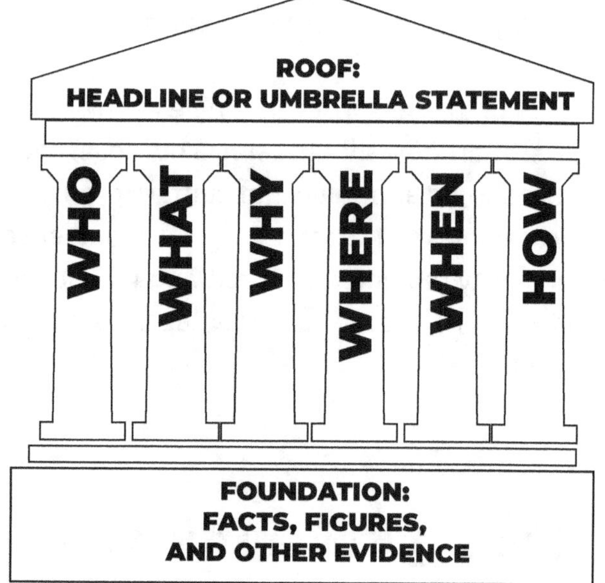

Your Audience: Prospective Employers

Pillar (Key Message):
- I'm a - self-starter with a strong work ethic.
  I like to come up with new ideas to
  streamline processes.

Foundation (Proof Points):
- Launched a mentoring program at
  company XYZ for new hires.
- Created a new system to improve workflow
  efficiencies by 30 percent.

As you build your Message house, grab a pen and paper and draw an illustration like the one on the previous page. Jot down your Uniquely Me Statement, pick an audience or two, then get to work on the pillars and foundation.

Maintenance matters

All houses need upkeep, and message houses are no different. If you neglect it, it grows old and eventually collapses. As your career progresses and changes, revise your key messages to remain relevant and swap in newer and more impressive proof points. And remember to be consistent: if you update your messaging on LinkedIn, do the same on your résumé, website, and wherever else your messages live.

Putting your messaging to work

Your key messages are a valuable tool, so apply them often. Job interviews, which are often a source of anxiety, are a great place to deploy them. You'll ace the interview and feel more confident.

Below, I've listed a handful of common questions that arise during job interviews. Take a moment to consider how you can respond to them using your key messages.

- **Motivation:** What led you to apply to our company? What excited you about the role?
- **Achievements:** What is your proudest accomplishment?
- **Extracurriculars:** What are you passionate about?
- **Ambitions:** Where do you see yourself 10 years from now?

In addition to answering with your key messages, have a few anecdotes handy, too. They can provide color and common ground. For example, you might tell the story of how you organized a day of service at your last job, volunteering at a local soup kitchen.

Five-Star Applications

Most job postings these days receive a blizzard of applications. It's not enough to simply have a good package — you need a stellar one. Here are four ways to stand out in the job application process:

• **Build a personal website.** There's no better way to showcase your accomplishments than with a website. You have as much space as you need, unlimited design potential, and the ability to share it with anyone, anytime. You can also share testimonials to boost your credibility. For those who cringe at the thought of building one, fear not. Tools like Squarespace and WordPress make website creation seamless, giving you a product that's as sleek as a big brand's website. Make sure to pick a professional and memorable URL (your name works great if it's available). And make sure to keep your website updated: an out-of-date website is worse than no website at all.

• **Create an online portfolio.** Websites are the first step; online portfolios are the next. This is an opportunity to provide a direct window into your skills and accomplishments with articles you've written, projects you've launched, and photos you've taken. Your portfolio should span multiple platforms, from LinkedIn to Instagram and beyond. These days, there are portfolio tools for every industry. Creative types use Behance and Dribbble; technical folks use GitHub; and prolific freelancers use Fiverr (which can double as a business development platform). Meanwhile, message boards and communities like subreddits and DeviantArt offer interactive opportunities, allowing for comments and conversation. Pick the platforms that dovetail with your work and audience, then get started.

• **Maximize your email signature.** That small space at the end of your emails is valuable real estate — the digital equivalent of waterfront property! Everyone you correspond with sees it, sometimes multiple times in a day. Be thoughtful and concise. Your website, your most active social media handles, your portfolio, or even a tagline are all great additions.

• **Create a video.** Did you know one minute of video is worth 1.8 million words? This popular statement about video was made by Dr. James McQuivey of Forrester Research. Put this to practice and share your Uniquely Me statement through video. It could simply be you talking to the camera or a reel showcasing past accomplishments. If you appear in the video, speak clearly, dress professionally, and film in a suitable location. And remember how short attention spans are these days — keep the video to 90 seconds, tops.

Ace Your Interview

Job interviews are a great opportunity for you to showcase your potential and skills. You have the power to make a lasting impression. Here are a few tactics for wowing your potential employers and making the most of your next interview:

• **Face time:** We live in an increasingly virtual world, but nothing beats real face time. If possible, opt for an in-person conversation. It will strengthen your connection and highlight your enthusiasm.

• **Virtual interviews:** If an in-person interview isn't in the cards, take your virtual interview just as seriously. Whether connecting on Zoom, FaceTime, or another platform, pick a spot with good backlighting (or use a ring light), clean up your background, and sit up straight. Make sure your computer is at eye level and dress professionally.

• **Study, study, study:** Never go into an interview unprepared. Spend ample time researching the company, the position you're applying for, and the person or people interviewing you. Scour the company website and social media accounts as well as the interviewer's LinkedIn profile. Consider checking out forums like Glassdoor and Reddit, where you can gather intel from employees at the company.

• **Present your best self:** Always dress sharp and bring a firm handshake. Be confident, enthusiastic, and personable. Remember, the interviewer wants to get to know the personality *behind* the résumé and cover letter.

• **Ask smart questions:** An interview is a conversation, not an interrogation. Recruiters and hiring managers expect you to come prepared with questions of your own. If you don't, you'll appear uninterested or unprepared. Some starters: "Can you share examples of projects a person in this role would work on?" and "How does the company support and encourage innovation and creativity?"

• **Dress rehearsal:** If you're nervous or this is one of your first interviews, consider doing a practice run with a friend or colleague. They can ask you questions you anticipate, and you can get the hang of asking your questions, too.

• **Tell stories, not lists:** Your résumé is a springboard, not the focus of the interview. Tell stories and anecdotes that enliven what's on your résumé. Did you increase sales at your last company? Explain what that experience was like.

• **Emphasize soft skills:** Soft skills like communication are essential no matter the job. Provide examples of how you're an expert communicator to show you're a well-rounded candidate.

• **Wrapping up:** Before wrapping up the interview, make sure the interviewer has all the details they need and clarify the next steps. Ask, "What are the next steps in the interview process?" and "Is there anything else I can provide?"

NOTE ABOUT SOFT SKILLS:

Remember, you're more than just a résumé. Attitude and soft skills rule the day. A recent Leadership IQ study revealed that 46 percent of new hires fail within 18 months, mainly due to poor interpersonal skills. These failures are due to an inability to accept feedback (26 percent) or manage emotions (23 percent), a lack of motivation (17 percent), or having the wrong temperament (15 percent). Surprisingly, only 11 percent fail due to inadequate technical skills. Enthusiasm and a can-do attitude are highly valued attributes as they boost team morale and project success, which impact the bottom line. Soft skills matter even more than hard skills. Those who bring a positive mindset, passion, and drive? They're the real winners.

> *The biggest mistake I see in the interview process is painting an overly rosy picture and avoiding discussions about failures and setbacks. Be authentic; we're human, and it's okay to fail. What intestinal fortitude did you have to get over the finish line? How are you going to identify the low-hanging fruit and make a positive impact on the business? How will you solve problems that keep your boss up at night? Do not focus solely on your development or personal gain. Instead, show me how you will contribute to the team's success. Two pet peeves: not taking notes during the meeting (which shows that you are not actively engaged) and being unprepared. While I'm not concerned about employment or skill set gaps, I do prioritize candidates who demonstrate deep knowledge of the company and the role they're applying for.*
>
> **– Joseph DiCarlo, SPHR, SHRM-SCP, Chief People Officer at Clarest Health**

20 Questions: What to Expect in the Interview

No two jobs are the same, even within the same industry. But there are several questions that tend to be universal. Here's what you can expect to be asked:

Can you tell me about yourself?

Can you walk me through your résumé?

Why are you interested in this position/company?

What are your strengths and weaknesses?

Can you describe a challenging situation you've faced at work and how you handled it?

How do you handle failure or setbacks?

What is your leadership style?

Can you provide an example of when you had to problem-solve on the job?

How do you prioritize your work?

What are your salary expectations?

Can you explain any gaps in your employment history?

Where do you see yourself in five years?

Why did you leave your last job?

Why are you looking for a new role?

Why should we hire you over other qualified candidates?

What is your greatest achievement?

How do you handle conflict or stress?

What keeps you motivated?

Can you provide an example of a time when you worked well in a team?

Do you have any questions for us?

Sparkling Samples: Cover Letter, Résumé, LinkedIn, and Thank-You Letter

It's been a productive few chapters. You've assessed your strengths, crafted key messages, and prepared for interviews. What next? Let's put all this into practice and start applying for your next big opportunity.

Your four essential tools will be your cover letter, résumé, LinkedIn profile, and thank-you letter. These materials are what recruiters and hiring managers expect to see first, and they're the mediums you'll use to deliver your Uniquely Me Statement and key messages.

If you remember just one thing from this section, let it be this: ***Always customize your materials to the role you're applying for.*** Select and insert keywords and phrases from the job posting and company website to show recruiters you're "listening" and highlighting what they're looking for. Data-driven bullet points that speak directly to a posting's prerequisites are the best way forward. Hiring managers and recruiters can sniff a template miles away, underscoring the need for personalization to avoid the impression of disinterest or lack of commitment.

Also, make sure your materials meet any requirements stated in the posting. If recruiters are looking for cover letters that are no longer than one page long, respect that. A two-page cover letter may well get tossed in the trash.

While your materials should always be customized, they don't have to be built from scratch. It's smart to have templates you can use as a foundation, which makes it far more efficient to apply for roles. A bit further along, I've provided a handful of templates you can start with. But first, a few words about each of your key materials.

The Cover Letter: Ditch the 1,000-word novel and aim for brevity instead. The sweet spot is somewhere between 250 and 400 words. This allows your biggest accomplishments to shine and highlights your communication skills.

Your cover letter should include a mix of achievements, motivations, and interests, ultimately answering the question, "Are you a good fit for this company?" Avoid clichés like "excellent communication skills," which don't prove anything. Instead, include a brief story from your career history proving your claim. Show — don't tell.

Lastly, you can use your cover letter to expand on anything noteworthy in your résumé, like an employment gap. Explain why you had to take a leave to help a sick family member or complete your degree.

The Résumé: Résumés should be quick and to the point — no more than a page. Make sure to use the active voice and action verbs ("Created," "Built," "Achieved"). And always back up assertions with hard data.

One of the most effective résumé formulas is the X-Y-Z method, which involves quantifying the impact of your achievements in a clear and measurable way: "Accomplished [X] as measured by [Y], by doing [Z]." By using this structure, you convey the value you brought to each role, making your résumé more compelling to potential employers. For instance, instead of saying, "Improved sales," you could state, "Increased sales by 20% within six months by implementing a new customer relationship management system." This approach doesn't just state your successes; it backs it up with proof, ensuring your résumé shines.

Space is limited, so prioritize experience that's relevant to the role at hand. There's no need to include your dog walking jobs from middle school.

If you're listing skills on your résumé without examples of those skills in action, it's a huge red flag for recruiters and hiring decision-makers. A common mistake for entry-level applicants is creating a functional résumé focusing on skills. It screams, "I don't have experience!" If you used or honed a skill as a student, a volunteer, or in an organized group, then this is experience. Use it!

– Steph Cartwright, Job Search Strategist at Off The Clock Résumés

LinkedIn Profile: An indispensable tool, LinkedIn serves as your digital résumé, highlighting professional accomplishments, skills, and career aspirations. Crafting a profile that stands out is essential to grab the attention of potential employers and recruiters, increasing the likelihood of nabbing sought-after job opportunities. In fact, LinkedIn is such an essential tool for today's job-hunting strategies that we devoted a whole chapter to it (see page 104).

The Thank-You Letter: This is the shortest of the big four, but no less important. Whether or not you send a thank-you could be the determining factor in your landing — or losing — the opportunity. Always send a thank-you within 24 hours of the interview. Make sure to express a mix of gratitude and ambition. And double down on why you're such a strong fit for the role. Just like the résumé and cover letter, shorter is better — a few paragraphs at most. While email is acceptable, you may want to consider going above and beyond with a handwritten note.

While I excel in packaging products, services, and people, I am not a résumé writer and believe in collaborating with the best of the best. For this section, I sought expertise from an esteemed résumé writing authority: Melissa Trager, Chief Resume Officer and Founder of Resume All Day.

Now, here are examples to get you started!

Michael Wilson
East 79th Street, New York, NY 10075
michaelwilson123@gmail.com | 123-456-7890

Dear Hiring Manager,

I'm very interested in working at Insert Company Name as a(n) Insert Job Name. I received my Bachelor of Business Administration degree with a concentration in Finance from the University of Michigan and have finance internship experiences. This, paired with my financial modeling and investment coursework, analytical skills, and strong communication style, makes me a strong candidate for this position.

Financial Markets and Investment Experience - During my internship at JPMorgan Chase as a Private Wealth Management Analyst, I assisted over 50 high-net-worth clients shape their investment portfolios. As part of a two-month project, I built a comprehensive financial pitchbook that included portfolio recommendations to maximize clients' returns, rewards, and risk assessments. My background in industry research and building discounted cash flow and comparable company analysis as an Equity Summer Research Analyst at KBW, a Stifel company, helped drive my investment strategy, resulting in a 15% return on investment.

Analytical Team Player - As a member of Michigan Ross's International Investment Fund, I collaborated with other finance majors to manage a simulated $1MM portfolio, applying principles from advanced finance courses such as Managing the Maze and Blue Fund. Similar to my responsibilities at KBW, I conducted in-depth analyses of the consumer-packaged goods industry, evaluating stock valuations and updating financial models to present stock recommendations to fund members to maximize the portfolio's value. My campus involvement and coursework have given me a strong foundation to start my finance career and contribute to Insert Company Name.

Interpersonal Communicator - As the Finance Director for Circle K, a community service organization, I partnered with student board members to allocate funds for mission-driven campus events and local events. I tracked expenditures and participated in monthly meetings with the national board to report expenses. My ability to calculate financials and communicate a story behind the numbers helped the club receive an additional $500 in funding for a signature event.

I'm excited about the prospect of working for Insert Company Name and believe that my experience makes me a great candidate for the Insert Job Name. I look forward to hearing from you to schedule an interview. If you have any questions about my résumé, please do not hesitate to contact me at (123)-456-7890 or michaelwilson123@gmail.com. Thank you for your time and consideration.

Sincerely,
Michael Wilson

Michael Wilson

New York, NY | michaelwilson123@gmail.com | 123-456-7890 | LinkedIn

EDUCATION

University of Michigan, Ann Arbor, MI
Bachelor of Business Administration in Finance, GPA: 3.82   Expected graduation May 2024
Honors: Dean's List 5 semesters, Ross Business School Excellence Scholarship Recipient
London School of Economics and Political Science, *Study Abroad Program*; London, Spring 2023

PROFESSIONAL EXPERIENCE

JPMorgan Chase & Co., New York, NY
Private Wealth Management Summer Analyst   June 2023–August 2023
- Evaluated 50+ high-net-worth clients' needs with wealth advisors and conducted market research to recommend investment strategies to support their financial goals.
- Analyzed 20 client portfolios, researching investments and macro-level economic trends to create a financial pitchbook for high-net-worth clients; investment strategy resulted in a 15% increase in portfolio returns.
- Collaborated with a cross-functional team of bankers and global investment specialists to conduct market research analysis and provide input to support financial product solution development.
- Participated in a weekly guest speaker series and mentorship program to grow professional network.

Keefe, Bruyette & Woods (KBW), a Stifel Company, New York, NY
Equity Research Summer Analyst   May 2022–August 2022
- Compiled and synthesized data from multiple sources on 15 telecommunications companies to identify industry trends, understand the competitive landscape, and assess capital and debt levels.
- Built and maintained financial models, including discounted cash flow (DCF) and comparable company analysis (CCA), to assess intrinsic value of target companies.
- Assessed stock valuations, created industry trend reports, and made recommendations to senior management.

LEADERSHIP EXPERIENCE & ACTIVITIES

Michigan Ross International Investment Fund, Ann Arbor, MI
Active Member   January 2021–Present
- Manage simulated $1MM investment portfolio of international securities by implementing rebalancing techniques and asset allocation to mitigate risks and maximize returns.
- Analyze investment opportunities, compile findings, and create investment pitches to present to club members.

Circle K, Ann Arbor, MI
Finance Director   October 2020–Present
- Oversee $8K budget, maintain books, present purchase summaries to national board, and organize community service opportunities.

RELEVANT COURSEWORK

Managing the Maize and Blue Fund   September 2023–December 2023
- Collaborated with student team to analyze, select, and pitch stocks from specific sectors, using financial research and modeling tools to inform portfolio management and investment strategy recommendations.

Capital Markets and Investment Strategy   September 2022–December 2022
- Conducted portfolio analysis and security valuation, built pricing models, and designed investment strategies across broad classes of financial assets and markets.

SKILLS & INTERESTS

Technical Skills: Advanced Knowledge of Microsoft Office Suite (Excel, Word, PowerPoint)
Languages: Fluent in Spanish, Beginner Knowledge of Italian
Interests: Marvel Cinematic Universe, Broadway, Yoga, Financial Modeling, Financial Market Research

MICHAEL WILSON LINKEDIN

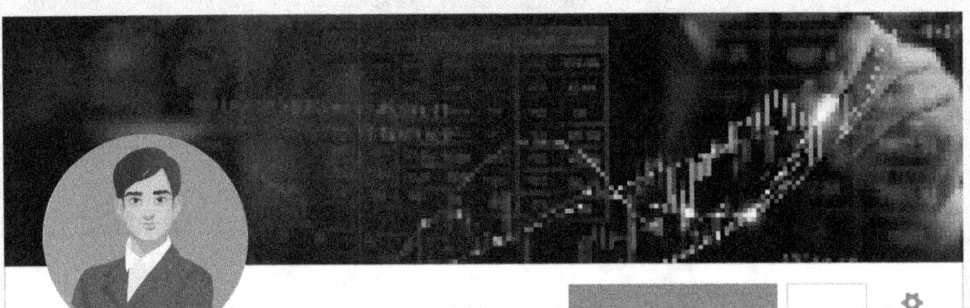

Michael Wilson

Financial Analyst | Wealth Management | Equity Research | Investment Analyst

About

I'm a finance student passionate about portfolio management and building strong client relationships, seeking a full-time opportunity beginning in Summer 2024. I have experience working for leading global financial services and investment firms and possess a solid foundation of investment research, market trend analysis, and financial modeling for strategic investment decisions.

Experience

JPMorgan Chase & Co.; Private Wealth Management Summer Analyst; New York, NY; June 2023–August 2023
- Assisted wealth advisor in managing 50+ high-net-worth client accounts by analyzing portfolios, researching market activities, and recommending investment strategies to maximize ROI and support clients' long- and short-term financial goals.

Keefe, Bruyette & Woods (KBW), a Stifel Company; Equity Research Summer Analyst; New York, NY; May 2022–August 2022
- Compiled and synthesized data to identify industry trends, understand competitive landscape, and assess capital and debt levels and built financial models to assess intrinsic value of target companies.

Michigan Ross International Investment Fund, Active Member; Ann Arbor, MI; January 2021–Present
- Manage simulated $1MM investment portfolio, analyze investment opportunities, and create investment pitches to drive maximum return on investment and mitigate risks.

Circle K, Finance Director; Ann Arbor, MI; October 2020–Present
- Oversee organization's annual budget, maintain accurate books, and report purchases to national board members; help organize and participate in community service opportunities.

Education

University of Michigan, Degree - Bachelor of Science, Field of Study - Finance, Start Date – August 2020, End Date – May 2024
London School of Economics, Semester Abroad Program, Start Date – January 2023, End Date – May 2023

Activities and Societies: Michigan Ross International Investment Fund, Circle K

Skills & Endorsements

Finance, Financial Analysis, Financial Reporting, Investment Strategies, Investment Research, Investment Portfolios, Financial Analysis, Trend Analysis, Microsoft Excel, Reporting & Analysis, Financial Modeling, Account Management, Client Relations, Communication, Cash Flow Analysis

> **Note:** *In Michael's case, adding activities to his professional experience section complements his financial background. The international investment fund simulates real-world scenarios relevant to potential full-time jobs.*

OLIVIA SMITH
COVER LETTER

OLIVIA SMITH

Wetherly Drive, Los Angeles, CA 90210 | oliviasmith@gmail.com | 789-456-1230

Dear Recruitment Director,

I'm very interested in working for Insert Company Name as a(n) Insert Role. I'm an Account Executive for BLK PR, a full-service PR agency specializing in brand development, influencer marketing, celebrity placements, and impactful media mentions. My experience in public relations, strategic thinking, and ability to build and maintain strong relationships make me an ideal candidate for this position.

Public Relations Experience - As an Account Executive for BLK PR, I support six celebrity client accounts. This involves regular meetings with the account team to stay updated on brand initiatives and identify growth opportunities. By building strategic media relationships and crafting compelling narratives, I have successfully secured national media coverage, including *The New York Times*, *Variety*, *Entertainment Tonight*, and *Good Morning America*.

Analytical Problem-Solver - In addition to crafting press pitches, I analyze campaign metrics and recommend strategy adjustments to help clients achieve their goals. As a PR Assistant at Walt Disney Studios, I extensively researched the influencer landscape and media trends. Using market research databases and social media analytic tools, I identified brand and influencer partnerships matching their target demographic.

Collaborative Communicator - Working under Pixar's Head of PR, I prepared for press events and communicated key information to the media. I helped plan four activations for *Elemental*, Pixar's new children's film. To secure press coverage, I liaised with the media, managed press lists, and distributed press releases. I compiled press clippings, tracked coverage, and generated media summary reports to capture the events' success. This experience enhanced my writing and communication skills, which I've applied throughout my PR career.

I am very interested in working for Insert Company Name as a(n) Insert Role, and I look forward to hearing from you to schedule an interview. If you have any questions about my résumé, please do not hesitate to contact me at (789)-456-1230 or oliviasmith@gmail.com. Thank you for your time and consideration.

Sincerely,
Olivia Smith

OLIVIA SMITH
RÉSUMÉ

OLIVIA SMITH

Los Angeles, CA I 789-456-1230 I oliviasmith@gmail.com I <u>LinkedIn</u>

PROFESSIONAL EXPERIENCE

BLK PR, *Account Executive,* Los Angeles, CA — August 2023–Present
- Draft communication materials, including press releases, media alerts, and communication plans for 6 VIP client accounts.
- Communicate with talent accounts and their teams to stay informed of clients' latest initiatives and proactively identify concerns; update media contacts to enhance press coverage and brand awareness.
- Build strong relationships with top-tier media outlets and coordinate event coverage; secure product launch placements by sharing engaging articles and creating marketing content.
- Drive the creative brainstorming process, developing unique story angles and pitches to achieve client goals and build brand recognition.

Walt Disney Studios, Public Relations Assistant, Burbank, CA — September 2020–July 2023
- Created weekly social media and press coverage reports, analyzed results to adjust PR strategies, and organized meetings with global press to promote TV and film releases.
- Supported screening events, facilitating coverage, maintaining guest lists, and sourcing vendors for décor and catering.
- Researched and identified 50+ brand partnership and influencer collaborations, increasing brand mentions by 25%.

Pixar Animation Studios, *Public Relations Intern,* Orlando, FL — June 2019–August 2019
- Collaborated with PR team to plan 4 events, write press releases, and prepare media kits for brand partners.
- Conducted market analysis and industry research to develop and present a new social media strategy to 4 executives.
- Attended marketing meetings to provide input on creative social media content strategies to improve awareness for an upcoming movie release targeting Gen Z.

Publicis Groupe, *Communications Intern,* New York, NY — June 2018–August 2018
- Prepared Media Summary reports to track competitors, social media engagement, and marketing campaign metrics.
- Launched 10 social media campaigns for food and beverage clients, generating 1MM+ impressions on Instagram.
- Expanded internal media contact database by 20% to drive broader outreach.

Pastabilities, *Social Media Manager,* Syracuse, NY — September 2017–June 2019
- Developed and executed social media plan to increase followers on Instagram and TikTok and collaborated with influencers to launch hashtag campaign to drive brand awareness.

EDUCATION

Syracuse University, *Bachelor of Science,* May 2020
S.I. Newhouse School of Public Communications, Major: Public Relations, Minor: Fashion Design, **GPA: 3.9/4.0**
Dean's List 5 semesters, Invest in Success Scholars
Semester Abroad Program: CIEE BARCELONA, Spring 2019

LEADERSHIP EXPERIENCE:

Zeta Phi Eta – Secretary; Syracuse NY — January 2017–May 2020
The Daily Orange – Head of PR, Syracuse, NY — September 2016–May 2020
Syracuse University – Social Media Manager, Marketing Department — September 2019–December 2019

SKILLS & INTERESTS

Technical Skills: Skilled in Microsoft Office Suite (Word, Excel, PowerPoint); Adobe Creative Suite (Photoshop, InDesign, Illustrator)
Social Media Skills: Proficient in Instagram, Facebook, Twitter, YouTube, and TikTok
Interests: Fashion, Beauty and Wellness, Travel, Content Creation, Brand Storytelling

OLIVIA SMITH

Executive at BLK PR | Entertainment Public Relations Specialist | Strategic Brand Partnerships

About

I am a high-energy Public Relations Account Executive with in-house and agency experience managing VIP talent and entertainment client accounts. I am an excellent communicator with a proven track record of building strong media relations and client partnerships. I am skilled in developing communication materials, pitching stories, writing press releases, managing events, creating press and influencer kits, and researching strategic brand partnerships to drive brand growth and awareness.

Experience

BLK PR, Account Executive; Los Angeles, CA; August 2023–Present
• Manage six VIP client accounts by communicating regularly with teams to stay informed of latest initiatives, prepare press releases and communication plans, and secure media coverage.
• Drive brainstorming process to develop creative narratives that exceed clients' brand goals.

Walt Disney Studios, Public Relations Assistant; Burbank, CA; September 2020–July 2023
• Conducted market research to identify influencer and brand collaboration opportunities.
• Assisted with screening events and created media coverage reports to track press mentions and social media.
• Organized meetings with key global press outlets to promote TV and film releases.

Pixar Animation Studios, Public Relations Intern; Orlando, FL; June 2019–August 2019
• Supported PR team in planning four marketing events, writing press releases, preparing media kits, and monitoring event media coverage by creating press clippings.

Publicis Groupe, Communications Intern; New York, NY; June 2018–August 2018
• Assisted with managing six client accounts by attending weekly meetings, preparing reports to track social media and marketing strategies, and launching ten social media campaigns.

Pastabilities, Social Media Manager; Syracuse, NY; September 2017–June 2019
• Developed and executed social media plan to increase followers on Instagram and TikTok and collaborated with influencers to launch hashtag campaign to drive brand awareness.

Education

Syracuse University, Degree – Bachelor of Science, Field of Study – Public Relations/Image Management, Start Date – August 2017, End Date – May 2020

Activities and Societies: Zeta Phi Eta, The Daily Orange, Whitman School of Management Marketing Department Social Media Manager

Skills & Endorsements

Public Relations, Press Releases, Social Media, Communications, Organization Skills, Interpersonal Communication, Teamwork, Marketing, Digital Marketing, Content Marketing, Writing, Content Strategy, Microsoft Word, Microsoft PowerPoint

Lorem ipsum dolor sit amet, consectet adipiscing elit

Lorem ipsum dolor sit amet, consectet adipiscing elit

Lorem ipsum dolor sit amet:

Name Surname
Lorem ipsum dolor sit amet

Name Surname
Lorem ipsum dolor sit amet, consec adipiscing elit

Name Surname
Lorem ipsum dolor

Lorem ipsum dolor sit amet, consectet

Lorem ipsum dolor
Lorem: 12 875

Lorem ipsum
Lorem: 7 612

Lorem ipsum dolor consectetur adipisc
Lorem: 55 211

JOHN MICHAELS
COVER LETTER

JOHN MICHAELS

East 72 Street, New York, NY 10021 | johnmichaels@gmail.com | 456-123-7890

Dear Hiring Manager,

As a Dietician for East Side Nutrition and Wellness, I use my expertise in sports nutrition and disordered eating to create personalized meal plans. I guide clients toward better health, mental well-being, and athletic performance. Working for Insert Company Name would enable me to expand this impactful work on a national scale.

Disordered Eating Experience - During my Dietetics internship at New York Presbyterian Hospital, I assisted Dr. John Johnson with clinical research relating to adolescent healthy diet and exercise habits for those with disordered eating. The study focused on using a positive, mindful approach to reframe thinking about food as fuel. I applied these insights to develop and lead a program for adolescents with disordered eating, conducting four weekly group therapy sessions on nutrition and reframing techniques. The program has grown to 50+ participants since its inception.

Sports Nutrition Connoisseur - Before earning my Master of Science in Nutrition and Dietetics, I worked as a Sports Nutritionist for the New York Giants, collaborating with the team's medical and nutrition staff. I developed customized programs to enhance muscle recovery and athletic performance, and I monitored the plan's progress to make necessary adjustments. This experience honed my skills in communicating complex food science principles and providing effective nutritional counseling.

Patient-First Mindset - Working in the New York hospital system expanded my nutritional training and patient care, exposing me to diverse patients with varied dietary needs. Providing quality patient care across geriatrics, pediatrics, and oncology has broadened my knowledge of nutrition plans, supplements, and targeted techniques for specific health concerns.

Thank you for your time and consideration. I am excited about the prospect of working for Insert Company Name. If you have any questions about my résumé, please do not hesitate to contact me at (456)-123-7890 or johnmichaels@gmail.com. I look forward to scheduling an interview with your team soon.

Sincerely,

John Michaels

JOHN MICHAELS, CNSC, CDN, RD

New York, NY | johnmichaels@gmail.com | 456-123-7890 | LinkedIn

PROFESSIONAL EXPERIENCE

East Side Nutrition and Wellness, New York, NY

Dietician   2022–Present

- Assess patients' nutrition needs and food patterns to develop customized meal plans, grocery lists, and educate on healthy nutrition practices to achieve health goals.
- Partner with clients to identify gaps in their eating plans and create actionable steps for improvement, specializing in sports nutrition and disordered eating.
- Develop and implement food services and nutrition counseling programs for adolescents with disordered eating to foster positive relationships with food, leading 4 cohorts annually.
- Conduct initial client intakes through in-person and telehealth meetings, expanding the practice's client base by 25% by offering evening virtual appointments.

NYU Langone Health, New York, NY

Clinical Dietician   2020–2022

- Provided quality patient care in intensive care and general medical, surgical, and pediatric units through nutrition screening, counseling, metabolic monitoring, and medical team communication.
- Assisted clinical director with staff scheduling for 20 nutrition professionals and developed educational material for nutrition staff.
- Served as Diet and Nutrition Committee member, attending meetings with the medical board and assuring compliance with state regulations.
- Communicated with health-care team members, including nurses and physicians, to ensure patients received optimal care and executed diet changes in partnership with food services team.

New York Presbyterian Hospital, New York, NY

Dietetics Intern   2018–2019

- Selected to participate in highly selective 16-person internship program, rotating through various units at 8 greater New York hospitals to learn, practice, and assume responsibilities of entry-level dietician.
- Helped counsel patients and families on nutritional principles, dietary plans, food selection, and preparation to improve quality of life.
- Planned and implemented nutritional care plans and evaluated effectiveness for adult nutritional support, GI, behavioral health, oncology, geriatrics, diabetes, cardiology, and general medicine.
- Assisted Dr. John Johnson with clinical research on applying adolescent healthy diet and exercise habits for those with disordered eating.

New York Giants, East Rutherford, NJ

Sports Nutritionist   2016–2018

- Designed customized diet plans for professional athletes to improve stamina and muscle recovery post-workout, monitoring body composition and metrics to make necessary adjustments.
- Provided counseling on proper supplementation and explained metabolic processes to increase athletes' understanding of optimal foods for specific activities.
- Arranged food services and developed travel menus, coordinating delivery logistics with caterers, hotels, and airlines to consistently meet players' dietary needs.

Assistant Sports Nutritionist   2014–2015
- Collaborated with doctors, nutritionists, and athletic trainers to provide comprehensive nutrition services to professional football players to optimize overall health, athletic goals, and training phases.
- Supported assessment and analysis of nutrition, body composition, and dietary intake to identify nutrition needs and build individualized programs.
- Conducted assessment and analysis of nutrition, body composition, and dietary intake to build individualized programs based on identified needs.

Sports Nutritionist Intern   2013

COMMUNITY INVOLVEMENT
New York University Nutrition Graduate Society, *President*; New York, NY   2018–2020
- Organized monthly guest speaker series to provide networking, career, and research opportunities for clinical nutrition program graduate students.
- Secured Jane Doe, renowned nutritionist at Mount Sinai Medical Center, to speak to members on private versus clinical practice career paths.

New York University Food Studies Graduate Society, *Member*; New York, NY   2019–2020
- Participated in monthly programs (food preparation workshops, farm tours, career panels) to expand cultural food knowledge and sourcing practices.

Cornell University Fitness Centers, *Personal Trainer*; Ithaca, NY   2011–2013
- Evaluated 3 students' fitness levels, personal goals, and athletic skills; conducted weekly 1:1 training sessions to monitor progress and ensure proper use of exercise equipment.

EDUCATION
New York University, New York, NY
Master of Science in Nutrition and Dietetics, Concentration: Clinical Nutrition, May 2020

Cornell University, Ithaca, NY
Bachelor of Science in Nutritional Science, Minor: Applied Exercise, May 2014

CERTIFICATIONS & LICENSES
Certified Nutrition Support Clinician, *New York University*, May 2020
Certified Dietitian Nutritionist, *New York State*, May 2020
Registered Dietician, *Accreditation Council for Education in Nutrition and Dietetics*, January 2017
Premium Health Coach, *American Council on Exercise*, March 2015

MEMBERSHIPS & PROFESSIONAL ORGANIZATIONS
Sports, Cardio, Wellness Nutrition DPG, August 2023–Present
American Dietetic Association, January 2022–Present
Greater New York Dietetic Association, September 2021–Present

SKILLS & INTERESTS
Technical Skills: Proficient in Microsoft Office Suite, NutriAdmin, Carepatron, Nutrition Maker, TheraPlatform
Interests: Football (NYU Flag Football team member), Weightlifting, Cooking, Kinesiology, Food Science

JOHN MICHAELS

Registered Dietician | Clinical Dietician | Certified Nutrition Support Clinician | Certified Dietician Nutritionist | Health Coach

About

As a sports fanatic and wellness-obsessed dietician, I offer a unique approach to assessing clients' nutritional needs and food patterns, setting healthy lifestyle goals to optimize performance and mental well-being. With advanced nutrition education and dietetics certifications, I specialize in providing personalized care in sports nutrition and disordered eating for adolescents and adults. My clinical experience with diverse patients enables me to deliver optimal care, develop customized meal plans, and execute diet changes, providing a holistic approach to diet planning and patient education.

Experience

East Side Nutrition and Wellness, Dietician; New York, NY; July 2022–Present
• Assess nutrition needs and food patterns of patients, develop customized meal plans and steps to improve health, and specialize in sports nutrition and disordered eating.
• Lead food services and nutrition counseling programs for adolescents with disordered eating to foster positive relationship with food.

NYU Langone Health, Clinical Dietician; New York, NY; September 2020–July 2022
• Provided quality patient care to patients admitted to intensive care, general medical, surgical, and pediatric units through nutrition screening, support, counseling, metabolic monitoring, and medical team communication.
• Helped clinical director with staff scheduling, developed educational material for nutrition staff, and served as member of Diet and Nutrition Committee.

New York Presbyterian Hospital, Dietetics Intern; New York, NY; May 2018–August 2019
• Helped counsel patients and their families on nutritional principles, dietary plans, diet modifications, food selection, and preparation to improve their quality of life.
• Participated in a selective rotational program across eight New York hospitals.

New York Giants, East Rutherford, NJ
Sports Nutritionist, 2016–2018
• Designed customized diet plans for professional athletes targeting stamina and muscle recovery post-workout and monitored body composition and metrics throughout the season to make necessary adjustments by providing counseling for proper supplements and arranging travel menus.

Assistant Sports Nutritionist, 2014–2015

Sports Nutritionist Intern, 2013

Education

New York University, Degree – Master of Science, Field of Study – Dietetics and Clinical Nutrition Services, Start Date – August 2018, End Date – May 2020
• Activities and societies: New York University Nutrition Graduate Society, New York University Food Studies Graduate Society

Cornell University, Degree – Bachelor of Science, Field of Study – Nutrition Sciences, Start Date – August 2010, End Date – May 2014
• Activities and societies: Cornell University Fitness Centers Personal Trainer

Licenses and certifications

Certified Nutrition Support Clinician, Issuing Organization – *New York University*, Issue Date – May 2020
Certified Dietitian Nutritionist, Issuing Organization – *New York State*, Issue Date – May 2020
Registered Dietician, Issuing Organization – *Accreditation Council for Education in Nutrition and Dietetics*, Issue Date – January 2017
Premium Health Coach, Issuing Organization – *American Council on Exercise*, Issue Date – March 2015

Skills & Endorsements

Nutrition, Nutritional Counseling, Sports Nutrition, Nutrition Education, Clinical Nutrition, Exercise Planning, Dietetics, Public Speaking, Clinical Research, Food Science, Meal Planning, Microsoft Excel, Microsoft PowerPoint

Note: *It's not necessary to list descriptions for Assistant Sports Nutritionist and Internship positions since they were 10 years ago; can pull from most senior role with the company.*

- Highlights substantial hands-on experience in machine learning through internships at prestigious companies like Microsoft and Adobe, demonstrating a mix of technical and interpersonal skills.

- Her role as the technical lead in Code the Change demonstrates her leadership, team management, and effective problem-solving skills, crucial for technical roles.

MACY KELLY
COVER LETTER

MACY KELLY

Appletree Lane, Atlanta, GA 30002 | macykelly@gmail.com | 456-789-1230

Dear Recruitment Director,

I am very interested in working for Insert Company Name as a(n) Insert Role. I am a senior at the University of Southern California and am on track to graduate in May 2024 with a Bachelor of Science degree in Computer Engineering and Computer Science. My machine learning experience, paired with my programming capabilities, understanding of IT infrastructure, and communication skills, make me an ideal candidate for this position.

Machine Learning Experience – My internships at Microsoft and Adobe focused on supporting engineering and product development teams in building machine learning models and conducting statistical modeling and analytic tests to improve machine performance. I used several programming languages to analyze large data sets, identify trends, and pinpoint discrepancies for model updates. At Microsoft, I improved model accuracy by 15% within three months. These experiences have deepened my interest in artificial intelligence research, natural language processing, and machine learning.

Problem-Solving Programmer – I'm active in Code the Change, a service-driven organization that develops technology solutions for nonprofits. My peers chose me as the technical lead, where I oversee five developers and handle roadblocks, programming inquiries, and debugging exercises. To launch a nonprofit's website before a major fundraising event, I used Agile to assign tasks and allocated time to perform website testing to meet the tight deadline. My focus on organization, proactive problem-solving, and prioritizing the client's goal to increase user engagement led to the successful website launch with optimized performance and modern design principles.

Verbal and Written Communication Skills – In addition to my computer science extracurriculars and schoolwork, I work part-time as an IT Support Specialist for USC Centers and Institutes, assisting students and faculty with IT support. I start by understanding the user's problem and clearly explain the steps required to resolve it. This transparency helps users appreciate the time it takes to resolve the problem. My collaborative communication style has resulted in positive customer experience and receiving the Employee of the Semester award in Spring 2023.

I'm very interested in working for Insert Company Name as a(n) Insert Role and believe that my experiences and strengths make me a great candidate for the role. I look forward to hearing from you to schedule an interview. If you have any questions about my résumé, please do not hesitate to contact me at (456)-789-1230 or macykelly@gmail.com. Thank you for your time and consideration.

Sincerely,

Macy Kelly

MACY KELLY
RÉSUMÉ

MACY KELLY

Atlanta, GA | 456-789-1230 | macykelly@gmail.com | LinkedIn

EDUCATION

University of Southern California, **Bachelor of Science**, May 2024
Computer Engineering and Computer Science
GPA: 3.9, *Dean's List, 5 semesters*

PROFESSIONAL EXPERIENCE

USC Centers and Institutes, *IT Support Specialist*; Los Angeles, CA — February 2022–Present
- Provide IT support by troubleshooting hardware and software malfunctions for university students and faculty in person and via remote access; deliver exceptional customer support by resolving 90% of IT issues within 1 hour.
- Assist with setup and configuration of computers, printers, and other IT equipment in classrooms and labs throughout campus and perform routine computer software/hardware upgrades.
- Document ticket requests and diagnostic tests in internal database to track process compliance and maintain records.

Microsoft Corporation, *Research Intern*; Redmond, WA — June 2023–August 2023
- Collaborated with research and product development teams to develop original research agendas exploring machine learning (ML), reinforcement learning (RL), and natural language processing (NLP).
- Developed and implemented machine learning models using Python and TensorFlow to analyze big datasets and identified key insights, which resulted in improving accurate model outputs by 15% compared to existing model.
- Helped advance current artificial intelligence programs by performing sentiment analysis, named entity recognition, and supported programmers with testing and debugging code.

Adobe Inc., *Machine Learning Engineering Intern*; New York, NY — June 2022–August 2022
- Built and implemented machine learning models to enhance image recognition capabilities within Adobe Creative Cloud products by collaborating with product management and engineering teams.
- Designed predictive models on large-scale datasets and conducted performance analysis to improve model accuracy and efficiency, leading to a 20% reduction in inference time.
- Applied statistical modeling, machine learning, and analysis techniques to develop product recommendations to enhance customer understanding and support business growth.

EXTRACURRICULAR EXPERIENCE & VOLUNTEERING

Association for Computing Machinery – *Events Coordinator*; Los Angeles, CA — September 2022–Present
- Develop a mentorship program that pairs engineering faculty with students, with 30+ participants per year.
- Organize 2 events per semester to foster relationships and mutual learning, achieving a 70% retention rate among first-year participants.
- Organize 5 introductory coding workshops, each attracting 50+ students.

Code the Change – *Technical Lead*; Los Angeles, CA — September 2023–Present
- Lead 5 student developers through 3 programming 501(c)(3) organizations' technology solutions.
- Build dynamic platforms leveraging HTML, CSS, and JavaScript to facilitate seamless interaction between users and nonprofit.
- Redesigned company's website using modern design principles and optimized performance through agile methodologies, resulting in 110% increase in user engagement and time spent on site.

Association for Women in Computing – *Active Member*, Los Angeles, CA — January 2022–Present

SKILLS, AWARD & INTERESTS

Technical Skills: Advanced Knowledge of Microsoft Office Suite. Python, Java, JavaScript, TensorFlow, scikit-learn, C/C++, SQL, NoSQL
Award: Girls Who Code Summer Immersion Program, Hackathon competition 1st place of 75 teams, June 2021
Interests: Rowing, Reading (read 30 books in 2023), Nature, Coding, Database Building

MACY KELLY

LINKEDIN

MACY KELLY

Computer Engineering Student | Machine Learning Intern | AI Researcher | IT Support Specialist

About

I am a driven computer science student passionate about problem-solving and collaborating with others to advance modern technology and artificial intelligence tools. I have experience interning for multinational computer technology and software companies and have a proven ability to apply programming knowledge to help nonprofit businesses as a Technical Lead for Code the Change. I am seeking internships for Summer 2024 in the machine learning industry to continue developing my research skills and enhancing existing models.

Experience

USC Centers and Institutes, IT Support Specialist; Los Angeles, CA; February 2022–Present
• Provide IT support by troubleshooting hardware and software malfunctions for university students and faculty in person and via remote access.
• Assist with setup and configuration of computers, printers, and other IT equipment in classrooms and labs throughout campus and perform routine computer software and hardware upgrades throughout the semester.

Microsoft Corporation, Research Intern; Redmond, WA; June 2023–August 2023
• Collaborated with research and product development teams to develop original research agendas, implement machine learning models, and analyze big datasets to advance current machine learning (ML), reinforcement learning (RL), and natural language processing (NLP) programs.

Adobe Inc., Machine Learning Engineering Intern; New York, NY; June 2022–August 2022
• Built and implemented machine learning models to enhance product features, designed predictive models on large-scale datasets, and conducted performance analysis to improve accuracy and efficiency.

Code the Change, Los Angeles, CA
Technical Lead; September 2023–Present
• Lead five student developers through developing three 501(c)(3) organizations' technology solutions leveraging HTML, CSS, and JavaScript.

Developer; September 2021–May 2023
• Redesigned company's website using modern design principles and optimized performance through agile methodologies to increase user engagement.

Education

University of Southern California, Degree – Bachelor of Science, Field of Study – Computer Engineering, Start Date – August 2020, End Date – May 2024
Activities and Societies: Association for Computing Machinery, Association for Women in Computing

Skills & Endorsements

Programming, Python, JavaScript, SQL, Agile Methodologies, IT Operations, Technical Support, Machine Learning, Artificial Intelligence (AI), Generative AI, Problem-Solving, Communications, Teamwork, Microsoft Excel, Microsoft Word, Microsoft PowerPoint

Lorem ipsum dolor sit amet, consectetur adipiscing elit

Lorem ipsum dolor sit amet, consectetur adipiscing elit

Lorem ipsum dolor sit amet:

Name Surname
Lorem ipsum dolor sit amet

Name Surname
Lorem ipsum dolor sit amet, consectetur adipiscing elit

Name Surname
Lorem ipsum dolor

Lorem ipsum dolor sit amet, consectetur adipisc

Lorem ipsum dolor sit amet
Lorem: 12 875

Lorem ipsum
Lorem: 7 612

Lorem ipsum dolor sit amet, consectetur adipiscing elit
Lorem: 55 211

Overcome Résumé Obstacles

Overqualification: Surprisingly, employers may reject you for being *overqualified*. This can be the case even if you have just two more years of experience than required in the job posting. Why? They expect your salary would exceed their budget, or else fear you'd grow bored of the role relatively quickly and resign. So, how should you position yourself for a role you're overqualified for but still want to pursue? Ensure your résumé highlights relevant experience rather than your most impressive accomplishments. Also, it's okay to acknowledge that your experience is beyond what's required — just make sure to emphasize genuine interest and commitment, too.

Employment gaps: Years — or even months — on your résumé with no employment and no explanation are a red flag to recruiters. If there are gaps, make sure to explain them honestly and confidently. It's okay to share that you were caring for your family or earning those final credits for a degree. You should also include any smaller projects you worked on during those periods, like freelance work, volunteering, or consulting.

ATS-FRIENDLY RÉSUMÉ CHECKLIST

Don't know what "ATS" stands for? If you're applying for jobs, you should! ATS stands for applicant tracking system, software that vets cover letters and résumés before they reach the desk of a human recruiter. The ATS meticulously looks for the right keywords and phrases, so be sure to include the right ones. How will you know how? Those same keywords appear in the job posting. Here's a checklist to make sure you're giving the ATS what it's looking for:

- Use the same job title as in the job posting.
- Include your location/city.
- Use bullet points.
- Avoid pie charts, graphs, and other visuals that the ATS may not be able to read.
- Use ATS checker tools such as Jobscan to confirm your résumé's alignment with industry jargon, keywords, and other norms.
- Seek balance. Avoid over-optimizing, since the ATS may view this as spammy.

THANK-YOU LETTER

Dear Ms./Mrs. xxx:

I enjoyed meeting with you earlier today and appreciate your time and insights regarding the Financial Manager position. Our conversation reinforced my desire to join Company ABC, especially given its focus on innovation and client-centric solutions. Your commitment to staying ahead of industry trends aligns well with my financial analysis and strategic planning background. I'm excited to apply my expertise to deliver exceptional service to your clients and drive growth.

The company's collaborative environment and focus on professional development are exactly what I'm seeking in my next role. With a proven track record of thriving in team settings and a commitment to ongoing learning, I believe I'm a strong fit.

Thank you again for your time and consideration. Please let me know if there's any additional information I can provide. I'm excited about the possibility of joining your team and look forward to the next steps in the hiring process.

Signature
Name
Phone
Email address

Name of Applicant
Address of Applicant
City, State, Zip
LinkedIn address

Before you click "send" on your thank-you letter, run through this checklist:

- ☐ Personalized
- ☐ Enthusiastic
- ☐ Concise
- ☐ Demonstrated interest in the company
- ☐ Grateful
- ☐ Good fit value (include talents, achievements, and long-term goals)
- ☐ Proper grammar/spelling

Remember: Consistently following up during the hiring process demonstrates your diligence, motivation, and strong interest in joining the company.

Email Etiquette

Ensure your note hits the mark:

- Have a clear and simple subject line.
- Determine whether to use a first or last name based on the company culture and the interview's formality.
- If you interviewed with more than one person, send a personalized note to each one or a single email to everyone.

Finish with Grace: Withdraw from other job searches after accepting an offer. If you'd like to remain in consideration for another position or continue interviewing with other companies or organizations, ask for a deadline extension from the employer that has offered you the job. Do not burn any bridges by remaining in a search after you have committed to an employer. That's a no-no! Many people have been involved in your search in various supportive roles; be sure to let them know about your success. Notify your references and anyone else who helped you and thank them for their assistance. Update social media profiles to reflect your new title or position.

BRANDAMENTALS

1 **Craft a powerful narrative.** The story of your career needs to be more than numbers and names — it needs to be a narrative. Use your Uniquely Me Statement, compelling key messaging, and lots of supporting evidence to get it right.

2 **Successful interviews take preparation.** Even the most charismatic applicants can't bluff their way through a job interview. Make sure to do your homework, prepare smart questions, dress sharp, and act confident.

3 **Invest in your application materials.** Your résumé, cover letter, and thank-you notes are key to landing the right job. Make sure they're up-to-date, compelling, and sleekly designed.

4 **Personalize!** Whether it's your cover letter, follow-up emails, or list of interview questions, always customize them for the job and company you're applying for. Recruiters can tell a boilerplate application or email from a mile away.

PART IV – LINKEDIN IS ALL THAT

LinkedIn is an essential resource for job seekers, recruiters, and hiring managers alike. It tops the charts as a career development tool. It's the world's largest professional network, with over 1 billion users in more than 200 countries. It's used for networking, job hunting, industry research, and news. Is it any surprise that LinkedIn gets its very own chapter?

Knowing how to leverage LinkedIn is indispensable for career growth — and a wise investment in your future. After all, your LinkedIn profile is likely the first thing a prospective employer or hiring manager will see. Whether you need to create a LinkedIn profile from scratch or revise your existing one, this chapter will help you make the most of this influential social network.

LinkedIn offers a range of opportunities, from marketing yourself to expanding your network. Here are just 10 incredible benefits:

1. Open doors to new opportunities, including internships, freelance work, and collaborations.
2. Network with professionals in your field, industry experts, and potential mentors.
3. Search for new jobs.
4. Showcase your professional achievements and skills.
5. Follow industry news and trends, like salary information.
6. Connect with potential customers or clients.
7. Join industry-specific groups and discussions.
8. Recruit top talent for your organization.
9. Access vast learning resources.
10. Conduct job market research.

Invest time in keeping your LinkedIn profile polished. Over time, it'll become a comprehensive portfolio, making it easy to showcase the highlights of your career journey.

One way to go to the top of the résumé pile is LinkedIn. Determine if you know someone who works at your target company and see whether or not they would be willing to share your résumé with recruiters. It's important to figure out another door into the company beyond the online application.

**– Elissa Barrett, Former VP
of Human Resources at HubSpot**

LinkedIn by the Numbers:

Why is LinkedIn so essential?

- LinkedIn is a community of 1B+ members, 67M companies, and 134K schools listed.
- 65 million people use LinkedIn to search for jobs each week.
- 28 million people have added #OpentoWork frames to their profiles.
- 140 job applications are submitted every second on the platform.
- Between 87% and 95% of recruiters frequently use LinkedIn.
- There was a 55% year-over-year increase in LinkedIn Premium sign-ups in 2024.
- 48% of hirers on LinkedIn explicitly use skills data to fill their roles.
- Six people are hired on LinkedIn every minute. That's 8,640 people per day.

Degrees of Separation

People in your LinkedIn network are called "connections." Connections can be first-degree, second-degree, and third-degree, and include fellow members of your LinkedIn Groups. People outside this circle may not be able to see or search your profile. You'll see the degree level option next to their name on their profile and in search results.

First-degree Connections are people who have accepted your invitation to connect or vice versa. You can contact these connections directly by sending a message.

Second-degree Connections are people connected to your first-degree connections. Think of them as colleagues of your colleagues. They exist beyond your immediate network, but you can send them an invitation by clicking "Connect."

Third-degree Connections are people connected to your second-degree connections.

LinkedIn caps the number of connections someone can have at 30,000, even for Premium accounts. Beyond this limit, you can't accept new connection requests, but others can still follow you. LinkedIn values quality over quantity and uses "500+" for users with more than 500 connections to discourage competition. If someone has fewer than 500 connections, you'll see the exact number. Connections are mutual agreements, while followers choose to follow you. To see your connections, go to "My Network," visit your profile's "Articles & Activity" section, and check your follower count. Influencers tend to rack up more followers than connections because of the 30,000 limit. And remember, seek depth over breadth in connections.

Get Noticed: Develop a Winning Profile

Your LinkedIn profile is your best chance to make an unforgettable first impression with job recruiters, hiring managers, and others. Ensure your profile is 100 percent complete and presents your most polished and professional image. A mediocre LinkedIn profile simply won't cut it.

First Things First: Customize Your LinkedIn URL

LinkedIn automatically assigns you a clunky URL when you sign up — a random string of letters and numbers that no one can remember. But you can update to a customized URL, like http://www.linkedin.com/in/yourname. If your name has already been snatched up, select a variation. Perhaps use a middle name or initial or add a number. An easy-to-remember URL will significantly boost your LinkedIn game. Share it widely, match it with your social handles, and hyperlink it in your résumé and email signature.

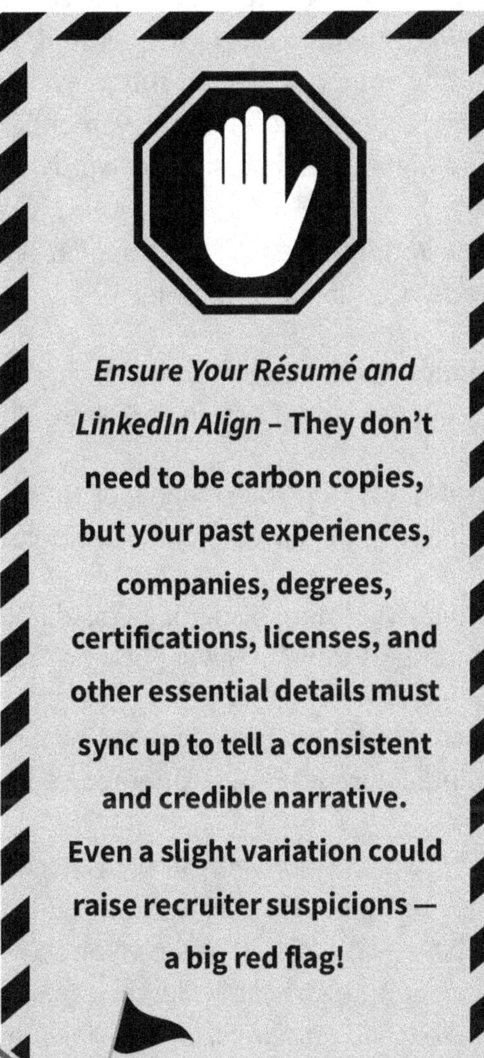

Anatomy of a LinkedIn Profile

Let's tackle your profile section by section:

HEADLINE

This is the first thing people see when they visit your profile, so use it to flaunt your superpower(s). With a 220-character limit, every word counts. Avoid the common mistake of simply stating your job title and company. Instead, treat your headline as a billboard for your unique skills, experiences, and achievements. Check out these stellar examples. (Remember: Your goal is to make sure LinkedIn's keyword optimization feature works in your favor.)

Max Walden: Website Developer at TechWave Solutions I Creating Innovative Solutions with Code I Certified Programmer

Philip Johnson: Horizon University Student I Aspiring Mechanical Engineer I Pursuing Excellence in CAD Design and Thermal Dynamics

Ashley Blank: Project Manager @ BuildRight Construction I Project Coordination I Resource Management I Commercial & Residential I Results-Driven Leader I Certified PMP

Olivia Waldman: Marketing Coordinator, HealthWell Pharma I Digital Marketing I Social Media I Creative Problem-Solver I Google Analytics Certified

Michael Adams: HR Manager, Unity Enterprises I Recruitment & Employee Specialist I Tech & Manufacturing I People-Oriented Leader I SHRM-CP Certified

Avoid generic phrases like "Recent Graduate," "Job Seeker," or "Seeking Employment" in your headline. Meanwhile, leveraging the #OpenToWork green frame on your profile is up for debate — is it a sign of desperation or ambition? While some recruiters I spoke with advised against it, the majority like the transparency it offers and see it as a valuable tool for both job seekers and recruiters. In fact, LinkedIn reports that signaling your job search can boost profile views by up to 40 percent. What's better, you can control who sees it by clicking "Recruiters only," ensuring discretion with your current employer. To activate this feature, click the blue circle under your headline, select "Open to finding a new job," and customize your selection with job titles, locations, and more.

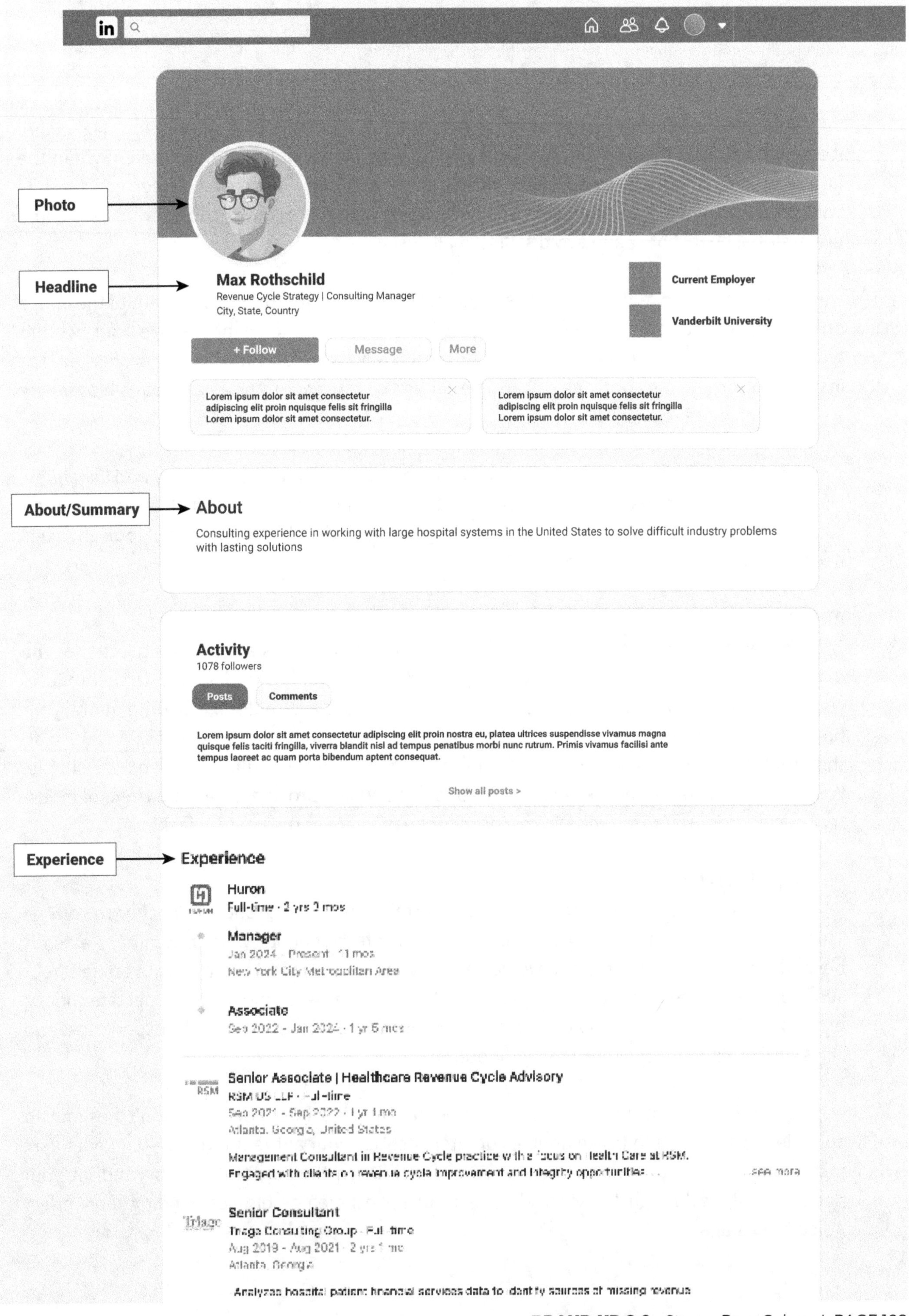

Photo
Headline
About/Summary
Experience

Max Rothschild
Revenue Cycle Strategy | Consulting Manager
City, State, Country

+ Follow
Message
More

Current Employer
Vanderbilt University

Lorem ipsum dolor sit amet consectetur adipiscing elit proin nquisque felis sit fringilla Lorem ipsum dolor sit amet consectetur.
Lorem ipsum dolor sit amet consectetur adipiscing elit proin nquisque felis sit fringilla Lorem ipsum dolor sit amet consectetur.

About
Consulting experience in working with large hospital systems in the United States to solve difficult industry problems with lasting solutions

Activity
1078 followers

Posts
Comments

Lorem ipsum dolor sit amet consectetur adipiscing elit proin nostra eu, platea ultrices suspendisse vivamus magna quisque felis taciti fringilla, viverra blandit nisl ad tempus penatibus morbi nunc rutrum. Primis vivamus facilisi ante tempus laoreet ac quam porta bibendum aptent consequat.

Show all posts >

Experience

Huron
Full-time · 2 yrs 3 mos

Manager
Jan 2024 - Present · 1 mos
New York City Metropolitan Area

Associate
Sep 2022 - Jan 2024 · 1 yr 5 mos

Senior Associate | Healthcare Revenue Cycle Advisory
RSM US LLP · Full-time
Sep 2021 - Sep 2022 · 1 yr 1 mo
Atlanta, Georgia, United States

Management Consultant in Revenue Cycle practice with a focus on Health Care at RSM.
Engaged with clients on revenue cycle improvement and integrity opportunities...
see more

Senior Consultant
Triage Consulting Group · Full-time
Aug 2019 - Aug 2021 · 2 yrs 1 mo
Atlanta, Georgia

Analyzes hospital patient financial services data to identify sources of missing revenue

PHOTO

Your profile photo plays a crucial role in making a positive first impression. Make sure it's a high-resolution headshot (400 x 400 pixels) with a neutral background taken within the last three years. It should also align with your professional image and career goals. While your phone's camera can produce a quality picture, you may want to consider investing in a professional headshot — and avoid selfies at all costs!

According to LinkedIn's guidelines, your face should occupy about 60 percent of the image once cropped. Crop the image from the top of your shoulders to slightly above your head to ensure your face takes center stage. Dress appropriately based on your specific profession. For instance, attorneys may opt for a suit and tie, whereas graphic designers can wear a blazer over a t-shirt for a more relaxed vibe.

To smile or not to smile? My vote is *smile*! It enhances your approachability and likeability. However, a more serious image might be in order for some professions — such as astrophysics. Lastly, don't forget to update your photo when your hairstyle, glasses, or overall look changes. Keep it fresh, current, and authentically you.

PROFILE BANNER

The blank banner above your profile picture is prime real estate, so don't settle for the default dull, gray box. Instead, choose a captivating banner or background photo that reflects your expertise and boosts your personal brand. The options are endless: a favorite quote, your proudest achievements, or even your contact details. You don't have to be a design whiz to do this. Tools like Canva make creating a polished banner with the required dimensions simple. You can also use platforms like Pexels and Unsplash, which provide a treasure trove of industry-specific stock photos: think stethoscopes for health care or runways for fashion.

ABOUT/SUMMARY

Your LinkedIn summary needs to answer the million-dollar question: ***Why choose you?*** Think of it as a canvas for painting your unique professional story. Your summary extends beyond the limits of a résumé or cover letter, allowing you to reveal more about yourself. Your summary should be tailored to your target audience — future employers, prospective clients, professionals, recruiters — and the job you're aiming for. Consider the specific experiences and skills your audience is seeking in a candidate.

Speak in the first person, just as you would in a job interview, and don't hesitate to sprinkle in personal tidbits like hobbies or interests. Use your authentic voice — LinkedIn isn't just about titles and achievements; it's about *you*. Ditch the corporate jargon and let your personality shine through. Use vivid adjectives and make it memorable (see "Finding Your Perfect Adjectives," page 32).

How should your summary flow? Here's a checklist for how best to structure it:

✔ Provide a brief introduction highlighting your professional identity and emphasize your value. For example: "I'm a marketing strategist with a track record of data-driven campaigns that fuel engagement and brand growth."

✔ Next, share your key skills, experiences, and achievements in paragraph form or a bulleted list (or alternate between those two formats).

✔ Finally, for a personal touch, use the remainder of your summary to delve into your professional aspirations and passions, revealing what drives and motivates you in your career.

For instance: "I'm dedicated to advancing health care through innovative solutions, driven by a deep passion to enhance patient care and well-being."

Even if you follow this structure, there are infinite ways to write your summary. And remember, this isn't the space for an exhaustive list — you'll have a chance to do that in the Experience section. Keep in mind that there is a 2,600-character limit for this section.

FEATURED SECTION (optional add-on)

This lesser-known gem below the About section lets you showcase media like blog posts, articles, and external links that make your profile more engaging and interactive. To access it, click "Add profile section" on your LinkedIn, then select "Featured" from the dropdown menu. Use this section to give visitors a quick snapshot of your work. Here's a sampling of what you might include: your résumé, videos you've produced or appeared in, articles about you, blog posts by you, relevant case studies, whitepapers, and links to relevant webinars, events, or podcasts. (Note: You can also add links, images, videos, and files to your Experience section.)

EXPERIENCE

The Experience section goes deeper than the About section — but beware of excessive details, a common mistake among job seekers. Keep it concise, crisp, and meaningful. Include your employment history, eliminate employment gaps, and quantify achievements with bullet points whenever possible. Because what's more impressive: claiming "deep knowledge of social media platforms," or boasting about "increasing social engagement by 40%"? Let's look at two examples:

Sales Manager
- Increased quarterly sales by 20% through targeted client outreach.
- Expanded the customer base by 15%, resulting in a revenue boost of $750,000.

Software Developer:
- Developed a new feature that reduced application loading times by 40%, enhancing user satisfaction.
- Resolved 100+ software bugs, leading to a 20% decrease in customer support requests.

If you lack relevant work experience, don't worry! You can highlight similar projects and volunteer work in your Experience section (and also in the dedicated Volunteering and Education sections further down on your profile).

Always focus on the skills and experiences most relevant to your target industry. Emphasize the aspects of your past that most align with your desired job, and, if needed, tailor your résumé for each job application.

Be sure to leave room for less relevant skills further down. While younger job seekers often worry about including unrelated roles — like past work in retail when pursuing engineering careers — it's advantageous. It showcases adaptability, work ethic, and valuable transferable skills. Hiring managers are like detectives, eager to connect the dots between your past experiences and the role you're applying for. Embrace your unique journey, and don't hesitate to explain any gaps in your work history, whether due to education, family, or other reasons, as it adds depth and personality to your professional story.

LICENSES & CERTIFICATIONS

Whether you hold professional licenses, specialized certifications, or industry-specific badges, this section showcases your commitment to continued learning and staying at the forefront of your field. For those concerned about limited work experience, spotlighting your certifications and licenses can set you apart and impress employers. It's important to also include certifications in your header, as many careers require them.

I'm a big fan of certifications as they boost confidence, trust, autonomy, and career prospects, especially in technology. Python certification is highly advantageous due to its widespread use in tech and at top companies like Google. While certificates validate proficiency and differentiate job applicants, real-world experience no doubt leads the way.

EDUCATION

This is where you paint a vivid picture of your academic journey. Start by listing the name of your educational institution(s), followed by your degree and major or field of study. Include the dates you attended or the anticipated graduation date. If you've received academic honors, scholarships, or awards, include them. You can also spotlight relevant extracurricular activities. Include your GPA (if it's impressive), as well as a brief description connecting your education to your career goals.

PROJECTS

In this section, spotlight your most impressive projects. Begin with an attention-grabbing project title and specify the project's duration. Craft a concise yet comprehensive project description, stressing the objectives, your role, and quantifiable results. Call attention to the skills and tools you utilized, emphasizing your expertise. If you collaborated with a team, give credit where credit is due and detail your specific role. Don't forget visuals for that extra wow factor.

VOLUNTEERING

Hiring managers and recruiters appreciate job applicants who demonstrate a commitment to their community. Many studies show that people who list volunteer experience on their LinkedIn profiles are more likely to get hired than those who don't. This section is an opportunity to demonstrate your skills and capacity for giving back. Start by introducing the organization where you volunteered, detailing your contributions and volunteering experience.

SKILLS AND ENDORSEMENTS

You can manage skills and endorsements in your profile's Skills section. Adding specific skills to your LinkedIn profile strengthens your profile and increases visibility for relevant opportunities. Endorsements build trust and credibility, similar to Amazon product reviews, validating your skills and making you more attractive to employers and collaborators.

Seek endorsements from colleagues, classmates, and past supervisors to validate your skill set. Focus on career objectives and select the most relevant skills to share. While you can list up to 100 skills, viewers can only see your top three, so choose strategically. Starting with 15 key skills is sufficient, as adding too many skills typically leads to fewer endorsements for each one. Endorsements require less effort than LinkedIn recommendations, which offer deeper insights into your strengths. Note that only first-level connections can endorse you. And don't forget to pay it forward and give endorsements yourself!

Reorder and pin your top skills on your LinkedIn profile to manage how they appear in the skills and endorsements section. By clicking the edit button, you can prioritize skills to better align with your professional narrative and highlight your specialties. It's a smart move to pin skills on your LinkedIn profile that include your keywords, as this reinforces your specialty to LinkedIn's algorithms.

RECOMMENDATIONS

Similar to skills and endorsements, LinkedIn recommendations demonstrate that your coworkers and peers value your contributions. They're like mini reference checks for potential employers, validating that you are the talented professional you claim to be. To request recommendations, scroll down to the Recommendations section located below the Skills & Endorsements section. Next, click on "Ask for a recommendation" and enter the person's name, your work relationship, and your position during the collaboration. Craft a warm, personalized message encouraging them to write a recommendation for you and provide guidance on what they should focus on.

For example, your recommendation request might look like this:

"Hi [Name], I hope all is well! I'm reaching out to ask for a LinkedIn recommendation to highlight my [specific] skills. I'm particularly proud of our work on [project name], and your insights would mean the world to me. I'd appreciate it if you write a brief recommendation that highlights our collaboration and the results achieved. And, of course, I'm happy to return the favor by writing a recommendation for you."

The most impactful recommendations often come from those who have seen your work up close and personal, such as direct managers or clients. Request new recommendations at least twice a year to ensure your profile reflects your current professional standing.

PUBLICATIONS

This section of your LinkedIn profile is for proudly displaying articles, research papers, books, or other publications that you've authored or co-authored. Share the title, a concise summary, and a link (if it's available online). This is your chance to showcase your subject matter expertise in your field.

INTERESTS

The Interests section displays top voices, companies, schools, newsletters, and groups you follow or subscribe to, highlighting your professional passions. Curate this section carefully, following industry thought leaders, subscribing to informative newsletters, and joining relevant groups. This keeps you informed and highlights your dedication to ongoing learning.

THE FINISH LINE

Completing your LinkedIn profile is about more than checking boxes; it's a strategic undertaking that influences career success. Not only will you stand out among the sea of profiles, but you will also increase your chances of appearing in search results. LinkedIn's algorithm prioritizes users with "All-Star" status (100 percent profile completion), ultimately making you 40 times more likely to appear in searches. You can see your completion status in the bar across the top of your LinkedIn profile.

While you're at it, pay attention to these often-overlooked details that can enrich your profile:

Former Name: If applicable, consider listing a former name, such as a nickname or maiden name, to increase your searchability.

Name Pronunciation: If your name is long or challenging to pronounce, use this feature to make it easier for others.

Location: Enter a strategic location for visibility, like a nearby metropolitan area instead of a smaller city or suburb. If you plan to relocate, mention your target city in your summary.

Industry: Select the most relevant sector that aligns with your profile, and if your expertise spans multiple industries, highlight them in your summary. This optimizes the discoverability of your LinkedIn profile for recruiters conducting industry-specific searches.

Contact Info: Include your email address so recruiters can reach out. Consider adding it to your profile banner for greater prominence. Avoid sharing personal cell phone numbers to maintain privacy. When it comes to additional social media platforms, only include professional ones related to your career.

A Few Words to Unlock LinkedIn's Search Magic

Want to make your profile a magnet for opportunities?

- LinkedIn's powerful search features allow you to search by keywords, location, past workplaces, hashtags, languages, and more. Combine these filters to create and curate a list of target companies, recruiters, and potential strategic partnerships. Evaluate these profiles, spot the active ones, engage with their content, and join the conversation!

- Embed keywords that define your skills in your LinkedIn profile so recruiters can easily find you. Add them to your Headline and About, Experience, and Skills & Endorsements sections. For example: "Finance professional skilled in **risk management**, f**inancial analysis**, and **portfolio optimization**, committed to delivering **data-driven solutions** to **optimize performance** and **profitability**." Check out profiles and job descriptions in your desired field for inspiration. And stay relevant by regularly updating information and keywords as applicable.

- LinkedIn's collaborative articles are highly recommended for those who want to amplify their professional visibility and reach a wider audience. These AI-powered conversation starters, covering a range of professional topics, are developed with LinkedIn's editorial team and enhanced by member contributions. This feature drives platform traffic, sparks engaging discussions, and helps users build their professional brand. Contributors can earn the prestigious "Top Voice" badge, showcasing their subject matter expertise.

- Companies frequently share job openings on LinkedIn. Be sure to search for job openings by industry, location, keywords, and other criteria. LinkedIn's "Easy Apply" feature streamlines the application process, making it a breeze to send your résumé to multiple job listings.

- LinkedIn profiles rank exceptionally well on Google due to their authority in search engine results. When employers Google your name, your LinkedIn profile will likely appear on the first page, above personal websites and portfolios. With a staggering 6.3 million Google searches every minute, don't neglect your LinkedIn!

Get Your Money's Worth: Membership Plans & Tools

Membership Plans

There are several different LinkedIn membership tiers available. Pick a plan that aligns with your goals, whether that's job hunting, sales, recruiting, or brand promotion. The primary LinkedIn membership plans (which vary in features and pricing) are:

LinkedIn Basic Account: This free, entry-level plan is ideal for those starting out on LinkedIn. It includes essential networking features, allowing you to connect with others, view profiles, and join groups. You must upgrade to a Premium account to access InMail messaging; without it, you can only directly message LinkedIn members you're connected to.

LinkedIn Premium Career: This plan is designed for job seekers and offers enhanced features, including InMail messages, key insights (salary, job, who's viewed your profile), and a résumé builder. LinkedIn Learning (details follow) and all other paid subscriptions are part of this package.

LinkedIn Premium Business: This is tailored for businesses and provides company page management. It offers the same perks as LinkedIn Premium Career plus job postings and advertising solutions to promote your brand, attract talent, and reach a wider audience.

LinkedIn Sales Navigator: Sales Navigator is the go-to solution for sales professionals, providing lead recommendations, advanced search filters, and seamless CRM integration. This paid subscription service enables sales professionals to identify and connect with potential clients and key accounts, offering industry insights and personalized outreach for a strategic sales approach. It empowers effective client targeting and engagement, driving lead generation and customer growth.

LinkedIn Recruiter: This plan is tailored to recruiters and talent acquisition experts. It boasts advanced search functions, candidate insights, and tools to manage and track job applicants. It also includes features to streamline the hiring process, including project management and guided search.

LinkedIn Learning: All premium plans include free access to LinkedIn Learning, a powerful resource for professional development featuring a vast library of courses. Completing a course earns you a certification you can proudly display in your LinkedIn profile's Accomplishments section. Access this resource by clicking the "Work" icon on your LinkedIn homepage.

Be sure to visit the LinkedIn website for the most up-to-date information on its offerings and pricing.

Dos & Don'ts

Below are essential dos and don'ts for LinkedIn success. If some seem familiar, that's because they are worth repeating.

DOs

Optimize your profile. Use relevant keywords — like skills and industries — to improve your visibility in searches.

Add value, not clutter. Regularly share informative articles, industry news, and insights to establish your expertise.

Stay engaged. Stay active by liking, commenting on, and sharing valuable content. Build relationships and follow industry leaders for the latest trends and insights.

Personalize your messages. Ditch those dull templates. When you message someone, personalize the note and highlight common interests for maximum impact. (See sample LinkedIn messages in the Networking chapter, page 137.)

Participate in groups. LinkedIn offers thousands of groups to explore. Find your niche, join the conversation, and share insights. Bonus: some groups post job openings!

Request recommendations. Ask colleagues and supervisors for recommendations to boost your credibility. Offer to return the favor.

Do research. Dive into company insights, track industry trends, and gather valuable intel on competitors, clients, and potential employers. All this intelligence gives you a significant competitive edge.

Broadcast language mastery. If you're bilingual and seeking global opportunities, add multiple languages to your profile.

Always include a current job, even when unemployed. When you're between jobs, you can creatively showcase your desired role while making it clear you are actively seeking opportunities. For example, if you're in marketing, you might consider something like "VP Marketing in Transition." If you're in the tech industry, you might consider something like "Cutting-edge innovator seeking opportunities."

Showcase your character strengths. Highlight qualities like leadership, resilience, teamwork, and initiative. Recruiters put these traits at the top of their list.

Add your LinkedIn URL to your résumé. Once you've customized your URL, highlight it on your résumé by placing it right beneath your name. This has become standard practice and will allow you to connect with potential employers easily.

Add hashtags to your comments. Since LinkedIn comments are now searchable, you can easily join relevant discussions and stay up to date with trending topics by integrating hashtags.

Beware of phishing. LinkedIn, like all platforms, is not immune to phishing attempts. Scammers may use deceptive emails to trick users into sharing personal information or donating money. Review and verify profiles you interact with, and always remain diligent.

> *LinkedIn is like a bank account. You make regular deposits, and it grows over time. Too often, I see folks take a "set it and forget it" approach, treating the platform like an online résumé and expecting recruiters to come knocking, or only showing up when they need something from a connection — or worse, a stranger! I worked with a recent college grad who heard he should do informational interviews. So, he had been diligently sending cold invites to random people on LinkedIn asking for advice and referrals. He was at a loss as to why no one was taking him up on his request. Informational interviews are a great idea, but leading with an ask is not. The best way to start getting active on LinkedIn is to show up regularly, even if it's only 15 minutes a day. Search for people in your field or roles that interest you, particularly those with an active post history, and start engaging by commenting. Look for alums from your school if you're a recent college grad.*

– Jennifer Fishberg, Career Storyteller and Job Search Strategist at
Career Karma Resume Services

DON'Ts

Leave your profile unfinished. An incomplete profile creates a negative impression. Fill out all relevant sections, aiming for All-Star status.

Send spam. Avoid sending generic messages or excessive connection requests. Get personal, and customize messages — quality, not quantity.

Overshare personal information. Maintain a divide between your personal and professional life on LinkedIn. Keep your cell phone number and political opinions private. Review and adjust your privacy settings to control what others can see. And remember that you can signal job openness to recruiters while discreetly hiding it from your current employer.

Go silent or stale. Consistency is a LinkedIn user's secret weapon. Timely responses to messages and inquiries are a must. Also, keep your profile updated, active, and engaging. An outdated LinkedIn profile is both a red flag and a missed opportunity.

Overlook group etiquette. Follow group rules and engage respectfully in discussions.

Copy-paste from your résumé. Unlike a traditional CV, your LinkedIn Summary should be narrative in form — a compelling story.

Brag. Avoid constantly promoting yourself or your products or services. Instead, focus on value sharing. Be honest and transparent about your skills, achievements, and experience; don't exaggerate or misrepresent.

> *Consider LinkedIn your ultimate search engine to find jobs, recruiters, professional contacts, and partnerships for career success!*

TOOLS

Here's a list of LinkedIn tools and features worth checking out:

- **LinkedIn Pulse:** A publishing platform for sharing long-form content and articles.
- **LinkedIn Groups:** Online communities where professionals can connect, discuss topics, and share insights.
- **LinkedIn Job Search:** A tool for finding job listings and opportunities.
- **LinkedIn Events:** A feature for creating and managing professional events and webinars.
- **LinkedIn Ads:** Advertising options to promote your business and target specific audiences.
- **LinkedIn Messaging:** A chat feature for connecting and communicating with other LinkedIn members.
- **LinkedIn Alumni Tool:** A feature to connect with alumni from your educational institution.

These tools and features cater to various professional needs, from networking and job searching to content creation and business promotion. Again, make sure to visit LinkedIn.com, as it is constantly modifying and adding new tools.

DID YOU KNOW?

Here are a handful of LinkedIn hacks:

- LinkedIn allows you to update your profile without notifying your network about the changes. If you don't want to share a specific update with your network, disable the option before saving the change.

- Turn on your "I'm interested" button to let recruiters and potential employers know you're open to hearing about new opportunities. LinkedIn will hide this open invitation from folks at your current company.

- Keep your message concise. According to LinkedIn, the shorter the InMail, the higher the open rate. Write just enough to pique interest and share links to your portfolio, website, and calendar. Look for any commonalities you may share with the hiring manager, such as both belonging to the American Marketing Association.

- If a member has chosen to view your profile in private mode, you won't be able to see their information — even if you have a Premium account.

- Respond to every message, job request, and connection invite on LinkedIn, even if it's just to decline. LinkedIn rewards active engagement. By interacting consistently, you'll likely see your LinkedIn performance improve.

- LinkedIn SSI (Social Selling Index), www.linkedin.com/sales/ssi, is a score that assesses your activity and engagement on the platform. It gauges your LinkedIn profile's strength from 0 to 100. While it isn't a guarantee of career success, a score above 70 is considered excellent. Boosting your SSI score increases your visibility, as the platform will show your content to more people and recommend your profile more frequently to recruiters and others.

- LinkedIn Career Explorer is a lesser-known tool that helps uncover potential career paths and job titles based on your skills. It offers insights to make informed career decisions, identifying trends and essential skills for career growth. Ensure your profile is complete before using it.

- To set up job alerts on LinkedIn, search for a job. At the top left of the job search results page, toggle the "Set Alert" option to "On" to create an alert based on your current search criteria. After setting the alert, you can manage it by clicking "Manage Alerts," where you can select how often you receive updates and through which channels, like email or app notifications.

- LinkedIn verification badges are a relatively new feature. They validate specific information, including your ID, work email, school email, and LinkedIn Learning license. There's no cost for verification. Once completed, these badges are visible on your profile, but you can remove them at any time.

LinkedIn is an absolute must for early-career professionals, empowering you to connect, learn, and effectively position yourself in your chosen field. It's much more than a social media platform; it can provide rich dividends for your career or business. Staying active on LinkedIn is essential even when you're not job hunting. Building your network and personal brand pro-actively benefits your current job and also makes your next job search smoother. Master the art of LinkedIn and you'll be unstoppable in your career journey.

One more thing: Check out the Networking chapter (page 137) to learn how to expand your LinkedIn reach more effectively, with sample messages and guidance on building winning relationships.

Remember these key points:

1 LinkedIn is indispensable. In today's digital world, professionals can't afford not to use LinkedIn. If you take personal branding and career success seriously, you need to take LinkedIn seriously, too.

2 Your connections matter. Networking is at the heart of LinkedIn. Who you're connected to on the platform could very well determine your next job, client, or hire.

3 Only stellar profiles stand out. LinkedIn has more than 1 billion users — which means competition is fierce. Optimize everything from your profile photo to your skills and endorsements.

4 Use LinkedIn wisely. Just like a physical workplace or networking event, LinkedIn has norms and etiquette. Be respectful, be professional, and don't spam your connections.

SECTION C: DELIVERY

PART V – AMPLIFYING YOUR CAREER THROUGH SOCIAL MEDIA

Contributed by: Kudzi Chikumbu

Do you ever wonder if social media could help you land your dream job or propel you to the next career level? Let's explore that together.

I'm Kudzi Chikumbu, and Stacey brought me in to discuss social media's powerful role in your professional life. Like many of you, I started my career with questions about the impact of social media.

My journey began in 2012 as an accountant at a top firm in South Africa, where my family and I moved to after my home country of Zimbabwe. Though grateful for the job, I found no joy in my work and felt a disconnect that left me yearning for more creativity, fun, and alignment with my passions.

In search of inspiration, I embarked on a transformative journey to several Asian countries, including Korea, Japan, and Thailand. I wanted to explore new places and feed my mind with inspiration. I captured my experiences in vlogs, and I shared them on YouTube. While I didn't achieve viral fame, the impact was profound in another way: other young Africans reached out to say my travels inspired them to travel and pursue their own adventures and dreams. This feedback was a turning point, prompting me to shift my career toward something that truly resonated with me — authentic creativity.

I took a bold step and applied to the Stanford Graduate School of Business, sharing my travel experiences and their impact in my application essays. Emphasizing personal authenticity and the power of social media, I was admitted, which marked the beginning of a new chapter in my life. The business school at Stanford University is one of the most challenging schools to get into. My life was on a new trajectory, thanks in part to online content creation. After Stanford, I secured a position at a leading tech company.

But the evolution didn't stop there. In 2018, while visiting Paris, I discovered a luxury scented candle on a shopping excursion that captivated me. This discovery led to the creation of "Sir Candle Man," my online social media persona and pages, where I shared my favorite candles and reviews. The authenticity of this venture resonated widely, leading to features in prestigious publications like *The Wall Street Journal* and appearances on shows like *The Drew Barrymore Show*. Sir Candle Man evolved from a simple social media account to a recognized personal brand, highlighting how a passion shared authentically can open doors to unimaginable opportunities.

Each step of my journey from an uninspired accountant to a fulfilled creative professional and influencer was underpinned by the strategic use of social media, which built an **authentic social résumé** that helped nurture my career growth.

Now, let's discover how you can leverage your social media not just to share your passions but strategically propel your career forward. What passions drive you? How can you convey them in a way that adds value to others and craft your **authentic social résumé**? Together, we'll uncover the answers. I'll share social media insights as if you were creating an incredible résumé that would make any recruiter notice you and any employer want you on their team.

Your social media presence isn't just a part of your personal life; it's a pivotal component of your professional growth.

Creating an Impactful Social Profile

Creating a compelling résumé requires impactful content, which might seem straightforward but is often overlooked. I've seen numerous résumés, including those of friends, that lack substantial content — what I call "not having enough meat on the bone." The essential first step is establishing a professional, public social media account. Again, think of your social media as an "**authentic social résumé**," where enough rich content allows others to form an opinion about your professional capabilities and potential for collaboration.

Reflecting on my own experiences, I realize that my travels across Asia not only enriched my life but also bolstered my résumé and application to the Stanford Graduate School of Business. These experiences provided vivid details highlighting my interests and adventures, proving pivotal in my application. The content gave color to my experience. You have to go on the trip if you want the adventure! Simply put, you need to undertake the journey to gather worthwhile content.

Years later, my venture into the world of candles and fragrances through Sir Candle Man wouldn't have been possible without sharing my interests online. I often meet aspiring creators in the fragrance industry who dream of success but have yet to take the first steps; many have minimal content posted or haven't started at all. Remember, success in creating requires active creation. If you want it, you have to go get it. In this case, you have to create it!

To kick-start your online presence, create a professional account, set it to public, and begin sharing.

Your Digital Presence: The Power of Content Pillars

Just as a well-structured résumé has clearly defined sections highlighting various experiences, a thoughtful social media presence should be similarly organized. Good recruiters look for specific skills and themes. Similarly, your social media should clearly display themes that align with your career goals. For your social media account, you can think of these as content pillars.

Now that you've started posting, it's crucial to strategize about what to post to advance your career goals. A quick web search on how to optimize your social media accounts will tell you to create a vision and support it with content pillars. These pillars act like the sections of your résumé, helping anyone who views your profile to quickly grasp your focus areas. The themes should be noticeable and pop out of the screen.

For example, a few years after launching Sir Candle Man, despite enjoying the process, I noticed the account's growth had plateaued. To address this, I started a candle review series — not to showcase expertise (as I was still learning about the industry) but to document my journey and discoveries. This was an intentional decision. I wanted to learn by doing. This shift engaged my audience and attracted attention from brands and media, including a feature by *The Hollywood Reporter*. My specific goal of highlighting my learning journey allowed me to progress. This demonstrates the importance of having focused goals and using my content to chronicle my learning path.

This approach helps build your social media presence. You don't need to be an expert from the start; you just need to be committed to your learning journey. Showing your development helps you show your commitment to a specific topic, company, or industry. For instance, if you aspire to a career in finance, you might highlight your participation in finance conferences, recommend finance books and podcasts, and celebrate any new industry certifications. This approach showcases your dedication to the finance industry as well as your efforts to develop expertise. Any good employer would see this growth in a positive light.

Ensure your social media profile clearly communicates your professional focus and journey. When people visit your profile, they should instantly understand your career trajectory and interests.

Delivering Value: How Social Media Can Serve Others

An impactful résumé doesn't just list qualifications — it demonstrates the unique value you can bring to a potential employer. Likewise, your social media presence should showcase the value you offer to your followers and potential connections. It's not just about why they should follow you but what valuable insights or services you can provide in return for their attention.

So, what do you do now that you've created your profile and started posting content? Once you've established your content pillars and gained some traction, the next step is to shift the focus from yourself to your audience. Think of this as turning the spotlight away from you and onto your audience. This means less of "look at me" and more "this is for you." This outward focus is key to thriving online and using your social media for career advancement. If you can master this, you will thrive online and use your account for your career growth.

During my travels, I initially thought my videos were just for personal joy and family entertainment. However, the underlying theme of seeking creative fulfillment resonated deeply with viewers, particularly those in early career stages seeking change. Many viewers, also in their early careers, connected with my sentiment. This connection transformed my travel vlogs into inspirational content, proving that value often lies in unexpected endeavors. What I thought was just a series of videos on my travels gave people a sense of being acknowledged and inspired them to go for their dreams. That is true authentic value.

This lesson was also vital when I developed Sir Candle Man. After initial success, the account's growth stalled as I tried to mimic viral trends. I even started posting about perfume to try something new to go viral. A breakthrough came from an unexpected interaction. One day, a new, highly anticipated perfume was announced. I bought it as soon as possible so that I could post my review before everyone else and hopefully go viral. The perfume arrived. I filmed my video, posted it, and went to bed with the expectation that I would wake up to a viral video. The video flopped, but a viewer pointed out a mistake in how I sprayed the perfume. I created a follow-up video to correct my technique and share the proper method for spraying perfume. To my surprise, this video went viral, highlighting a simple yet widespread need for practical, everyday advice. This second "how to" instructional video served a need that even more people had — how to use their everyday products. The content was useful and actionable for a lot of people.

This experience underscores a crucial point: delivering value often means filling widely relevant knowledge gaps. Give people content that helps their lives and that can help your career. For instance, if you're aiming for a career in real estate, address common questions and concerns. Share insights on buying homes, securing loans, or property management. Content that solves problems or eases challenges is highly valuable and sets you apart. Showing that you add value to someone else's life will set you and your authentic social résumé apart.

Ensure your social media output is not just informative but genuinely beneficial. Providing value is the cornerstone of building an influential and authentic social résumé.

Guardrails: Ensuring a Professional Online Image

A standout résumé showcases your achievements and indicates that you would positively represent a potential employer within their industry. Similarly, your social media should demonstrate that you are brand-safe and could serve as a commendable representative or spokesperson for a company. Would your next employer be proud to have you on their team? Are you a good representation of the company? Could you be a trusted company spokesperson? You should think about your social media presence in the same way as you build your "authentic social résumé."

Even before my acceptance into Stanford, which was powered in part by my content creator journey, a friend and I ran an emerging YouTube channel in South Africa that discussed pop culture and young African entrepreneurs. Although we occasionally explored edgy topics, we steered clear of negative, polarizing discussions. This decision was influenced by advice from our fathers, who cautioned against potentially divisive content that could polarize our audience and tarnish our brand. This approach proved wise, especially in today's climate, where past social media posts can resurface and damage reputations — the proverbial "canceling," as they call it. While it's important to have opinions, they should be expressed in a way that carefully considers long-term personal and professional repercussions. You don't want your past content to impact your present and future opportunities. For example, while employers shouldn't (and, in many places in the world, can't legally) discriminate against you because of your political leanings, they can still use it to form an opinion on your character. You can proactively own the narrative by posting professional content while considering its long-term impact.

Although reviewing candles as Sir Candle Man seems straightforward, even the act of lighting a candle can sometimes be auto-flagged by platforms for promoting unsafe behavior. Maintaining a brand-safe profile means adhering to community guidelines for any platform you are on to avoid accumulating strikes against your account, which could impact its standing.

When building your authentic social résumé, consider whether your content truly represents who you are and whether it would enhance your appeal to potential employers. Scrutinize your posts, photos, and videos to ensure they are free from provocative, harmful, or bullying content. Remember, future employers might review your public profiles, so keeping them polished and professional is crucial.

Ensure your social media accounts reflect
the best version of yourself and adhere
to community standards to maintain
good standing.

Authenticity: Embracing Uniqueness to Stand Out

The most memorable résumés jump out at recruiters not because of fancy fonts or colors but because the candidate's unique qualities and accomplishments shine through. It's about how you stand out. This is the same on social media. What makes you different? What makes you indispensable? Let's explore how to forge a notable and noticeable presence.

Although I often felt uninspired during my days as an accountant, I always looked for ways to inject creativity into my routine tasks. I've always been like this. I like to imagine more fun ways to do things that feel routine. In the world of accounting, I was an auditor, and at the beginning of every client's project, we hosted a planning meeting. Typically, this meeting would have a very long document that was tough to get through, given the length and the dense content. During a client planning meeting, I introduced an interactive, full-size physical board for brainstorming rather than relying on the typical lengthy digital document. This novel approach not only made the meeting more engaging but also left a lasting impression on my superiors, reinforcing the value of doing things differently.

This inclination to stand out was also central to my business school applications. In my application essays, I spoke about my intention to use the power of media to help people see themselves and live more authentically. I didn't just talk about my intentions; I demonstrated them through my travel videos, which showcased my commitment to using media to inspire others to live authentically. Very few, if any, student applicants have my unique story and have taken those exact steps to make their application come to life. Be fearless and be different. My unique approach resonated deeply, distinguishing my application from others.

The lesson was further cemented during my time as a teaching assistant for Allison Kluger (also a contributor to this book and the person who introduced me to Stacey) and the renowned Tyra Banks at Stanford. In the personal branding class, Tyra imparted a crucial insight. She said that in order for a personal brand to stand out, you don't always have to be better; you need to be different. "Different is better than better." I live by this. Yes, be good, but be different.

This philosophy has guided me as Sir Candle Man. In the crowded world of home fragrances, I distinguish myself not by claiming expert status but by being a learner and sharing my discoveries in everyday language that resonates with a broad audience. I explain what I smell in regular language and not by using deep industry jargon. Most people can relate to that authentic desire to learn and explore a new interest. My direct communication style and unique perspective as a Black gay African man in the niche luxury fragrance market further amplify my distinctiveness. There are very few creators who look and sound like me. I stand out. Lastly, in the world of aesthetically pleasing home and perfume content, most creators only show their personal spaces but don't speak to their audience. I speak straight to my audience. My approach allows me to have a strong connection with my community and to stand out. This has, in turn, led to significant achievements, including launching successful products, writing my book, *Let It Burn*, and becoming a speaker in the beauty industry. That is the power of standing out.

So, how can you stand out? Simply by being your authentic self. The importance of being authentic is often repeated because it is fundamentally true. Why is that? It's simple. There's only one you. You are unique, like a fingerprint, and by embracing your genuine self — polished and value-driven — you can leave your mark on the work and elevate your authentic social résumé above the crowd. Reflect on what you post online. Does it truly represent you? Don't be afraid to diverge from the norm. It's better not to follow the crowd.

Being your authentic self is not just good advice — it's a strategic move. Authenticity makes you memorable and can significantly elevate your professional profile.

Navigating Setbacks: Turning Mistakes into Opportunities

Every professional faces challenges, and in job interviews, you're often asked about weaknesses or difficult situations you've encountered. The way you respond to these questions can significantly impact your chances. Similarly, your approach to setbacks on social media can either bolster or undermine your professional image. This shouldn't scare you because you can easily prepare for this.

Sometimes, a post may be received differently than intended, leading to negative reactions. While such scenarios are less than ideal, they present an opportunity to demonstrate resilience and accountability. For example, in the fragrance influencer community, I've seen creators successfully navigate controversies, whether related to partnerships with problematic brands, misguided marketing campaigns, or subpar products. These experiences, while challenging, are not career-ending if handled correctly.

Here's how to turn negative feedback into a constructive path forward:

1. **Apologize Sincerely:** Owning up to your mistakes is crucial. Directly addressing your audience helps maintain their trust and clears the path for future interactions. This is how you maintain trust with your audience and future employers who may see your content.

2. **Overcommit to Improvement:** Clearly articulate how you plan to enhance your content or business practices to avoid similar issues in the future. Concrete steps and commitment to change are vital. Your employer needs to know you can make plans to improve mistakes.

3. **Follow Up:** Keep your audience updated on your progress. This transparency shows you are serious about your commitments and value your followers' trust. This shows your employer that you are accountable.

Have you ever posted something that got a negative response? Are you scared to post in fear that people may not like what you share? Negative feedback is a part of the social media landscape and any career journey. If you're apprehensive about posting due to potential backlash, remember that the key is to start engaging and learning from the process. Mistakes happen — we are all human. But with a thoughtful response strategy, you can manage most missteps and even use them as growth opportunities.

Most mistakes aren't permanent. With the right approach, you can recover and even strengthen your professional reputation.

Building Connections on Social Media

An effective résumé not only highlights your skills but also your ability to foster relationships with managers, team members, cross-functional colleagues, and industry peers. Your professional network is an integral part of your résumé; the connections you've made and maintained can significantly enhance your value to future employers. This concept extends seamlessly into social media, where your followers, who you follow, and your interactions contribute to your online persona, impacting your career progression either positively if you are strategic or negatively if you do not optimize correctly.

My journey of sharing my life online underscores the power of a strategic social presence. My online creative endeavors helped build a network that led me to unexpected business opportunities. Several years after sharing my travel experiences — which I initially used for my Stanford applications — I was discovered by a talent manager in Los Angeles through my videos. This connection led to a referral to a talent agency specializing in paid speakers, opening up opportunities I had never anticipated. Little did I know that my videos would help me grow a network, which, in turn, would help my career.

Similarly, my venture as Sir Candle Man enhanced my network further. By posting about different candle brands and tagging founders and industry influencers, I engaged with a community that reached out, shared knowledge, and offered insights. This network became instrumental when I wrote and published a book on the power of fragrance, allowing me to draw upon a wealth of industry expertise. I acknowledged their contributions in my book, solidifying those relationships and fostering a supportive community that continues to benefit my career.

Who will you tag in your content as you build your authentic social résumé? Who are the people you want to meet? Who are the people you know that you can make content with to show the vastness of your network? As you build your authentic social résumé, consider who you might tag in your posts. Who are you following so that you can watch and engage with their content? Think about the industry leaders you aspire to connect with and the peers you can collaborate with to showcase your network's breadth. Your online interactions should be thoughtful and strategic, aimed at watching, learning from, and engaging with the right people to enhance your professional landscape.

Harnessing Your Authentic Social Résumé

In today's digital age, crafting an "authentic social résumé" on social media is not just beneficial — it's essential for career growth. This chapter has guided you through various strategies for effectively using social media to enhance your professional life.

Here's a summary of each step:

1. How to Start: Launching Your Professional Presence Online

Get Started: The journey begins with establishing a public, professional profile that sets the stage for your ongoing engagement. Take the first step and create that first post.

2. Defining Your Digital Presence: The Power of Content Pillars

Define Your Content Pillars: Develop clear content pillars that reflect your professional interests and expertise, making it easy for others to understand your career focus and goals. Having a clear strategy will light up the path to career growth.

3. Delivering Value: How Your Social Media Can Be of Service

Provide Value: Transform your social media into a resource by sharing valuable, practical content that addresses the needs and interests of your audience, enhancing their lives and your professional reputation. Turn the spotlight away from you and onto other people.

4. Being Professional: The Importance of Being Brand-Safe

Be Polished: Ensure that your profile does not include any content that may show you in a negative light. Adhere to community guidelines. You own and should protect your online image.

5. Authenticity: Embracing Uniqueness to Stand Out

Be Authentic: Stand out by embracing and expressing your unique personal and professional identity, which attracts engagement and opportunities that align with your true self. The more authentic you are, the more magnetic you are.

6. Navigating Hurdles: Turning Mistakes into Opportunities

Manage Challenges: Learn how to effectively manage and recover from social media setbacks, demonstrating resilience and a commitment to maintaining a professional image. Everyone makes mistakes; it's all about how you handle them.

7. Community: Networking and Engagement on Social Media

Network Effectively: Utilize social media to expand your professional network by connecting and engaging with relevant individuals and groups within your industry.

Each of these steps lays out the path you need to follow. The approach is a step-by-step plan for how to use social media in your early career growth. You will build a great audience, connect with industry professionals, and become a trustworthy voice that your dream employer will want on their team. As you embark on or continue your journey, remember that the digital world offers vast opportunities for those who are strategic, thoughtful, and genuine in their engagements. Use what you've learned to make meaningful connections, stand out in your field, and propel your career forward. Good luck, and may your path be fruitful and your progress steady!

PART VI – NETWORKING FOR SUCCESS

It's all in who you know. Your network is your net worth.

This may appear to be cliché career advice to some, but any successful professional will tell you: it's all true. The stronger your professional network, the more likely you are to succeed. Take it from me: having a robust network is the primary factor behind my business success. The people in my network have opened doors and offered invaluable advice and support every step of the way.

But don't make the mistake of thinking networking is about shaking as many hands or collecting as many LinkedIn connections as possible. Your network includes colleagues, mentors, investors, and professionals in your industry. Truly effective networking is about genuine relationships and trust. It's about quality, not quantity.

I've met two of my most valuable strategic business partners and lifelong friends through networking. You might assume it happened at a typical conference, but that's not the case! One connection was made in the ladies' room, and the other in an elevator. The lesson here is simple: start a conversation anywhere — you never know where it might lead!

Networking is one of the most essential job search strategies and a skill you should hone and practice every day, no matter your field or profession. If you still need convincing, just look at the numbers:

- 88 percent of professionals consider networking to be crucial in furthering their careers (GrowMap, 2020).
- 82 percent participated in networking at least once per month (*Harvard Business Review*, 2020).
- 85 percent of job vacancies are filled via networking (*Forbes*, 2021).

Even in a digital world, networking is best done in person. To deeply connect with a colleague, mentor, or potential client, ditch the screen and grab a cup of coffee or a bite of lunch. That's the secret.

No matter how daunting networking might seem, mastering this skill is well worth the effort. When done correctly, networking can completely transform your career. Whether a business owner or a job holder, a robust network will take you farther and faster than you could ever go alone. Think of networking as a puzzle; each connection you make is a piece that completes the picture of your success. You can also liken networking to an intense effort to scale a mountain, but trust me, the view from the top is worth every step.

Here's the thing: There's nothing that replaces live interactions. So don't hide behind the screen; you've got to make this personal. I'm a big fan of grabbing a cup of joe. There's nothing quite like building connections in person. Here's the secret sauce: identify the individuals you're eager to connect with. Once you've been properly introduced, invite them to a coffee or lunch. It's the key to forging meaningful relationships.

This chapter offers guidance on connecting with industry professionals, recruiters, mentors, strategic partnerships, and more. You'll learn the nuts and bolts of networking, from that first handshake to a major opportunity down the line. Now, let's get started expanding your network!

The Why Behind Networking: 10 Reasons to Network

Networking isn't just a buzzword; it's the secret sauce for success as a young professional! While the merits of networking may seem straightforward, like growing your professional circle, see these compelling reasons to make networking a daily practice:

- **Career opportunities:** Networking increases your visibility in your industry, opening doors for better job offers, bigger promotions, and new clients.
- **Knowledge sharing:** Some of the best business lessons you will learn in your career come from experienced professionals. Your network is a gold mine of learning opportunities.
- **Mentorship:** You can connect with mentors who will guide and support your career journey.
- **Industry insights:** Stay updated on industry trends and developments with a strong network.
- **Personal growth:** Networking enhances communication, negotiation, and interpersonal skills.
- **Collaboration:** Networking can lead to partnerships and collaborative projects.
- **Build confidence:** Meeting new people helps boost self-confidence and reduces social anxiety.

- **Access to resources:** Networking provides access to resources, such as workshops, seminars, and training.
- **Diverse perspectives:** Interact with individuals from various backgrounds and perspectives and receive constructive feedback.
- **Hot tips:** A strong network allows you to access insider information, such as unpublicized job postings and industry trends, giving you the upper hand in staying well-informed.

And here's one more for good measure: **friendship and support.** Building a professional support system also results in lasting friendships. Within my inner circle, I count several friends who originated from networking.

> *The bottleneck most job seekers experience is getting the first interview. Online job postings are a black hole these days. But people don't know there's a viable alternative: networking. Turning strangers into advocates is a universal life skill that nobody ever teaches you. Yet, all of your employers expect you to have it. And not having it limits the impact of working professionals as much as it does job seekers. If you ask a stranger on the street if they're good at networking, people tend to overevaluate themselves. They'll say, "I'm pretty good at it. Whenever I'm put on a team, some of those people become my friends." But I call that reactive networking, or cooperation. We learned that in kindergarten. That's not proactive networking.*
>
> – Steve Dalton, Founder and CEO of
> Contact2Colleague and Author of *2-Hour Job Search*

Networking 101

It should be crystal clear by now: be sure to shmooze rather than snooze! But what are the tricks of the trade? Here are a few key tips for beginners:

■ **Build social capital now.** Don't wait until you need a network to create one; you can't pull one out of thin air at a moment's notice. Any ambitious professional should make networking a part of their daily activities. Just like personal friendships, genuine professional relationships develop naturally over time.

■ **Be strategic.** Ensure you're connecting with like-minded professionals who share your goals and interests. Building meaningful connections with the right people will open doors that propel your career forward. Choose your connections wisely to make the most of your professional journey — focus on relationships with those who can help you achieve your aspirations.

■ **Ensure all networking relationships are mutually beneficial.** Networking isn't about "me, me, me." It's about both parties. Even if you feel you have little to offer your professional contacts, that's most likely not the case. You never know how you can assist them: it might be through a helpful introduction or a resource recommendation. Always ask if you can do anything for them. At the very least, it shows you are willing to return the favor. A close contact of mine concludes each email with the question: "How can I serve you?" This personalized touch not only underscores his dedication to service but also reflects his commitment to nurturing meaningful connections.

■ **Become comfortable introducing yourself.** While you shouldn't recite a script, you should practice and be eloquent when answering questions like "Tell me about yourself," or "What do you do?" These are opportunities to deploy your Uniquely Me Statement and key messages. When making a first impression, be concise and confident. Here's an example: Michael is seeking freelance work in marketing and has just arrived at a networking event where he hopes to connect with potential clients. His pitch goes like this: "With 10 years in marketing, I'm all about engaging and activating audiences. Whether it's copywriting or ad campaigns, I bring strategy, creativity, and precise execution to every project."

■ **Have a game plan.** Don't go into a networking opportunity without a plan. Decide beforehand what you want to achieve, such as career exploration or making new connections. Regardless of your goal, always build rapport before making an ask. When a potential opportunity arises, your contact may be willing to refer you.

■ **Go pro.** Consider joining professional associations or industry organizations. Many provide valuable resources and networking opportunities, including events, discounts, mentorship programs, and access to job boards. A bonus is that these can expand your industry knowledge.

■ **Be open to new experiences.** Networking pays off when you're willing to say "yes!" You'll be pleasantly surprised by what a positive outlook can bring you. Agreeing to weigh in on an idea, accepting a challenging project, or assuming new responsibilities could be what lands you your next job.

■ **Volunteer your talent and time.** Networking isn't about the bottom line. Some of the most impactful and essential networking happens through volunteering — it's a great way to meet new people and build new connections. Fellow volunteers and nonprofit staff can often serve as potential career and mentorship sources. And think big: consider leading a community service event yourself to showcase your leadership skills.

■ **Express gratitude.** Showing appreciation is an essential element of professional networking. When a contact provides you with an idea, advice, or an opportunity — no matter how small — take the time to say "thanks." You can send an email (or, even better, a handwritten note). Here's an example for inspiration:

> Hi Michelle,
>
> It was great meeting you at the networking dinner yesterday. I appreciate you taking the time to tell me about your role and sharing advice as I pursue a similar career. I'm interested in the entry-level position you mentioned and plan to apply. I'll be sure to keep you posted on the outcome.
>
> With gratitude,
> Sara

■ **Maintain relationships.** Professional relationships are like plants — they need care and attention or they'll wither. But instead of water, use consistent communication. When you make a new contact, follow up with them in two days. Here are a few ideas to stay in touch: invite them to another event you're attending. Comment on their recent LinkedIn post. Send them a holiday card. Share relevant industry news. In terms of frequency, aim for four to six times a year — this way, you will be top of mind if an opportunity arises.

■ **Practice makes progress (not perfect).** "Perfect" networking skills — just like "perfect" anything — are unattainable. Instead of striving for networking perfection, aim for improvement. Networking is a new skill set for many, and it will likely feel awkward at first. However, practicing your Uniquely Me statement and key messages and exposing yourself to varied networking opportunities will build confidence. Every scenario can be a time to practice — from Starbucks to the career seminar to the water cooler.

> *Find a mentor who can guide you through career challenges and help you release your inner superhero. Better yet, form your own personal board of directors — individuals with different competencies. Surround yourself with those you can tap into for advice and learn from.*

Asking for an Introduction

Networking is about meeting new people, and your existing network is often your most valuable asset for making new connections. But asking a contact for an introduction can be intimidating. So, how do you go about it? Here are a few essentials for "introduction" success:

■ **Pick the right contact.** The person making the introduction should be someone you trust: a close business colleague or friend, a family member, or an existing or past mentor. Warm introductions are better received than cold outreach — but don't let that stop you from trying. Seek common ground, like the same alma mater or career paths. LinkedIn is an excellent resource to find out about a person's work, education, and interests.

■ **Explain why you're requesting an intro.** Since you're asking for a favor, make it clear why it matters to you. Explain why connecting to a particular person will help you professionally, such as considering an open role. For example: *Hi Mia, It was great seeing you at Izzy's birthday party last week. As you know, I'm actively looking for a job as a paralegal and noticed that you are connected to Susan Fields, Hiring Manager, ABC Law, through LinkedIn. ABC Law is at the top of my list of job opportunities, and I'd appreciate an intro to Susan if you feel comfortable doing so. Many thanks for your support. Best, Samantha*

■ **Give them a script.** To make it easy for them to make an intro, give them a "plug and play" blurb to pass along to their contact. Your mutual contact will be more willing to help if they don't need to put in much effort and can simply copy, paste, and send. This also gives you the power to control the narrative. Let's take the above example of Mia and Samantha and expand on it: *I know that you're traveling extensively and that this is a big ask, so I've included a short blurb to make the intro as easy as possible (and, of course, feel free to edit as you see fit): Hi Susan, My close friend and schoolmate, Samantha Mann, is very interested in the paralegal opening . . .*

■ **Say "please" and "thank you."** Remember that you're asking someone to use their precious social capital, so always be polite and respectful with your ask. Also, remember that there is a chance your contact may feel uncomfortable making the introduction. Regardless of the outcome, thank your contact for their time and effort and keep them posted on how the conversation went.

■ **Be concise.** When you're in contact with your target, get to the point. Your initial message should be two to three sentences maximum. Thank your go-between and move them to BCC (if the conversation is over email). This is also your chance to mention common ground, so scan their LinkedIn and other public profiles to find similarities. Then, offer two to three specific dates and time ranges to meet by phone, Zoom, or in person. Ensure they know you are flexible and can accommodate their schedule and preferences. Once they confirm, send them a calendar invite.

■ **Warming up a cold outreach.** If you don't have the luxury of a shared contact and introduction, get creative. Mention a shared interest. Or create an eye-catching subject line to increase the chances of them opening your note. Equally important is customizing/personalizing your message. A generic invitation without a personal note is not the way to go; your chances of getting a response from a personalized message are much higher. Add humor if that fits with your personality. Also, adding a question at the end of your message is an excellent technique to give the prospect a reason to respond.

Example 1 (connection in common):

Hi Sally,
I noticed that we're both connected to Jeanne Morse. I also saw on your profile that we both interned at Company ABC.

Example 2 (no connection in common)

Hi Max, I came across your profile after seeing your post about AI and health care. I'm currently exploring opportunities in the health-care field and considering a career transition. It's a rapidly evolving sector that aligns with my interests and strengths. Please let me know if you would be willing to share your insights with me. I would appreciate any guidance you can provide. Thanks!

If your early attempts at a cold outreach — or even a warm one — are unsuccessful, don't fret. Striking up a conversation with a stranger is hard work, especially in today's cluttered and noisy digital world. Stay optimistic, respect people's boundaries, and remember that practice makes progress!

Networking with a Twist

Networking is an art, not a science. Outside-the-box networking can sometimes be surprisingly effective in making meaningful connections. Here are some creative networking tips to test out:

Offer genuine compliments: Start conversations by complimenting someone's work, achievements, or attire. It creates a positive impression.

Host your own event: Organize a small meet-up, webinar, or workshop related to your field. This will position you as an expert and attract people interested in your niche.

Create a unique business card: Design a memorable business card that reflects your personality or interests. It can be a great icebreaker. I know this firsthand: our tagline at my PR and marketing agency is "Make Yourself Perfectly Clear." And so, our business cards are just that — transparent! My business card leaves a lasting impression. Even if some forget meeting me, they never forget the card itself. Consider using digital alternatives to paper business cards like Popl, HiHello, Wave, or Linq. Or do a mix of both: a QR code to your printed card that leads directly to your LinkedIn.

Send a clever follow-up: After meeting someone, send a follow-up message with a personal touch, like a relevant article or an offer to help with a specific project they mentioned. Better yet, why not drop something off or send it in the mail? I can't begin to tell you how successful my own technique is: a small, pizza-shaped chocolate sprinkled with M&Ms, accompanied by a note reading, "Thanks for a slice of your day."

Network at unexpected places: Networking doesn't have to happen at traditional events. Attend workshops, hobby clubs, or even charity events where you can meet people with common interests.

Ask unique questions: Instead of the usual "What do you do?" ask more intriguing questions, like "What's the most exciting project you've worked on recently?" Also, be an active listener. People appreciate those who genuinely listen and understand.

Join online forums and communities: Participate in online forums or communities like Reddit, where you can share your expertise and connect with professionals worldwide.

Create personalized content: Write articles, create videos, or start a podcast about topics in your industry. It establishes you as an authority and is a magnet for new connections.

Help others first: Offer assistance or information without expecting anything in return. It builds goodwill and often leads to reciprocity.

Send handwritten notes: Send a personalized, handwritten note after meeting someone at an event. It's a memorable gesture in our digital age.

Leverage alumni networks: Connect with alumni from your college or other institutions. Alumni often have a strong camaraderie and are willing to help fellow graduates.

Learn an uncommon skill: Pick up an unusual talent or hobby that sparks conversations and sets you apart at networking events. Why not beekeeping or rock climbing?

FIVE PRO TIPS FOR NETWORKING SUCCESS

Networking can be a game-changer, but it doesn't always come naturally. That's why we've condensed the essentials into these five best practices for you:

Be strategic: Don't rush in mindlessly. Craft a networking strategy with clear goals and tactics. For example, to build a robust LinkedIn network, set weekly targets, such as connecting with 10 industry leaders and sending five personalized requests daily. Tailor your strategy to your unique circumstances and strengths. Remember, less is more at the start — focus on just one, two, or three key goals.

Come prepared: Networking events move fast. Do your homework by researching attendees and preparing icebreakers to kick-start conversations. Many conferences use event apps (e.g., VOW) that have attendee directories.

Communicate effectively: Make your limited time count. Give your full attention, ask thoughtful questions, and find common ground. Look for opportunities to build camaraderie.

Add value: Always give more than you ask. Connect others in your network, provide feedback, or offer your expertise.

Maintain relationships: It's not just about adding more contacts; it's also about nurturing existing relationships. Share opportunities, engage with their content, and celebrate milestones. Keep in touch with those who helped in your job search. Building deeper connections can be as simple as showing support on social media or recommending them for opportunities.

Turning Coffee Chats into Career Gold

I'm a big fan of meeting in person because a simple coffee can become career gold. But that transformation requires careful planning and maximizing networking opportunities. Here's a step-by-step guide to show you how:

Prepare with purpose: Research the person you're meeting. Understand their background, achievements, and interests. I recommend that you connect with them beforehand on LinkedIn so you can both familiarize yourselves with each other's professional history.

Set clear goals: Define your objectives for the coffee chat. Are you seeking career advice, mentorship, job leads, or industry insights?

Choose the right venue: Select a comfortable and quiet location for the meeting. A coffee shop or the corner table of a restaurant can work well.

Share your story: Share your background, career aspirations, and challenges. Be authentic and open about your goals. Highlight your skills and achievements without coming across as boastful.

Forge a connection: Find common interests or connections outside of work to establish a personal connection. Remember details about the person's life and interests to strengthen the relationship.

Engage actively: Listen attentively to what the other person is saying. Show genuine interest in their experiences and insights. Ask open-ended, engaging questions to keep the conversation flowing. Inquire about their career journey and the challenges they've faced.

Request knowledge, not favors: Instead of asking for immediate job opportunities, request advice or insights related to your career path. Questions like "What would you have done differently in your early career?" can lead to valuable discussions.

Offer value: Be prepared to offer something in return. Share relevant resources, articles, or industry news that might interest them. If you have knowledge or resources that could be helpful to the other person, offer them without expecting anything in return.

Follow up: As mentioned above, promptly send a thank-you email after the meeting expressing gratitude for their time. Mention any key takeaways from the conversation that were particularly helpful.

Stay in touch: Maintain regular contact. Share updates on your progress and demonstrate how you've acted on any advice they gave you during the meet-up. If appropriate, ask for introductions to others in their network who may benefit your career. Career opportunities take time, so be patient and continue nurturing the connection.

Pay it forward: As you progress in your career, be willing to mentor or help others in the same way you were supported.

> View rejection as a stepping stone. Expect noes. Brush them off, and don't let it slow your stride. Be bold! All-star networking means stretching out of your comfort zone. Opportunities won't fall from the sky; you need to create them.

Your LinkedIn Networking Checklist

In a previous section (Part IV), we perfected your LinkedIn profile and covered the must-know features and membership plans. Now, the actual game begins! Here's your checklist to harness the full potential of LinkedIn:

✔ **Join and participate in LinkedIn groups:** It's time to find your tribe. There are thousands of groups to choose from, so be selective. Use the LinkedIn search bar and select the "Groups" filter to find relevant ones. Then, handpick the ones that align with your goals. Use interest-based or professional groups to connect with like-minded professionals, potential employers, and industry peers. Dive in and start mingling! Participating in these online communities will polish your skills, showcase your expertise, and grow your network. An added bonus: LinkedIn allows you to send messages for free to fellow members of the same group.

✔ **Get noticed:** Be a lively presence! Comment, share insights, and ask questions in groups. Regularly interact by liking, commenting, and sharing posts. Remember, networking is a two-way street.

✔ **The message matters:** Always include a personal message with your invitation to others. Explain why you're interested in connecting and how you may know each other. You only have 300 characters, so make every word count.

✔ **Mind your etiquette:** Follow proper etiquette when sending requests and messages to strangers. Thoughtful notes always win. Start by connecting with those you already know and follow industry leaders. Use LinkedIn's alumni tool or search for keywords to identify relevant connections.

✔ **Approaching recruiters:** Focus on building relationships with recruiters in your field or industry. Consistent follow-up will set you apart in their busy inboxes and keep you top of mind for fitting opportunities.

✔ **Quality over quantity:** When posting, less can be more. Post content that is relevant to your network; otherwise, you risk the chance of losing them. Consider posting a couple of times a week (no more than once a day). Also, don't just accumulate connections; nurture them.

✔ **Optimize your profile:** Periodically revisit and optimize your profile. Keep it updated, showcasing your latest achievements, skills, and experiences.

LinkedIn is your stage; with this checklist, you're set to shine!

Go beyond standard networking. Also think "inside the office." Connect with colleagues from other departments to build exposure and relationships, enhancing career prospects both internally and externally. Most importantly, keep those connections thriving! Your network is more than a career stepping stone; it's a community driving personal and professional growth.

Networking can completely transform your career. Whether you're a business owner or a job seeker, a robust network will take you farther and faster than you could ever go alone. Here's to growing your network.

BRANDAMENTALS

Remember these key points:

1 **Networking is indispensable.** Don't make the mistake of thinking it's optional.

2 **Your networking should be strategic, not tactical.** It's not about the quantity of relationships you build; it's about quality. Make sure you're connecting — and staying connected — to the right people.

3 **Practice makes progress.** Networking is a skill that takes time to master. Always practice and strive for improvement, not perfection.

4 **Network online and off.** LinkedIn is a valuable tool for growing your network, but make sure to get out from behind the screen, too. The best connections are made in person, over a coffee or a shared project.

Insider Tips for Job Search Success from 50-Plus Career Experts

Navigating the job market, especially early in your career, can be daunting. But fear not — this chapter is packed with insider secrets to job search success. I've gathered insights from over 50 career experts, including HR pros, recruiters, and LinkedIn experts, who weigh in on how to stand out and get hired. Here's their collective wisdom just for you:

Take up space in the room. Everyone has a right to share their ideas and contribute. You are important and worthy, and you do matter. Seeing ourselves deserving of space creates a healthy inner world, which enhances our outer world. Self-doubt and not believing you are smart enough can lead to not taking up space. When you choose not to take up space, you remove yourself from opportunities, conversations, and processes. Don't be a wallflower. Ask questions. Have a presence. If you're invited to a meeting, let your voice be heard. Recognizing your worth can be transformative, leading to greater confidence, meaningful connections, and the ability to impact your personal and professional life significantly.

Claude Silver, Chief Heart Officer at VaynerMedia, NY

Recognize that HR is essentially the gatekeeper. Their job often is to eliminate candidates, not push them forward. Try to get past the HR "filter" to speak with a decision-maker directly. Job hunting can be best accomplished through strategic networking and research. Look up decision-makers on LinkedIn or the company website to learn about them. Reach out to them by email (easy to derive), determine a common thread (e.g., both interested in field hockey), and request a 15-minute phone call to express interest and share your background. Many people who are job hunting don't take this strategy and don't have the chance to speak with a decision-maker early in their search. Doing this can lead to greater opportunities and set you apart from the competition.

David Lewis, CEO at OperationsInc, CT

It's essential that applicants show they are forever learners. Learning doesn't stop when the degree is garnered. With changing approaches and new technologies that disrupt the next thing, someone getting into the workforce must demonstrate a willingness to continue learning, growing, and adapting.

Elissa Barrett, Former Vice President of Human Resources at HubSpot, MA

Master your "long pitch." A long pitch is something you use in job interviews or informational meetings. It is two minutes in duration and answers why rather than what. A common mistake that people make with their long pitch is they sell themselves — you have the entire rest of your interview to sell yourself. This is the time to establish rapport and likability with your interviewer. To help you deliver an effective long pitch, I've developed the FIT Model. FIT stands for Favorite Part, Improvement Desired, and Transition Made. Here's an example: My favorite part of being a chemical engineer was learning how to break down big problems into smaller pieces. But the improvement I desired was applying that rigorous logic to a wider variety of challenges. So, the transition I made upon graduation was entering the strategy consulting industry with AT Kearney.

Steve Dalton, Founder and CEO of Contact2Colleague, Author of 2-Hour Job Search, NC

Have your résumé ready to go! Many companies open job postings for only 24–48 hours and receive thousands of applicants. I've seen candidates so busy perfecting their résumés that they miss this window of opportunity. Make sure your résumé includes keywords that match the position you're applying for to successfully pass through ATS filters. Always respect the interviewer's time: You need to be fully versed on the job description, even if it's just a phone screening. A person who has no questions has not prepared. Do your homework, find out about the company, and come up with at least 10 questions in advance.

Kerry Flynn Barrett, Founder and CEO of Flynn Barrett Consulting, NY ocus on your accomplishments, rather than your responsibilities, at every step of the job application process. Your résumé, cover letter, and interview answers should be filled with specific examples of how you've made a positive impact in your previous roles. Whenever possible, include hard numbers to help decision-makers envision what you can do for them if hired. Instead of making a vague statement like "Worked as a cashier," you should describe your impact: "Assisted 25+ customers daily, accurately handling $3,000+ in cash, check, and credit card transactions." Show you're constantly improving and collecting new skills and knowledge relevant to your industry in your application.

Aaron Case, Senior Digital Content Writer at Resume Genius, NY

---

ne of the red flags that I notice in résumés is adding outdated skills. For example, some candidates may list "Microsoft Office Suite Proficiency" as a skill. In today's technologically advanced landscape, certain skills, such as basic computer proficiency or familiarity with common software, are considered fundamental and assumed. Including these on a résumé no longer distinguishes a candidate. Mentioning out-of-date skills is a common trick to give the impression that one has a wide range of abilities, but in reality, these skills have lost their significance and don't contribute to setting a candidate apart. A résumé must highlight relevant, impactful skills that accurately represent a candidate's value in the modern workplace.

Harrison Tang, Co-Founder and CEO of Spokeo, CA

---

ecent college graduates should highlight their extracurricular, leadership, and volunteer experiences on campus. Individuals should not be discouraged or feel they aren't qualified for full-time opportunities if they haven't landed an internship in their desired field. Students can demonstrate their qualifications for full-time positions in their chosen industry through major capstone projects, leadership roles, or summer work experiences. When crafting a résumé, carefully review the requirements section of the job posting and pay attention to the skills listed. Think about how you use the skills in your classes and extracurriculars and use similar wording to describe your responsibilities on the résumé.

Melissa Trager, Chief Resume Officer and Founder of Resume All Day, NY

A winning résumé highlights relevant hard and soft skills. Hard skills encompass learned abilities such as writing, math, and proficiency with computer programs. In contrast, soft skills are interpersonal traits such as communication and collaboration that make you a good employee. Recruiters value hard skills such as project management, data analysis, software development, and digital management. They value soft skills such as adaptability, creativity, critical thinking, resilience, empathy, and problem-solving. Also, maintain clarity and conciseness in the employment history section. Limiting the detailed employment summary to a maximum of 10 years of experience helps keep the focus on recent and relevant roles. List relevant details such as titles, dates, accomplishments, employer locations, and educational background. Confusion about employment history, such as missing dates, will prompt the recruiter or hiring manager to move on quickly.

Matthew Warzel, President of MJW Careers, NC

The one question that will always be asked in the interview process is: "Do you have any questions for us?" Prepare a list of three to five questions for the interviewer(s). They should clarify job roles/responsibilities, seek to understand the team's passion, and explore opportunities for personal and professional growth. This approach showcases your enthusiasm, preparedness, and commitment.

Jackson Cooper, Adjunct Professor of Nonprofit Management and Arts Administration at Seattle University, WA

ChatGPT can assist with your résumé and cover letter by improving content, formatting, and language usage. A user can provide their current résumé and ask ChatGPT for feedback on how to enhance it. An example prompt might be: "Could you review my résumé and suggest improvements to make it more compelling for job applications in the software engineering field?" Similarly, users can provide details about the job they're applying for and ask ChatGPT to help craft a personalized cover letter. An example prompt might be: "I'm applying for a marketing coordinator position at XYZ company. Can you help me draft a cover letter that highlights my relevant experience and skills?" ChatGPT can offer specific advice on content structure, wording, and overall presentation to help users create impactful, tailored content. ChatGPT can also assist with interview preparation by simulating mock interviews.

Brittany Dolin and Nicole Dayan, Co-Founders of Pocketbook Agency, CA

There are two essential strategies young professionals should focus on. First, volunteer for the hard work that nobody wants to do. You will gain invaluable experience and take the burden off your manager, setting the stage for recognition, advancement, and increased opportunities. Second, high emotional intelligence will set you apart. Self-regulated, empathetic, and socially adept people make others like them. As I often say, "I hire for attitude, I train for skill." If you can do these two things as an early professional, you'll write your meal ticket.

Joseph DiCarlo, SPHR, SHRM-SCP, Chief People Officer at Clarest Health, NY

Your perfect career is about honoring who you truly are. If you feel dissatisfied in your career, it may not be just about your tasks but how your job aligns with your core values, like balance or integrity. Many people leave their jobs because they dislike their boss, showing that the "how" matters as much as the "what." With over 20,000 job titles and skills becoming obsolete every five years, finding the right career can feel overwhelming. Just because you've spent years in one job or industry doesn't mean you're stuck there forever.

Ashley Stahl, CEO, Wise Whisper; Host, You Turn Podcast; and Author of You Turn: Get Unstuck, Discover Your Direction, and Design Your Dream Career, CA

The top qualities young professionals need to possess are integrity, decisiveness, good judgment, the ability to form and execute a vision, confidence, and selflessness. Without the ability to be selfless, you will never get people to follow you to a place where they wouldn't go by themselves.

Dr. Paul A. Dillon, Founder, Dillon Consulting Services and Adjunct Professor at the Sanford School of Public Policy at Duke University, NC

There's a growing emphasis on soft skills in today's job market. While companies are willing to upskill or reskill employees to fill technical skill gaps, recent hiring efforts focus on finding candidates with the right mix of soft skills, which are considered harder to teach. Your résumé should highlight skills such as adaptability, effective communication, conflict resolution, and the ability to collaborate with colleagues to solve problems, meet goals, and add value. For remote work, it's crucial to demonstrate your ability to thrive both on-site and from home by highlighting previous telecommuting experience and the accomplishments you achieved while working remotely.

Amanda Augustine, Career Expert at TopResume, NY

Focusing on numbers is essential. It's no longer enough to simply list your job duties. You need to quantify your accomplishments. Instead of writing, "Oversaw the accounting team," try "Developed and implemented a new accounting department training program that increased productivity by 19% in six months." This is what I call your CAR story: Challenge, Action, Result. Numbers, statistics, and percentages grab attention and provide undeniable proof of your achievements. These quantifiable results make a compelling case for why you're a strong hire.

Marc Cenedella, Founder and CEO of Ladders, NY

Speaking negatively about a past job or supervisor is a big no-no! Instead of leading with the negative, share what you learned from that experience or what motivates you in a job. Turn it into a positive. For example: "My previous job made me value independence and autonomy. I find that I work better when I can be creative, and I enjoy working for supervisors who empower me to do my best."

Debbie Douglas, Director of Recruiting-Talent Acquisition at Paramount, NY

You will stand out if you specifically explain how your work affects those around you. Tell stories about how you add value to your organization and coworkers. Share how you volunteer on committees, display leadership, and mentor younger professionals or students.

Mark Anthony Dyson, President of Mark Dyson Consulting and Host of The Voice of Job Seekers Podcast, IL

To get to the top of the application pile, early-career professionals should have one or two relevant internships, work experiences, or school projects on their résumé that demonstrate a similar skill set to the role they are applying for. Tailoring different résumé versions to each job is also a smart strategy. To ensure visibility when recruiters search for talent, it's essential to include the right keywords on the résumé, such as specific technologies, software, project types, industry experience, and skill sets. Recruiters often use keyword searches on LinkedIn and other platforms, and AI technology increasingly relies on these keywords to pull candidate profiles. Therefore, a detailed LinkedIn profile with bullet points explaining responsibilities in previous roles is a must. I come across many LinkedIn pages where candidates list only job titles and company names without explaining their role, making it difficult for hiring managers to assess fit, which often results in them passing on that candidate.

Danielle Aranya, Lead Recruiter at Creative Circle, NY

Job candidates must pay close attention to their online presence to ensure their digital footprint shows them in a positive and professional light. Early-career professionals should consider developing a website or portfolio to strengthen their online presence. I believe enthusiasm is underrated yet essential for candidates to stand out during the job search process and advance their careers. Enthusiastic individuals typically demonstrate a willingness to learn and adapt, which is crucial in today's ever-changing work landscape. They approach challenges with a can-do attitude, fostering a collaborative and innovative team culture. Enthusiasm can be infectious, uplifting team morale and encouraging others to engage more deeply with their work.

Dr. Mark Farrell, FIA, CEO of ProActuary, UK

Contrary to popular belief, understanding how to leverage flaws to your advantage is more important than a perfect résumé. Every job applicant has obstacles to overcome, some more complicated than others — particularly for those whose résumés raise red flags. Take charge of your story and change the negative to the positive. Positivity is a crucial professional trait since it plays a major role in creating a positive work atmosphere. Optimism increases the likelihood that you will work toward the solution rather than focusing on the problem. Positive individuals frequently have a can-do mentality, which advances the objectives of the business.

Steve Feiner, Managing Editor, Tech Jive and CEO, ABF Group, CA

There are three things that make a college graduate or young professional stand out. First, having one or two internships with well-known companies, ideally in a field they are looking to work in. Second, holding a master's degree can significantly enhance their appeal. Lastly, it's essential to have a LinkedIn profile. If these elements are absent, having a well-formatted résumé with a clear summary of career goals and how their college course-work has prepared them for the role they are applying for is important. Also, bulleting relevant projects, charity work, or events from their college experience can add value to their application.

Nicole Aranya, Talent Acquisition Senior Manager at FanDuel, NY

One of the biggest traps I see early-career job seekers fall into is creating an overly broad résumé to cast the widest possible job search net. This typically has the opposite of the desired effect. If you don't know how or where you fit, how should a potential employer know? Sometimes, this lack of résumé targeting is a FOMO thing. In other cases, it's a matter of not taking the time to do your homework and connect your unique skills and values to the problems you want to solve. The combination of self-knowledge and data from employer research gives you the tools to create a clear brand and to articulate how your superpowers position you to help that employer move the ball forward. Your target job listings can be a goldmine of information, not just about the kinds of skills that will help you stand out but about an employer's values and whether they align with yours.

Jennifer Fishberg, Career Storyteller and Job Search Strategist at Career Karma Resume Services, NJ

To impress decision-makers, focus on three key aspects: demonstrating impact by providing concrete examples of your achievements, highlighting adaptability and resilience in overcoming challenges, and cultivating an authentic online and offline professional presence. During interviews, blend preparation with authenticity. Understanding a company's culture and how your unique skills fit into that picture is crucial. It's not just about ticking boxes; it's about demonstrating how your individuality and perspectives add value to the team and the organization. Integrity and accountability are also paramount. They speak volumes about a person's character and potential as a long-term asset to any team.

Tara Furiani, CEO at Not the HR Lady, TX

During the job search process, tapping into alumni from the undergraduate or graduate school you attended is a valuable resource. Use LinkedIn's Alumni Search tool to identify graduates who now work in roles and/or for employers that interest you. Examine those alums' LinkedIn profiles to understand what they did during their student years to prepare for their current work. Reach out to these alumni and ask for informational interviews to build relationships and learn more about their journeys from college to career.

Carli Fink, Founder of Foreseeable Futures, Ontario

Early in one's career, it is common to compare oneself to others further along professionally. This often results in exaggerated résumé accomplishments and LinkedIn profiles full of cliché words that leave a saccharine taste. Instead of worrying about the lack of major accomplishments, offer authentic impacts. Don't "fake it until you make it," as recruiters want to hire people who are real. When sending a LinkedIn message to connections, don't agonize over the perfect language. It should be short and sweet, like: "Great meeting you at the networking event last week" or "Hope you are doing well since graduation and enjoying life in NYC." In most cases, the reason you didn't get the job isn't anything you did wrong. So, instead of taking it personally and feeling dejected, look at it as an opportunity to build your connection with an employer.

Denise Fowler, Founder of Career Happiness Coaching, Washington, DC

It's easy to tell when a candidate is "robo-applying" to job openings, and we question whether this person read the job posting. It's important to reflect on why you're applying to a particular job or company, what aspects of the company attract you, and how your skills align with the role. Candidates must demonstrate their uniqueness and good-fit values throughout the job search process, starting with the application. When you reach the interview stage, your questions must show you did your homework. While many emerging professionals ask what the company culture is like, there are far better questions. For example, the applicant can share what they have learned about the company and ask, "I noticed that you have five employee resource groups on your website, which is so exciting to see. Can you share more about these groups and what prompted the company to create them?"

Lindsey Garito, SHRM-SCP, SPHR, AVP at Large Health-care Organization, NY

....

Résumé red flags include something that appears too good to be true. For instance, I often see résumés of people who claim they released a major product at Facebook (or a similar company). Once I dig in during the interview, it is evident that they claim ownership without clarifying their actual contributions. This lack of transparency erodes trust; any good interviewer can always sniff this out. When it comes to the job search, don't ask for a job or referral on LinkedIn. Instead, ask for guidance and advice. If you make a strong impression on this person, they will likely offer to help. When a desirable job opening arises, reach out by personal email to the hiring manager and let them know you applied and why you want the job. It's almost a sure thing they'll look at your résumé if you do this.

Nicolas Garfinkel, Founder of Mindful Conversation, WA

....

A lot of job seekers want to work fully remotely or hybrid. It's important to do research and have perspective of where the market stands: today's companies are mostly operating in a hybrid fashion. If you want to work 100 percent remotely, recognize this may mean a longer job search for you. Balance being open to flexible (hybrid) work situations, doing your research to understand what is typical or reasonable to ask for while also staying grounded in what you know you want in your next work experience. Also, I find that job seekers are more so seeking flexibility, empathy, and understanding from employers rather than needing to be fully remote, so focus on asking questions during interviews that help you understand how employers handle flexibility when it is required, rather than only focusing on their remote policies.

Rachel Serwetz, CEO and Founder of WOKEN, NY

The biggest red flag when reviewing a job seeker's LinkedIn or résumé is the absence of quantifiable metrics. According to our data, this single factor is the most predictive of whether a résumé will result in an interview. Include even approximate metrics or estimates to demonstrate to the hiring manager your focus on what matters: measurable impact. Since hiring managers sift through hundreds of résumés for each open position and spend approximately 60 seconds on each, including measurable impact will make their job easier and increase your chances of getting noticed.

Stephen Greet, CEO at Beamjobs, NY

Red flags that recruiters and hiring managers look out for include short tenures (especially jumping between jobs in different industries), unexplained gaps, exaggerations, inconsistencies in expectations (i.e., previous jobs versus current aspirations), and inconsistencies between LinkedIn and the résumé. Job seekers will always make a strong impression if they are professional, know what they want without coming across as arrogant, can explain themselves succinctly, show their relevant and transferable skills, and show that they have done their homework.

R. Karl Hebenstreit, PhD, PCC, Principal, Perform & Function, LLC, CA

When crafting your résumé, focus on the top three accomplishments from each position to highlight your overarching contribution to the organization. These can also serve as valuable talking points during interviews. Take a few minutes to complete the verification option on LinkedIn to build trust among recruiters and employers. Additionally, sharing causes (e.g., animal rights, social impact, children's rights) that are important to you can establish common ground with others. Stay active on LinkedIn by following organizations and leaders in your field, commenting on feeds, and sharing your knowledge, activities, and articles of interest. Some recruiters will submit your LinkedIn recommendations alongside your résumé for the hiring manager's review, so don't sleep on this one (ask for endorsements). Signing up for job alerts keeps you informed about available opportunities in the market. Compare your profile with industry colleagues you admire to uncover areas for improvement in positioning yourself. Lastly, use analytics to your advantage by monitoring profile views, search appearances, and engagement on your posts and adjust as needed. These steps enhance your visibility, credibility, and competitiveness in the job market.

Christy Honeycutt, SVP of Strategy Development and Execution at AppyHere, TX

One common mistake is not fully answering an interviewer's questions. Also, soft skills like communication, professionalism, and eagerness to learn set candidates apart. I've personally hired individuals who lacked technical skills but had the soft skills and motivation I was seeking. Companies are happy to train individuals who are ready and willing to learn and work hard.

Crystal Kardys, Managing Partner at L21 Solutions, NY

Job search success comes down to self-awareness and identifying your skill set, strengths, and interests. Those with this understanding have an edge over those who are unclear about their direction. When transitioning careers, it's essential to determine how your skill set aligns with the new role and demonstrates your ability to adapt. By knowing yourself and focusing on your skill set, you can position yourself for success. It's not about achieving perfection; it's about embracing failure as a natural part of growth. When people share stories of their challenges, I'm more interested in hearing about their failures and how they handled them. I want to know the details: what went wrong, how they fixed it, and whether they learned from it. In an interview, highlighting a failure and demonstrating how you turned it around shows resilience and growth.

Michael Kerrigan, Director of Human Resources/Head of HR Americas and APAC at Interactive Brokers, NY

Don't underestimate the power of curiosity. Asking insightful questions clarifies your understanding and shows you're actively thinking about how you can contribute to the role and company. Candidates who show they can navigate change and are resilient stand out. An eagerness to learn indicates a growth mindset, which is essential for personal and professional development. Be genuine in your interactions: authentic candidates create a connection and trust, which are vital in any working relationship.

Chris Kille, Founder of Elevate Outsourcing, MA

Virtual interviews have surged in popularity, especially formats entailing blank screens with text prompts, where neither the interviewer nor the candidate is visible. These encourage objectivity in assessing candidates' responses. Candidates are typically presented with around 10 questions, often starting with an inquiry about their background. While redo options exist, it's best to limit their use due to time constraints. Software can assess intonation, eye movements, and facial expressions, so ensure you maintain clear and confident communication and practice with similar software beforehand.

Naomi Koller, Naomi Koller Careers, NY

Leverage LinkedIn strategically by shifting your focus from quantity and job titles to your ideal employer and company. Use LinkedIn to engage with and follow their company pages, filter employees, and concentrate your networking efforts on individuals within those organizations to ultimately get your foot in the door. Before diving into this strategy, ensure your profile clearly communicates your career goals to viewers. Replace generic headlines like "Student" or "Graduate" with a concise statement that demonstrates your understanding of the desired role's objectives or how your transferable skills make you a great match for those roles.

Steph Cartwright, Job Search Strategist at Off The Clock Resumes, WA

AI search engines like Perplexity AI and Google's Gemini are invaluable for job seekers by synthesizing vast amounts of information into easily digestible chunks. These tools provide quick boosts in learning in-demand skills or credentials for particular roles or industries, emerging trends and best practices impacting a specific profession, salary averages, and role-specific interview questions. If you want to learn critical information to support your job search efforts but don't have a ton of time to devote to conducting research, then it's definitely worth leveraging AI search engines!

Keith Spencer, Career Expert at FlexJobs, PA

Embrace Your Journey: Entering the workforce can be scary. Before discounting your "limited experience," remember that your coursework, extracurricular activities, internships, and volunteer experiences are transferable. Soft skills and knowledge gained from these experiences can set you apart. Most graduates need more practical experience, and hiring partners are aware of that. They want to see your preparation, questions, and engagement. They are willing to train you and invest, but you must show them you're serious and not just "looking for another job."

Grace Meidanis, Consultant, Talent Acquisition Leader, MA

....

While preparation is crucial, how you show up is equally important. I've come across candidates who appear impressive on paper, but during a Zoom call, they're either slouched on a couch or barely visible due to poor lighting. For recent college grads, I'm not solely focused on experience; I'm interested in their skills, passions, hobbies, and extracurricular activities. It also comes down to how well a candidate will integrate into the organization's culture and the actual team they'll be working with. Above all, I look for teachability in a candidate.

Linda Low, Director of People & Culture at ESG, Boston, MA

....

My top LinkedIn recommendation is to build friendships. Note that I'm not using the word "networking," although they're one and the same. Many young professionals don't like the word networking, so I clarify that it's about building professional friendships. My mantra is "Be a Friend First," which I use in my LinkedIn headline. Come to LinkedIn with that mindset rather than asking, "Who will hire me?" or "Who will buy from me?" This will help you get, keep, and advance in the job.

Sandra Long, Author of **LinkedIn for Personal Branding** *and* **Jumpstart Your LinkedIn Profile,** *TEDx Speaker, CT*

....

eady Set Switch: For career switchers, getting in front of decision-makers can be the toughest part of the job search, and everything you've done up to this point has prepared you to succeed. There are three things an interviewer is looking for: Abilities (the "What"), Fit (the "How"), and Motivation (the "Why"). Motivation (the "Why") is the single most important factor of the three and the ultimate decider, particularly for those transitioning careers. Hiring managers dig into your motivation by asking, "Why do you want this job, at this company, at this time?" While it can be asked in a number of ways, what you need to be able to convincingly articulate is why you're choosing to make a career change and what specifically about the job/company is of interest to you. Craft a career story that demonstrates your commitment to the role, aligns with your career path, is genuine, communicates your value, and highlights why you are the right fit for the role. When you keep in mind the hiring process is about elimination (not selection), you begin to realize how important these three factors are in the interview.

Dr. Dawn Graham, Author of Switchers: How Smart Professionals Change Careers and Seize Success, NY

e targeted in your job search strategy and make it personal. Your résumé is a marketing tool and needs to instantly capture the attention of recruiters by being tailored to your desired job and employers. There's no need to recapture the skills listed on your résumé in the cover letter; this is your chance to explain the "why" behind your application and highlight your personality and alignment with the company's needs and values — and demonstrate you did your homework. Young professionals need a voracious appetite for learning. You can't master by observing; mastery comes from doing and hard work, sometimes requiring long hours. You can and should work a 60-hour work week while you don't have a mortgage or family obligations. Remember, those extra hours are an investment in yourself to master your craft, not merely putting in hours for an employer.

Allison Madison, President and CEO at Madison Approach Staffing, NY

When it comes to climbing the company ladder, there are several steps you can take in the short term. Start by learning about every facet of the company and its industry. Consistently act and dress appropriately for the next promotion, creating the perception that you're suited for advancement. Hitch your wagon to a star: Find a mentor who's moving up and actively support their goals, leveraging their guidance and influence to propel your career forward. In addition, demonstrate your capabilities and capacity to grow by doing the jobs no one else is willing to do. For the long term, be active in the industry and aim to gain a positive reputation. When going for a promotion, be ready to articulate a compelling business case for deserving the job. How will your promotion contribute to the company's profitability, cost savings, efficiency, or productivity? While you may deserve a promotion, it's essential to communicate its benefits to the company and consider how it will advance the interests of those recommending it. In simple terms, if you want them on your side, what's in it for them?

Barry Maher, Principal, Barry Maher & Associates, CA, and Author of Filling the Glass

Spending 15 minutes daily developing a growth mindset is a success multiplier. Your career will benefit from being known as the person who embraces challenges, persists through setbacks, and enhances performance and productivity. Here's a daily sprint to develop this crucial skill: Start the week by choosing a focus related to your field. Learn about it for 10 minutes Monday to Thursday. Then brainstorm how to apply it to your work for 5 minutes. Summarize and share your insights on Friday. This exercise will increase your visibility and position you as a proactive problem-solver, effective communicator, continuous learner, and emerging leader.

Lisa K. McDonald, Founder and President of Career Polish, IN

Never talk about a problem you had in a previous role, with a previous team or manager, or while in school. You have never had a bad experience — only learning experiences. If we hear that you had a bad experience, we are going to assume that you are the problem and that you may be a toxic employee. Don't start telling us about your history; start with your most recent experience and work backward. Once you're out of college, we're not interested in what you did in high school or high school summers. Don't try to be someone you're not. If you're quiet, you can be quiet and still have a great interview. We want to know who we are going to be working with! Don't tell us anything personal, but do tell us what your personality will be once we start working with you.

Amy Feind Reeves, Career Coach and Author of
Hire A Hiring Manager, MA

One of the biggest mistakes on LinkedIn is not taking advantage of messaging. Identify the hiring lead on LinkedIn and stand out by sending a personalized message to the recruiter or hiring manager, significantly increasing your chances of being hired. To make a lasting impression on decision-makers, job seekers and aspiring professionals should prioritize two essentials. First, quantify your achievements to demonstrate tangible results. Instead of merely saying, "I managed Client X," share specific accomplishments, like "Achieved a 60% increase in YoY traffic growth while managing Client X." Second, go the extra mile and reach out to people in the company. If applying to a non-sales job, your proactive interest stands out. If applying to a sales job, you've already lost the job if you haven't reached out proactively.

Andrew McLellan, CEO at Trellis Consulting, UT

Reviewing job descriptions is an essential piece of the job search puzzle. Make sure your résumé includes skills and keywords from your target roles. Lacking direct experience for a particular role is okay; if you have completed relevant coursework, it may apply to the job. Quantify results whenever possible. For instance, if you saved your company $300,000, spell that out! If you worked with a $50-million client, mention it, and if you have Fortune 500 clients, name-drop (as long as it's not proprietary information). Adding numbers or context wherever possible enhances your résumé's impact. Building trust and relationships is the most valuable soft skill for career success and will pay dividends in so many ways.

Colleen Paulson, MBA, CPRW, Founder of Ageless Careers, Pittsburgh, PA

Whether you're an entry-level employee or an executive, remember to bring three essential qualities to the table: humility (nobody likes a know-it-all), knowledge (in other words, experience), and curiosity (asking insightful questions). These prove you are thinking about the business. Don't hesitate to ask clarifying questions like, "Can you explain that?" Drawing on my own experience transitioning from a Fortune 500 company to a family-owned business, don't discount your transferable skills. Skills like leadership, planning, and strategic insight are in all roles and should be communicated. Position your strong management skills as assets that can be applied in just about any corporation or industry.

Frank Giuliano, SHRM-SCP, HR Executive, NY

Talent search has become robotic, losing the human touch that often leads to successful hires. Many recruiters manually review the first 100 résumés before resorting to technology, prioritizing personal insight over automated filters. It's on a first-come, first-served basis, so jump on opportunities before the tracking system enters into play. Advancements have made mass résumé blasting effortless, flooding the hiring process with generic applications. When someone tells me that they've applied to over 1,000 jobs, that tells me their career search is unfocused and that they are using a one-size-fits-all résumé. Recruiters can spot these cookie-cutter résumés a mile away. While incorporating job-specific terms is beneficial, it's essential to highlight your unique attributes to avoid being dismissed as a keyword spammer. Résumés overloaded with keywords may bypass filters but won't get past the human eye. It's an unfortunate waste of time for both parties.

Angela Priest, Co-Founder and COO of Alma.Me, Denver, CO

If you think a LinkedIn Profile is a résumé, think again. LinkedIn offers two major visual opportunities: the banner space above your Profile and the Featured section, allowing you to have a carousel of visuals, such as a brief introductory video on you. Being visual is important, particularly if you are targeting employers in advertising, technology, or with a start-up. LinkedIn is getting more crowded, with over 1 billion members posting more than ever. You have to figure out how to be visible on a platform that is the place where professionals network online. Can you put time and thought into your posts and comments so that your connections see you as a valued colleague? Or will you rely on AI to generate frequent posts (an option I don't recommend)?

Bruce K. Segall, Founder of Marketing Sense for Business, NY

Your job is to sell yourself. Likeability is everything when it comes to job interviews. Confidence is critical; avoid showing uncertainty, such as saying, "I want to get my foot in the door" or "I'll do anything," which conveys desperation and a lack of direction. Instead, demonstrate your enthusiasm and suitability for the role. Always come armed with a couple of questions. Questions I like include: "What are two or three characteristics that will make someone successful in this job?" and "Is there anything that gives you pause about my background?" (which shows you are bold and take feedback well). Remember, the person who really, really wants the job outshines the others and gets it!

Linda Glass Shapiro, Principal at Cavit Group, Washington, DC

Networking and information interviews are the cornerstone of any successful job search. Building relationships and gaining industry insights through informal chats are invaluable. I encourage young professionals to engage in these conversations early and often. They underscore the importance of curiosity and openness to learn and can dramatically increase job prospects.

Tracy Shroyer, PhD, From Corporate to Classroom; Professor of Business & Career Development Coach, OH

The most important thing you can do is start networking at a young age. Business relationships take time, and farther down the line, it will be people you have shared experiences with who will bring you opportunities. This is long-term thinking. If you want a "secret weapon," invest time to establish relationships, helping others without expecting anything in return. Twenty-five years from now, nobody will have a better network than yours. Also, never meet or call another person without closely reviewing their LinkedIn. You want to learn about their career and see if you have shared experiences, common friends, or other things that can help you in a personal conversation ahead of time. It is okay to tell someone, "I saw on LinkedIn that you once worked at XYZ company. . . . My first job was with XYZ." The idea is to find things to talk about that come naturally so your conversation will flow better and help you build that all-important relationship.

Thom Singer, CEO at Austin Technology Council, TX and author of The ABC's of Networking

We're finally getting to the place where employers understand people need to take time off of work for various reasons. However, it's still a good idea to fill any résumé gaps of more than six months with a short description. "Family health care," "cross-country move," and even "professional development" are all acceptable. You can provide more details during an interview, but be concise! It's equally important to highlight achievements. Recruiters want to see what you accomplished in addition to your duties. Use numbers to stand out and show the scope and scale of your roles. For example, instead of "track invoices," write "track and reconcile invoices for a $2.5M business unit, ensuring accuracy and providing detailed reports to senior leaders."

Anna Kate Anderson, Founder of Anna Kate Anderson Executive Résumés, Illinois

Early-career professionals should showcase work outside of school to stand out. For instance, if the candidate is a software engineer and has won a hackathon, consider including this in a portfolio. Hiring managers and recruiters would find this impressive. Similarly, volunteering or leading a volunteering event or organization should be highlighted. Many companies like hiring candidates who have vertical experience in their industry.. If an individual did not receive a job offer from their internship, they should consider applying to that company's competitors.

Marsh Sutherland, Lead Recruiter at Vizit, MA

....

Navigating the job market can feel overwhelming. But armed with these insider tips and expert advice, you're well-equipped to forge ahead confidently. Remember, each insight in this chapter aims to enhance your career journey. Whether refining your résumé, mastering interviews, or building a five-star network, these tips empower you at every step. Apply these gems to your unique style and watch your career dreams become your future LinkedIn headline.

PART VIII —
THE ENTREPRENEUR
IN YOU

For some, entrepreneurship comes naturally. It did for me! I grew up in a very entrepreneurial family. My parents had successful businesses in the fashion industry and, later, in real estate. I've always been a risk-taker and love to confront new challenges. I started my first business at age 14 — a home waitress service — with my friend Jen. Driven to make more than the standard hourly babysitting rate, we placed an ad in the local newspaper with the headline: "We Set, Serve & Clean Up. Let us help you at your next party." The only expense was the purchase of a white uniform, bought secondhand. We increased our earnings by 500 percent and were booked for months with repeat business.

The lesson? Learning the fundamentals of business early has big advantages. You develop a skill set you can use for the rest of your life: time management, creativity, and networking. These skills are applicable across a wide range of careers.

Before taking a deep dive into this chapter, let's cover some definitions. An "entrepreneur" is an individual who starts their own business, often based on their idea. Meanwhile, "entrepreneurship" is the overall process of launching a business. Entrepreneurs are both born and made. Likewise, entrepreneurship is a blend of innate traits — problem-solving, resilience, risk tolerance — and learned skills.

"Entrepreneur" means different things to different people. Some may picture a future tech mogul tinkering in their garage; others may picture the owner of a mom-and-pop shop on Main Street. Contrary to popular belief, entrepreneurship is not about having a million-dollar idea. It's about having the passion and perseverance to turn that idea into a reality. It's about being your own boss. And it's about building something from the ground up.

Entrepreneurship presents a diverse array of possibilities. Tech entrepreneurship is characterized by rapid scalability and innovation; social entrepreneurship solves complex issues; and serial entrepreneurship is about building, expanding, and then starting all over again. There's even intrapreneurship or corporate entrepreneurship — less risky varieties that allow you to innovate within the safety net of an existing organization. This reminds us that you don't need to have your own business to be an entrepreneur.

Entrepreneurship is on the rise. No matter how you define or perceive it, the general concept of entrepreneurship is becoming more and more popular. The intersection of several trends — like remote work and e-commerce — has made starting a business more accessible than ever before.

Entrepreneurship Matters

Like brands, entrepreneurship isn't about "me, me, me." It brings tremendous value to the wider world, like:

- Fueling job creation, wealth, and a thriving economy.
- Providing new and disruptive services, products, or technologies that improve society.
- Sparking social change and enhancing quality of life.
- Solving complex problems through innovation.

Entrepreneurship by the Numbers

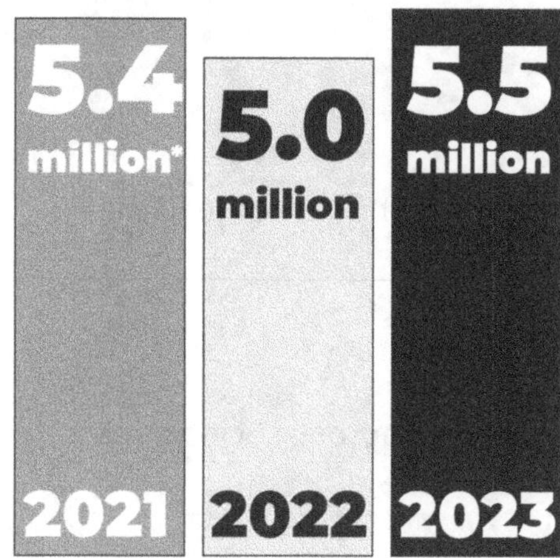

55% of adults have started a business at some point in their lives, and

26% have started two or more businesses.

(Global Entrepreneurship Monitor)

31 million entrepreneurs in the US, which is about **16%** of the adult workforce and **9.29%** of the population

(Global Entrepreneurship Monitor)

Side Hustle Facts

- **34%, or one in three, Americans have a side hustle.** *(Zapier)*
- **The US side hustle market is valued at over $2.58 trillion.** *(USA Today)*
- **The average monthly income from a side hustle is $810.** *(Bankrate survey)*

582 million entrepreneurs across the globe

(GEM: Global Entrepreneurship Monitor)

85%
of jobs that will exist in 2030 haven't yet been invented.

(Institute for the Future)

33%
of small businesses get started with less than

$5,000.

(SBA)

Around **20%** of small businesses fail in their first year.

(US Small Business Administration)

13
million women own their own businesses in the US.

(WBENC: Women's Business Enterprise National Council, 2024)

42%
of US businesses are women-owned.

(WBENC, 2024)

Profile of an Entrepreneur

The entrepreneurial bug bites many young people, and for good reason. Starting your own business can be a gratifying experience. But what exactly does it take to be a successful entrepreneur? There's no one-size-fits-all answer to this question, but certain traits are common among successful entrepreneurs. Whether you're interested in starting your own business or want to become more entrepreneurial in your current job, read on for a quick overview of some essential attributes of successful entrepreneurs:

Grit – Perseverance and determination to see ideas through, no matter how hard things get.

Purpose – Clarity on what you stand for. Commitment to your purpose needs to be steadfast.

Risk-taking – The ability to stretch out of your comfort zone and confront challenges head-on.

Motivation – An insatiable appetite for achieving success.

Passion – A burning desire to turn an idea into reality.

Flexibility – The ability to adapt to change. As the business and market shift, you must go with the flow.

Creativity – The ability to live in a state of constant curiosity and envision new possibilities.

Networker – A commitment to building meaningful relationships.

Positivity – A growth mindset. (Refer to Part II, Page 70) for a reminder of the importance of a growth mindset.)

Resourcefulness – The ability to optimize your resources and do more with less.

Take note: If you've got the grit, passion, and a knack for business, it doesn't matter where you come from or how old you are — you're in the game!

Idea to Empire in Five Steps

No two entrepreneurs have the same journey. But as an angel investor, I've learned there's a common sequence of steps you can follow to help transform your idea into an empire. Let's dive in.

1 **Pick a lane.** Every entrepreneur dreams of success. But to achieve it, you first have to *define* it. Ask yourself: What does success mean to you? Consider your aspirations, risk tolerance, market dynamics, potential competition, and more. Conduct an honest assessment of your passions, skills, limitations, and resources — and then follow a course that makes sense. Will this be your supplementary or primary source of income? How big do you want to grow? Are you seeking profits, impact, or something else?

2 **Identify a need.** The very best start-ups fulfill an unmet demand. In other words, you shouldn't be building a solution in search of a problem. Researching and validating your business idea is crucial; a product will only succeed with a market eager to buy it. After market research, start networking with industry experts and speaking to potential investors. Begin defining your target audience through interviews, focus groups, or surveys, pinpointing their needs, wants, and pain points. Explore whether special licenses or additional education are required for your venture. Then, once you deeply understand the market and your audience, build a proof of concept or minimum viable product (MVP).

3 **Develop your product.** This step is where you bring your idea to life, so pay close attention:

■ **Choose a name.** A strong name should be short, simple, and SEO-friendly. To get the creative juices flowing, use ChatGPT or other generative tools.

■ **Choose a structure.** Your business structure affects everything from taxes to personal liability to your operation. Choose wisely from this list, and consult an attorney and a certified accountant before finalizing your decision:

- ☐ A **Limited Liability Company (LLC)** combines limited liability protection with pass-through taxation, offering flexibility in management and taxation.
- ☐ An **S-Corporation (S-Corp)** and a **C-Corporation (C-Corp)** differ primarily in taxation and ownership structures. S-Corps have pass-through taxation and limit shareholders to 100 US citizens or residents with only one class of stock, whereas C-Corps can have unlimited shareholders and multiple stock classes and are subject to double taxation on profits and dividends.
- ☐ A **Sole Proprietorship** involves one individual owning and operating the business, offering simplicity in management but making the owner personally liable for all business obligations.
- ☐ A **Partnership** involves two or more individuals sharing ownership and responsibilities in a business, with options for general or limited partnerships.
- ☐ A **Corporation** is a separate legal entity offering limited liability protection to shareholders and the ability to raise capital through stock and bond sales, subject to double taxation on corporate profits and dividends.

- **Protect your brand.** Make sure you're buttoned up: compliance with all relevant laws, regulations, and industry standards is essential. Obtain licenses and permits, study labor laws, and prioritize data privacy. Safeguard your intellectual property through trademarks, patents, and copyrights. I strongly advise nondisclosure agreements (NDAs) at the outset to maintain confidentiality.

- **Build the plan.** A detailed business plan is indispensable. List out your goals and strategies, map a market analysis, and outline operational structure and financial projections. HR considerations — like staffing, compensation, and benefits — are also integral components of a business plan, along with marketing and operational details. Marketing should *never* be an afterthought — "build it, and they shall come" does not work! Experiencing business plan writer's block? SCORE and HubSpot are excellent platforms for finding templates.

- **Network like crazy.** Every successful entrepreneur understands the power of relationships. Growing your network unlocks more resources, opportunities, and support. Seek mentors, peers, and investors — relentlessly. Join professional groups like Entrepreneurs' Organization or Young Entrepreneur Council and consider creating your own advisory board.

- **Figure out financing.** If you're an entrepreneur, "Math isn't my thing" is no longer an acceptable phrase. It's time to embrace numbers! Assess start-up costs, expenses, and funding options (see sidebar on page 179). Formalize your budgeting and bookkeeping and learn how to decipher balance sheets and income statements. You don't need to be a certified CPA, but you do need a firm understanding of pricing strategies, cash flow management, and tax preparation.

- Establish systems. Entrepreneurs need order to succeed. Choose the right tools to tame chaos, like accounting software, project management websites, creative suites, and so on.

4 **Blast off.** Three, two, one — liftoff! For a spectacular launch, several stars need to align: customer acquisition. Sales and PR plans. Competitive yet profitable pricing strategies. Key performance indicators (KPIs) to track progress. And a positive company culture built on collaboration, innovation, and a customer-centric mindset. With these as your North Stars, you can chart a path toward success and sustainability from the get-go. Also, who doesn't love a party? Plan a big bash for day one and invite business leaders and local dignitaries.

5 **Pursue profitability.** It should go without saying: the lifeline of a successful new business relies on steady cash. However, many new ventures don't turn a profit in their first year, so having a financial cushion is a must. Start with ample cash reserves, but aggressively pursue profits soon after. You don't want the constant pressure of managing short-term loans. When I launched my firm, my very first hire was a bookkeeper. I highly recommend bringing in an accountant or bookkeeper from day one to help stay in the black.

Some other financial tips to remember: Always keep personal and business finances separate. Quantify factors like desired earnings, the necessary client base for profitability, and weekly time commitments. And contemplate worthwhile investments, including new equipment and employees. One thing that is an absolute must is to keep tabs on market dynamics and competitors. Leveraging trends enables entrepreneurs to grasp customer motivations and refine products accordingly.

Pitch Perfect

Successful entrepreneurs' secret weapon is their pitch — their answer to the question, "Why me and my business?" I've heard countless pitches over the years: some really good, several not so good, and a good deal that made me want to scream. Well-crafted pitches tell an easy-to-understand and compelling story about the potential to scale a start-up.

For a deep dive into pitches, I turned to my friend Sandy Wollman, Co-Founder and Managing Director of the Westchester Angels in metro New York. First, he shared the basics:

The format. A good pitch has two parts: a slide deck (usually a PowerPoint) and a verbal presentation. An effective slide deck enhances what you say rather than distracting from it. Pitches are not business plans, so less text is better. You want to pique interest, not delve into fine print.

The process. All angel groups have the same basic four-step process. First comes the *virtual application*, where investors can weed out the worst. Then comes *screening*, which is a (usually) virtual presentation and your first chance to nail the pitch. Next is the *investor meeting*, where you'll pitch again — most likely in person. And last is *due diligence*, where investors dig in. The process can take weeks or months. Rest assured: you *will* be tested.

Next, Sandy shared advice for entrepreneurs ready to make their big pitch:

Relax and be confident. Practice, practice, practice your pitch so you can deliver it in your sleep.

Less is more. Your slide deck should be simple. White spaces, pictures, and bullet points allow investors to stay focused on your verbal presentation.

Open BIG. A bold statement on the first slide immediately grabs your audience's attention. Here's a recent one that stuck in my head: "Loliware: Advancing the Planet Towards a Plastic-Free Future with Products That Will Disappear."

Stand in their shoes. Your pitch should cater to your audience's point of view, *not* yours. What would you want to hear if you were an investor?

Be transparent. Remember, you are pitching experienced business professionals. So, if you don't know the answer to a question, don't bluff. It's okay to say, "I don't know," or "I'll get back to you."

Mention marketing. No matter what stage your idea is in, investors will want to hear something about your go-to-market strategy. How are you going to sell your product or platform?

Have multiple decks. Some angel groups allow a four-minute pitch, others 10. Learn the time allotted beforehand and customize your deck accordingly.

Try video. Angel investors tend to like short-form videos, especially if they communicate your impact so far.

Anticipate questions. Determine likely questions ahead of time and then practice smart, concise answers.

Look at your audience. You're pitching people, not a screen. Stay focused on the investors in front of you.

FUNDING OPTIONS:

Once you've refined your idea and developed a solid business plan, your next priority is funding to launch your business. Even the most brilliant idea won't go far without adequate capital. Here are several funding options worth exploring:

Friends and family: Initial funding or loans from friends and family can be immensely helpful; trust levels are high, and interest rates are low.

Bootstrapping: You can also tap into personal savings, which provides autonomy — no investors or outside interference demanding quick profits.

Crowdfunding: Platforms like Kickstarter, Indiegogo, GoFundMe, Fundable, and Wefunder allow you to collect numerous smaller donations rather than relying on one or two big investors.

Angel Investors/Venture Capital (VC) firms: This option provides a significant initial investment in exchange for equity. These types of investors also provide guidance, mentorship, and connections. Platforms like the Angel Investment Network are an excellent place to start.

Government programs: The US Small Business Administration (SBA), a federal agency, offers loans to start-ups with favorable terms, including lower down payments and extended repayment periods. There are also federal grant opportunities. Check out Grants.gov, which boasts over 1,000 grant programs.

Seek a co-founder: Teaming up with a like-minded partner means a smaller piece of the pie and more capital and human resources.

10 QUESTIONS EVERY ENTREPRENEUR MUST ANSWER:

1. What problem are you passionate about solving?
2. Who is your target audience?
3. What is the demand for the product/service?
4. How will you fund your venture?
5. What unique solution or value proposition do you offer?
6. How will you differentiate your product or service from competitors?
7. What resources, skills, and expertise do you need to succeed?
8. What are your short- and long-term goals?
9. Do you have a solid network and mentors to provide guidance?
10. How will you measure success?

Why Businesses Fail

Entrepreneurship is not for the faint of heart. Approximately 50 percent of businesses fail within the first few years, with only around 15 percent of start-ups achieving significant success.

Here are the top three reasons why:

1) **Running out of money.**
2) **Lack of demand for product/service.**
3) **Poor management team/infrastructure.**

An Entrepreneur's Brand

Earlier, I said that an entrepreneur's secret weapon is their pitch. Well, they have a second one: their brand. The right branding can make an ambitious idea a reality — and the wrong brand can sink even the most innovative idea. Here are some best practices to build a positive brand:

> *Innovation is the new competitive advantage. In the ever-changing world of entrepreneurship, adaptability is the language of success — it's essential for thriving amid shifting landscapes, client whims, and marketing fads.*

Relationships over revenues. For authentic entrepreneurs, it's about more than just the money — it's about the customers, too. Make sure that shows. Brands should communicate with empathy, asking their audience, "How can we help?" Socially responsible companies are particularly important to Millennials and Gen Zers. Ultimately, people make decisions based on trust.

Be genuine. Don't hide your authentic self or leave your passion on the sidelines. Humans don't want to connect with a logo — they want to relate with other humans. Give customers a glimpse of the people behind the business, talk like a real person (not a robot), and own your mistakes.

Let others speak for you. Did you know approximately 95 percent of customers read online reviews before making a decision? Gather social proof of all types: testimonials, reviews, ratings, follower counts, influencer endorsements, subscribers, and fans. Then, leverage this proof on your website and across social media.

Stay relevant. Create high-value content for your audience; make sure it passes the "Who cares?" test. Your articles, blog posts, videos, and other content need to be incredibly shareable, engaging, and actionable.

Invest in Education

It's never too late to pick up new skills. Your nearby colleges and business schools likely offer entrepreneurship programs, certificates, and degrees, often tailored to individuals at different stages of their entrepreneurial journey. Meanwhile, platforms like Udemy and HubSpot Academy offer courses and certificates on business growth, sales, digital marketing, and even podcasting. See the resource section for additional ideas (pg. 223).

Did You Know?

If you're thinking of launching a business or curious about what it involves, read on for some inspiring entrepreneurship stories and tips. You never know — you might be the next Richard Branson or Oprah Winfrey!

Top dogs. Tesla executive Elon Musk is currently the wealthiest person in the world, with a net worth of $263 billion, followed by Jeff Bezos, Founder and Executive Chair, Amazon ($209 billion) and Mark Zuckerberg, CEO and Chair, META ($201 billion). Other billionaires with the largest net worths include LVMH's Arnault, Microsoft's Bill Gates, and Oracle's Larry Ellison. Eight of the top 10 billionaires made their fortunes in technology, with Arnault and Berkshire Hathaway's Warren Buffett as exceptions. (Investopedia, Nov. 2024)

Garage genesis. Twelve companies worth more than $1 billion were founded in garages, and they're not just tech companies. Mattel, Maglite, Harley Davidson, Disney, and Yankee Candle all got their start in the garage.

- Hewlett-Packard was started in a garage in 1939. Today, the garage is a private museum known as the "birthplace of Silicon Valley."
- Ten miles from the HP garage, Steve Wozniak created Apple's first computers in 1976.
- Bill Gates and Paul Allen started Microsoft in a garage, and Larry Page and Sergey Brin started Google in a garage in 1998.
- Disney's first film studio was started in a Los Angeles garage in 1923.

Maximum disruption. Some entrepreneurs, known as "first in a category," are innovators who redefine whole industries with groundbreaking ideas.

- Sara Blakely: Blakely revolutionized the undergarment industry by creating Spanx, a line of undergarments designed to smooth and shape women's bodies. She invested her savings into developing the product and eventually turned it into a billion-dollar company. Blakely's initial steps involved extensive research and development to perfect the design and functionality. Her breakthrough came when she secured shelf space in major department stores, effectively launching Spanx into the market. Spanx quickly gained popularity, becoming a staple in women's wardrobes worldwide. Today, Spanx offers many products beyond shapewear, including leggings, bras, and activewear.

- Brian Chesky: Chesky revolutionized hospitality by enabling homeowners to rent their spaces to travelers. Alongside Joe Gebbia and Nathan Blecharczyk, Chesky founded Airbnb in 2008 during a design conference when they struggled to afford rent in San Francisco. Seizing an opportunity, they rented air mattresses and offered breakfast, sparking the idea for Airbnb. They created a website, "AirBed & Breakfast," attracting three guests who paid $80 each per night. Recognizing the potential, they expanded beyond air mattresses, developing a platform for global accommodations. Today, Airbnb boasts millions of listings worldwide, disrupting traditional hospitality.

Early success. Think you are too young to consider entrepreneurship? Think again. Some entrepreneurs launched a business before they were under the age of 16:

■ **Moziah "Mo" Bridges** – Mo launched Mo's Bows, a stylish handmade bow tie collection, in 2011 at age nine. Two years later, he appeared on ABC's *Shark Tank*, and investor Daymond John became his mentor. In 2017, Mo signed a seven-figure licensing deal with the NBA to feature the NBA's logo on his apparel.

■ **Ben Pasternak** – Australian Ben Pasternak developed his first app, a brain teaser game called "Impossible Rush," at age 15 in 2014. The app peaked at number 16 on the US App Store (iOS) charts with millions of downloads. In 2018, he co-founded SIMULATE, a nutrition technology company featuring a plant-based signature product called NUGGS.

■ **Ashley Qualls** – At age 14, Ashley launched whateverlife.com, which was initially conceived as a personal portfolio. It quickly evolved to provide free Myspace layouts and tutorials for teens. In the first few months, she generated $70,000 in sales, primarily from advertising revenues.

■ **Hillary Yip** – Hillary is the CEO of MinorMynas, which she founded at age 10 in 2016 — making her one of the youngest CEOs worldwide. MinorMynas is an online educational platform for children that facilitates language learning through live video calls and chat features.

Girl power. Some of the world's most successful entrepreneurs are women. You'll recognize these names:

■ Oprah Winfrey – She grew up on an isolated farm in Mississippi and is now a television mogul worth billions of dollars.

■ Beyoncé – This top-selling solo artist has millions of dollars in endorsement deals and a $60 million contract with Netflix.

■ Tory Burch – The founder of her namesake fashion company, Tory Burch has a $1 billion net worth.

What's Your Niche?

Everyone has skills and passions — and every skill and passion can lead to a potential business venture. Maybe it's writing, interior design, or teaching French. Here are just a few niches where you might pursue your entrepreneurship journey, organized by category. (Note: Specific training, licensing, or certification may be required.)

REAL ESTATE/CONSTRUCTION:

Real estate agent: Establish yourself as the go-to expert on rentals, sales, beachfront homes, smart homes, or whatever other real estate interests you.

Property management: Consider scaling your own property portfolio or offering management services like rent collection and tenant support.

Cleaning service: Skilled, reliable cleaning solutions for both residential and commercial sectors are always in demand, especially if they're eco-friendly.

Professional organizing: Decluttering and optimizing spaces is a true calling for some people — are you one of them? Start by building relationships with real estate agents who can refer new homeowners.

Home improvement: Whether you want to put your green thumb to work, grab a paintbrush, or craft custom cabinets, handymen (or women) are always in demand.

BUSINESS/FINANCIAL PLANNING:

Franchise: Purchasing a franchise offers the advantages of a proven business model, brand recognition, and extensive support/tools. Analyze market demand and competition to ensure success.

Financial advisor: Do you have a knack for understanding the market? Offer your expertise to individuals and help them achieve their financial goals.

Accounting services: If you look forward to filling out your taxes, extend your expertise to individuals and businesses seeking assistance with accounting, bookkeeping, and more.

Business/Consulting: With a consulting business, you can work with a wide range of businesses on various business problems. You could help new entities get off the ground by creating business plans, conducting market research, and organizing a management structure.

CREATIVE ENDEAVORS:

PR/Marketing: Take it from me, a 25-plus year agency owner: agency ownership is a roller coaster ride — but worth every bump. Services include branding, media relations, graphic design, logo development, social media management, community management, website development, search engine marketing, advertising, and more. And yes, you need to be right- and left-brained.

Photography/Videography: Professionals in photography and videography thrive on visual storytelling. And headshots, weddings, corporate events, and sizzle reels never go out of style.

Art: Artists have several options at their disposal, including selling commissioned pieces, teaching classes, licensing designs, and participating in exhibitions or art fairs. Successful artists establish a strong brand, cultivate a loyal customer base, and effectively market their work.

TRAINING/COACHING VENTURES:

Personal training: Health and fitness is a space with almost unlimited opportunity. Everyone wants to be in shape! Fitness trainers can offer one-on-one appointments, online coaching, and group fitness classes.

Nutrition: There's a growing demand for nutrition services in various sectors, like pediatrics, sports, and lifestyle. Practitioners can offer personalized meal plans and coaching and form partnerships with fitness centers or health-care providers.

Career coaching: Career coaches assist individuals in identifying and honing their skill sets, managing career transitions, crafting cover letters/résumés, preparing for interviews, and more. They are sought after in both high- and low-unemployment environments.

Tutoring: Tutors provide valuable assistance in various subjects and test prep to supplement students' learning. They can also capitalize on opportunities for supplemental income by creating and offering online courses, meeting the demand for remote learning options.

HOSPITALITY:

Private chef: The booming private chef service market creates culinary opportunities for bespoke dining experiences. Whether for intimate dinner parties or extravagant events, personalized culinary experiences are a sure bet.

Catering: Aspiring entrepreneurs entering the catering realm can focus on intimate gatherings, large-scale events, or both. With the expanding demand for quality catering services, diverse dietary preferences, and seemingly unlimited event themes, ample opportunities exist.

Food trucks: Mobile restaurants have the upside of lower up-front costs. Select a sought-after cuisine, equip your truck accordingly, and build a loyal following.

Great Side Hustles

Some of us moonlight as entrepreneurs — and that's okay! Side hustles offer lower risk and always have the potential to evolve into thriving businesses. They can also provide valuable skill-building opportunities without having to be a full-time student or intern. Still, there's no such thing as "quick cash" — side hustles take time, talent, and energy. Here are a handful of ideas:

- Academic tutor
- Music teacher
- Computer support
- Pet photographer
- T-shirt designer
- Farmers market vendor
- Errand-running (e.g., dry-cleaning, grocery shopping)
- Airbnb host
- Dog walking
- House-sitting
- Grocery delivery
- Lawn care
- Copywriting
- Data entry
- Party entertainment services (e.g., clown, magician, balloon artist)
- Garage sale organizer
- Home energy auditing

Let's end on a quirky note. "Entrepreneur" often conjures images of tech founders and savvy investors — but plenty of entrepreneurs are offbeat, too. Here are a few concepts that may not have occurred to you:

- Specialty coffee roasting
- Sustainable packaging design
- Virtual reality therapy for anxiety
- Virtual reality fitness
- Online vintage clothing marketplace
- Hydroponic indoor gardening kits
- Personalized home brewing kits
- Urban beekeeping services
- Digital detox retreats
- Interactive murder mystery events
- Urban farming subscription

1 Entrepreneurship is common. If you're nervous about taking the leap, remember that plenty of others have. In the US, in 2023, 5.5 million new business applications were filed.

2 Follow a blueprint. Entrepreneurs are creative, but they don't wing it. Follow tried-and-true steps like market research, developing a pitch, and cultivating investors.

3 Invest in your brand. Brands — both personal and business — are essential to an entrepreneur's success. Don't neglect them.

4 There is no shortage of opportunities. No matter your skill set — dog walking, fitness, copywriting, or piano — there's a way to parlay it into a successful business venture.

PART IX – YOUR REPUTATION IS EVERYTHING

Contributed by: Allison Kluger

Reputation is intrinsically tied to your personal brand. The difference between the two is you can control your personal brand and choose how to represent your identity, express yourself, and promote yourself on social media or in person. You can create slogans and brand promises and do demonstrations to convince the public that what you believe about yourself or your company is true. Reputation is more about how others perceive and react to your personal brand offering. Your reputation is shaped by others' opinions of you and by people's reactions to your words and actions.

We all have a lens into how we see ourselves: friendly, stoic, creative, quiet, demanding … the list goes on. However, do others perceive us as we think they do or should? And therein lies the rub. We can happily believe we are kind, generous, or tolerant, while someone observing or interacting with us may have a completely different perspective. *To accurately know how you wish to arrive, it's crucial to know where you currently stand.* Your reputation affects your personal brand, whether you like it or not.

Here's an example of how perception is changeable and how a reputation can start outside your control:

Scenario: A man is catching a taxi in New York City one busy morning. It is raining, and he is afraid of being late for an important meeting. He walks up and down the street, looking for an open taxi. He is not alone. There are other desperate New Yorkers also searching for a taxi. Finally, the man steps into the middle of the street and flags down a cab on its way to a woman standing past him waiting on the corner. He stops the taxi mid-block and rapidly hops into the backseat. He feels victorious and responsible. He braved the wretched downpour to catch an elusive taxi to get to his appointment on time so he could satisfy his work commitments. In his mind, he is the hero of his story. The other people on the street in the rain never factored into his consideration. However, the wet, disgruntled woman who saw the taxi heading toward her does not perceive this man the same way. Instead, in her mind, perception, and reality, this man is selfish, unaware, rude, and aggressive. Both their perceptions are accurate.

According to Elon Musk, CEO of Tesla, "Perception becomes reality." If this is true, then this wet, bedraggled woman will never think that the man who took her taxi is anything other than awful. So, what to do? This man didn't even think about the woman's situation. He was so focused on his goals. The answer is surprisingly basic: be aware of how your actions and words affect the people and world around you. Sounds pretty simple, right? But this means looking around, checking out a situation, anticipating pushback, and consciously adjusting your behavior. The reward is that if you are someone who can flex and self-reflect, you will be viewed as a better leader, a better partner, a better friend, and a better human. And this ultimately plays into curating the personal brand you want to authentically embody.

Reputation as an Echo

I have always said that your reputation is like an echo. It precedes you into the room before you get there. Once you leave the room, your reputation lingers among the comments and feelings others have thought and said about you when you are not around to hear them. One summer, I was reading Elena Ferrante's *The Story of a New Name*, and I saw this passage: "He was absolutely the first person to show me in a practical sense how comfortable it is to arrive in a strange, potentially hostile environment and discover that you had been preceded by your reputation, that you don't have to do anything to be accepted, that your name is known, that everyone knows about you, and it's the others, the strangers, who must strive to win your favor and not you theirs." (Source: Elena Ferrante, *The Story of a New Name*, p. 154, 2013)

Synthesized, this means that your reputation is your currency and your calling card. Let's say I am going to speak at a conference, and my contact has set the stage for me with the various stakeholders: "Wait until you meet Allison. She is an expert in reputation and personal branding. She has great stories, and her experience in the television industry and teaching at Stanford Graduate School of Business has given her a unique perspective on how to communicate effectively. She's also very warm and funny. You'll love her." Automatically, I will be greeted by people who are already programmed to welcome, trust, and appreciate me. I have done no work yet. My reputation — what is said about me when I am not in the room — has done all the work. Now, of course, I must live up to that reputation, or else there will be a disconnect, disappointment, and ironically, the person who praised me initially may find that *their* reputation suffers if it is perceived they described me in an unrealistic manner.

Takeaways:

1 A good reputation based on your past work and experiences can pave the way for even better opportunities.

2 If you do not show up the way someone else has promised you will, you may hurt someone else's reputation and damage your reputation in the process. This is why we must all be careful when connecting people. We must vet them carefully. Remember that you will be held accountable if you vouch for someone you don't know well. How you leverage your reputation in the service of others is just as important as how you show up in person.

THE CONTINUUM OF REPUTATION

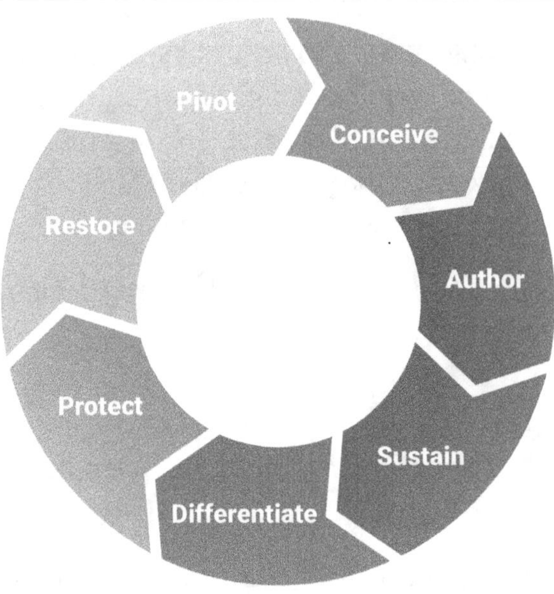

(Source: JD Schramm and Allison Kluger, 2014)

You are never stuck in a reputation sinkhole! Introducing **The Continuum of Reputation:**

My colleague and teaching partner at the Stanford Graduate School of Business, JD Schramm, and I created the *Continuum of Reputation* as a visual representation of how everyone curates, maintains, and changes their reputations constantly. In order and going clockwise to the right: We initially **conceive** of the reputation we want to be recognized for — a hard worker, innovative, commanding, and so on. We **author** that reputation by walking the walk, showing up each time, and demonstrating how we embody this reputation. We **sustain** this reputation by appearing consistenly in whatever arena we work or live in. Once we get comfortable with our reputation and are not questioned but rather trusted for who people think we are, we try to **differentiate** ourselves.

For example, a person may be in medical school, and their reputation is that they can handle emergencies well, function on little sleep, and interact with residents and doctors in a respectful and professional manner. Once that reputation is sustained, this person might veer toward a differentiated specialty in OB-GYN or pediatrics. This person has built the foundation of their reputation so that they will be supported and encouraged when they want to stand out.

There's a chance something might happen, and you will need to **protect** your reputation. It could be a bad Yelp review or a negative client interaction, but it's enough to make you feel derailed or misunderstood. So, you will **restore** your reputation by turning up consistently and staying true to your original values and the behaviors that you are known for. Or you might proactively post a message or make a statement reaffirming who you are and why this review is wrong or unfair. Either due to a negative experience or because you want to elevate your reputation, you may then decide to **pivot** your reputation. This could be acknowledging what went wrong and how you plan to improve things or entering a new area of expertise. The good news about the reputation continuum is that you are never stuck. You can keep evolving. The reputation continuum does not necessarily follow the order above. You can go in and out of the continuum many times at different stages.

Power of First Impressions on Reputation

Making a first impression is not a choice; it's inevitable. What you do, what you say, what you *don't* say, what you wear, how you interact, and so on, will leave people with some sort of impression, so be strategic. A first impression is the first point of contact. The first point of contact is where and when a reputation begins. Think back on a time you attended a high school reunion, college reunion, or an annual business event. Can you remember any comments such as:

"I remember the first time I met you. I was lost and couldn't find the business school. You actually walked me there."

Or

"The first time I met you, you were in conversation with a few colleagues, but you stopped, asked my name, and welcomed me to join the group."

Comments like these lead to a strong reputation and a first impression bias that can last for years. When people first interact, they can make a positive, neutral, or negative impression. To make a negative impression, you usually have to try to be controversial or belligerent. Many times, there is a strategic reason for showing up this way. More often than not, though, you choose to be neutral. That means hanging back, not extending warmth first, waiting for someone to talk to you, or biding your time until you join a conversation. Nothing is wrong with being neutral except that you are missing an opportunity to create a positive first impression. This positive first impression can lead to a long-lasting connection or relationship, such as a business partnership, mentor/mentee, investor, advocate, best friend, or spouse. You also increase the odds of your reputation evolving past this first moment of contact. The recipient of your positive engagement can then spread your positive attributes to a secondary or tertiary audience. Reputation goes viral in this manner.

Decoding First Impressions

How people take you in immediately can be called a "thin slice." This means that people can make a reasonably accurate judgment about you in less than five minutes. In my class, I talk about seven factors people automatically notice when first meeting you:

1) Gender
2) Age
3) Ethnic background/Skin color
4) Bearing (how you stand and move and your posture)
5) Appearance (face, hair, clothes, accessories)
6) Eye contact (hostile, submissive, open)
7) Speech (tone, pitch, rate, accent)

The first three factors — gender, age, and ethnic background/skin color — are descriptors that you can't control. They represent you. These factors are clues that your audience uses to make sense of you and to categorize you. This is not to diminish you but rather to help them efficiently recognize you in some manner that makes sense to them. The following four factors — bearing, appearance, eye contact, and speech — are all aspects of who you are that you can control and require some action on your part. The more aware you are of how you present verbally, vocally, and visually, the better impression you can make. This is where you can apply strategy and forethought, which can be a reliable tool you can flex.

Takeaway: Because you will take people in and others will take you in through minimal information, you can now prepare and practice for these first impression events. Will you lead with warmth or curiosity? I tend to lead with active listening, so the first impression I try to make on others is one of being committed and present. Injecting humor is another tool I use because humor is a unifying force. I speak clearly, use sustained eye contact, try to offer positive comments, and often offer help. I have a limited amount of time to create a positive impression, and I want to be memorable in a good way. Thinking beforehand about how you want to come off in a new environment is not inauthentic. It is proactive and thoughtful. You can bring the qualities you are most proud of or feel you need to flex to the forefront and see whether they create the impression you are hoping for.

SCENARIO:

Context: It was the first time during my years at the Stanford Graduate School of Business (the GSB) that, as a lecturer, I was invited to sit on the dais with all the tenured professors during the graduation ceremony. All the professors were decked out in robes with colorful sashes and regalia that signaled their years of experience and many degrees. I wore a plain, black robe with a predictable black mortarboard. Although I was invited because I had been teaching for five years and my classes were popular, I felt like an outsider. The fact that I was a younger woman helped, as diversity is always appreciated. I immediately felt excluded from the camaraderie apparent in the existing groups. So, I practiced what I preach and approached a small group of older male professors.

Allison: "Hi, I'm Allison Kluger. I teach Strategic Communication, Reputation Management, and Strategic Pivoting for Your Next Chapter. I am excited to join you today. How many years have you each been part of this ceremony?"

They each answered and were a bit frosty. I kept going.

Allison: "And what classes do you each teach?" (This was risky as I feel they assumed I should, of course, know this by their reputations.) Yet, they shared about their classes as I made mental notes. From there, I spoke of what I knew of their classes, mentioned articles I had read by each of them, and mentioned positive comments from my students about these classes and them as educators. Before long, we were all having a legitimate and pleasant conversation. I was finally able to inject this last comment:

Allison: "I want to say that teaching at the GSB is a genuine pleasure for me. I wake up happy each day to get to campus and interact with my students. Although I spent 25-plus years in the media before joining the GSB, I feel this is where I am meant to be. I am honored to be sharing this with all of you today. You are all so prestigious and legends, and I've really enjoyed getting to know each of you better today."

I have been part of the graduation ceremony and the processional for the last five years. While I still sometimes feel like an outlier, I am recognized, included in the conversation, and acknowledged by my colleagues, who are far more esteemed than me. The first impression I was trying to create upon that first meeting in a new environment years ago was one of curiosity, kindness, genuine appreciation, and confidence. This took effort initially and helped pave the way for future events on campus when I would see these same people again.

Fixed Biases

While numerous titles exist on the types of biases that can affect reputation, I often discuss first impression bias.

First impression bias can go both ways in terms of someone liking you or not liking you.

First Impression Bias:

A positive first impression:
If I am invited to a gathering at the GSB by some of my students, I will often meet students who

have heard about me but haven't yet officially met me. If we have a positive exchange and chat about life, classes, and relationships and enjoy each other's company, that will become a first impression bias. If that student ends up in a future class of mine, the likelihood is that they will feel excited to have me teach them. The first impression of me is positive, and they assume that this is the Allison Kluger who will show up consistently in class.

What if the first impression is not so great?

This is a true story involving one of my clients. "Max" was driving into San Francisco to meet with a group of investors considering investing in his software start-up. Traffic was crazy, and he was worried about being late. A car cut in front of him, and he honked and honked at the woman driving the car. She angrily honked back, and he stuck his hand out the window and gave her the finger. Fortunately, Max made it to the meeting on time with just a few minutes to spare despite feeling frazzled. As he entered the room for introductions and to begin negotiations, who did he see but the woman he had honked at and given the finger to? He realized immediately that she, in turn, recognized him just by the way her expression changed when he was introduced to her. No, this was not an episode of the NBC sitcom *Seinfeld*, where awkward encounters abound.

Max stepped outside the room, called me, quickly shared what happened, and asked how he should handle this situation. Should he play it off as though he did not recognize her or say something? I advised him that exercising transparency and accountability was a better route and might actually end up leading to a better connection with her, and I offered him some messaging suggestions. Max hung up and approached the woman. This is what he said: "Hi, it seems we have already met in a less-than-sterling manner. I am so embarrassed by my behavior. I was so worried about being late for this meeting that I gave in to my frustration. I apologize sincerely, and I hope we can move past this." According to Max, the woman didn't say much but offered a pat response, "Oh, it's fine. I was frustrated, too."

The big question is: did Max get the investment? No. This woman was the lead investor, and even though Max says it ended up being an interesting conversation with a lot of positivity, ultimately, this group passed. There is no doubt in my mind, or in Max's, that Max created a first impression bias that this woman couldn't get past. No matter how charming, apologetic, and smart Max was, she kept remembering the finger he gave her. She probably assumed that Max was a hothead, and if that was how he handled stress, she would not want to invest in his company.

> **Takeaway:** First impression bias can work in your favor or, in some cases, against you.

Repairing a Negative Reputation

I have shared many ways that we need to be cautious of inadvertently hurting our reputations. But I have also shared that you are never stuck in a bad reputation. So let me tell you a guaranteed way to change your reputation from negative to positive. The answer is: you behave your way out of a bad reputation.

You may have a reputation for being slow to warm, late, indecisive, an exacting boss with little empathy, or someone who constantly interrupts others. The great news is that you can change this reputation with some effort.

SCENARIO:

Let's say you have a reputation for always showing up late. At first, people accept this and may find it quirky and funny and part of how you are perceived. But then, your lateness gets tiresome and not so amusing. You are essentially signaling that your time is more important than others and that you are not being respectful. This is becoming problematic and negatively affecting your reputation. The solution: commit to arriving 10 minutes earlier for every meeting going forward. The first time you show up 10 minutes early, expect to hear, "Hey, why are you here early? You're always late." And you answer, "I know, but I'm going to be early from now on." The response could be rolled eyes, laughter, or even, "Yeah, good luck with that!" You show up 10 minutes early again for the next meeting. This time, you are met with, "Oh, still doing the early thing, huh?" And you answer, "Yep, still showing up early."

The skepticism may continue, but you keep showing up to every meeting 10 minutes early. What happens is that your reputation for being late starts to fade, and this new behavior of showing up early takes over. After five or six meetings, no one even mentions your reputation for always being late anymore. You are showing up consistently in a new manner that creates a brand-new reputation that makes you proud. You have behaved your way out of a negative reputation. Remember, however, if you are not consistent and you revert to being late, you can undo all the positive steps you have made. The power is within you to change people's perceptions.

> **Takeaway:** You are never stuck in a bad reputation. Even if there is a fixed bias against you or a first impression bias, showing up consistently the way you want to be seen will eventually change others' perceptions and expectations of you. Depending on the behavior or reputation you want to tweak or alter, it may take time, but it can be done.

To quote Socrates, "*Regard your good name as the richest jewel you can possibly be possessed of — for credit is like fire; when once you have kindled it you may easily preserve it, but if you once extinguish it, you will find it an arduous task to rekindle it again. The way to a good reputation is to endeavor to be what you desire to appear.*"

I have saved for last one of my favorite reputation frameworks that I teach in class, the **Trust Radar** featured in Daniel Diermeier's book, *Reputation Rules*. I use this framework to coach students and clients on how to analyze a reputation crisis, current news story, or personal reputation issue. It is simple and highly effective. Usually, reputation crises involve you or your company losing trust in a public way. The trust radar is your solution for how to rebuild trust. The word I, and most people, associate with a strong reputation, is trust.

According to Diermeier, empathy, transparency, expertise, and commitment are the four pillars to rebuild trust and, in many instances, to recover from a reputational incident. Let's break this down (see illustration on page 199). The radar has four axes, and at the top of it is **empathy**. This means that the first step is showing empathy for whoever feels that they were harmed or hurt by this incident. You take full accountability and show that you're very sorry for the hurt caused by naming the injured parties and how they were hurt.

To the right of the radar is **transparency**. This means you can't just say, "No comment." You have to share what you know and give context as to why something happened and what you will do moving forward. Once people understand the context, they are more likely to feel seen and heard and understand the "why" behind actions taken. In the Tylenol Scandal of 1982 in Chicago, a serial killer put cyanide into Tylenol capsules in random bottles of Tylenol. Seven people were killed. Johnson & Johnson did not hide this truth. Although they didn't know why this happened, they said, what we know now is that we can't accurately ascertain how many bottles of Tylenol have been tampered with, so we are removing every bottle of Tylenol off the shelves nationwide and giving refunds as well. They didn't keep the public in the dark; they shared what they knew and took action, which led to their creation of the "Tamper-Proof" bottle cap.

On the bottom of the radar is **expertise**, which means that you will put whoever is the most appropriate person and the most senior person at the forefront to fix this. If someone needs to write a post, an article, or a press release, it usually should be the most relevant person or the person who created the problem. If a television or radio appearance is required, the top person must take the lead and signal how seriously this incident is being taken.

Finally, on the left side of the axes is **commitment**. This means you're committed to ensuring everything gets fixed the way it should and to providing a timetable so that people know what the expectations are. Saying, "We'll take care of this," or "Don't worry, it will get done," does not mean anything without clearly setting up guarantees and guidelines for when results can be expected and seen. If you can hit all these four axes of the Trust Radar, you can repair a reputation.

The Trust Radar works for personal reputations. If you have mistreated someone, embarrassed someone, not delivered on a promise, or misled someone, these four pillars will help.

You have committed to being the keynote speaker at the graduation of an elite university. But two weeks before the event, you realize that you need to cancel because your summer trip, which your spouse planned, was inadvertently scheduled for the same week the graduation takes place. Because you did not add the graduation date to the family calendar, your spouse made travel plans that are not refundable. Your four kids are counting on you to be there, and your spouse is livid at the thought you might not be able to travel with them. The university has promoted your keynote for several months through emails, signage, and press releases. You worry that your reputation will take a hit as being unreliable and not caring enough to honor your promise. Yet this trip is the last family trip before one of your four kids goes away to college. What do you do? You use the Trust Radar.

Step one: Empathy. You call your contact as soon as possible and explain the situation. You acknowledge that you are creating a difficult situation for them and how frustrating it must be for them as they planned to have you speak well in advance. You say you realize that a graduation keynote is extremely special, and you are honored to have been asked. You sincerely apologize for putting them in a bind and offer to help rectify this situation. Empathy and understanding help take the sting out of disappointment, especially if you genuinely show remorse and understanding of how your actions impact the university and your point of contact, who will probably take the heat for your canceling. This is only part of how to handle this.

Step two: Transparency. You take full accountability and share that this is entirely your fault. You have been juggling so many personal and business obligations that you simply forgot to put the date on your family calendar, only on your personal calendar. As a result, your family made nonrefundable travel plans. You explain that it is not necessarily the cost but that the graduation is smack in the middle of your trip, and your spouse cannot manage the kids alone. You acknowledge that you are embarrassed and simply overextended and that if there were a way to reschedule, you absolutely would have done that. Finally, you write a statement that can be released to the students, faculty, and public: "I am incredibly disappointed that I won't be able to be the keynote speaker at this year's graduation. Due to an error on my part, I double-booked this day and cannot honor this commitment. However, I am determined to find an alternative speaker who will deliver the wisdom and advice expected at such an illustrious occasion." This statement takes away any assumptions that the university screwed up. It shows candor and accountability, and it shows that you recognize the importance of graduation.

Step three: Expertise. You say that while you know that they promoted you and were expecting you, you are happy to make suggestions and help get another speaker to take your place. You will focus on this immediately and ensure they feel happy with whoever replaces you. You leverage all your contacts to make this happen.

Step four: Commitment. You don't rest until you find someone to replace you and help connect the new speaker to the university. You even offer to pay the expenses to fly this person in if that helps. You write a personal introduction that can be read at the graduation in lieu of your absence. You check in, even while away, to make certain everything goes off without a hitch.

If you achieve the four pillars of the Trust Radar, the illustration below will show a full diamond reaching each axis's highest point. If you don't deliver as successfully on each pillar, your diamond will be low in some areas and higher in others. Below is a successful Trust Radar.

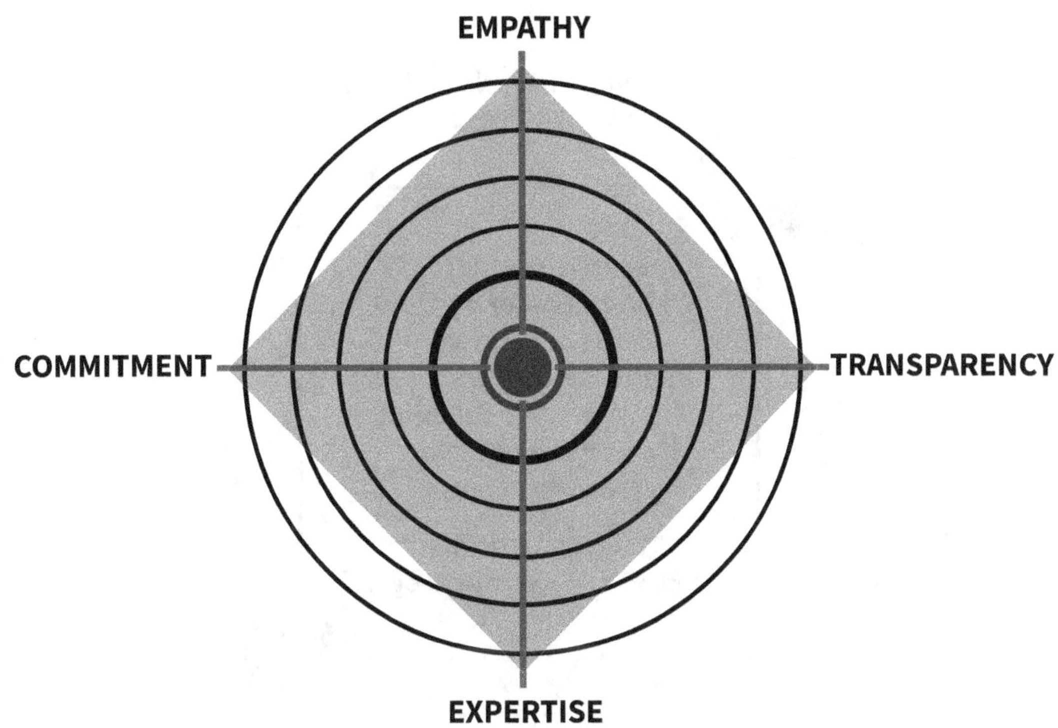

In closing, reputation is an intrinsic facet of your personal brand. It goes hand in hand with how people assess you and take in your "brand promise," whatever that may be. How people perceive you is often more important than what you know to be true about yourself. If you are not landing on others the way you think you are, the onus is on you to figure out how to create a perception aligned with your reality. When you can do this, you can create more personal and professional success and open yourself up to amazing and lucrative opportunities.

PART X – THE POWER OF EXECUTIVE PRESENCE

Contributed by: Allison Kluger

How does executive presence impact your personal brand? The ability to convey confidence, trust, credibility, and authority is what shapes a personal brand. If you want to be a leader at work or even among peers and family, all these facets, which signal "executive presence," apply. Surprisingly, traditional skills, seniority, and titles are less impactful in terms of executive presence than the ability to exhibit and inhabit these personality traits. If you want to stand out and differentiate yourself, personal branding is the key to making an impression that lasts. Executive presence is the most essential tool in curating a personal brand that people can trust.

I always start my Strategic Communication class at the Stanford Graduate School of Business by saying: "You can have a great idea, a great product or a great campaign, but if you can't communicate it successfully to others, then you are standing alone in the corner with a great idea, a great product or a great campaign. "

This dovetails beautifully with what Sylvia Ann Hewlett, author of *EP, Executive Presence,* writes about a study on executive presence:

- 66 percent say presence is key to career growth.
- Presence accounts for 26 percent of what it takes to get promoted beyond skills, intelligence, and experience.
- After two years of research, 40 focus groups, and a national survey, Hewlett contends the **three pillars of Executive Presence** are:
    - ☐ Appearance
    - ☐ Communication
    - ☐ Gravitas

I will break down each of these pillars for you. But first, a story.

I had recently graduated from the University of Pennsylvania. It was one of my earliest weeks at my first job as an associate producer at ABC's number one morning show, *Good Morning America,* when a senior producer, Sonya, saw me crying at work. I don't remember why I was crying, but I do recall it was about a personal issue. She pulled me into her office and closed the door. Sonya was petite and blonde with an English accent, and she terrified me. She was powerful, and I admired her from afar. Now, I was suddenly in her sights and sensed this would not be a great conversation. She told me, "Allison, I don't ever want to see you crying at the workplace. Do you know why?" I intuitively knew why, but all I could murmur was, "Uh-huh." Sonya ignored me and continued as if I hadn't made a sound. I realized it was a rhetorical question. "You're young, attractive, and female, Allison, and nobody will think you're reliable, and nobody will trust you to do the job, and nobody will give you responsibility. Do you understand?" (Another rhetorical question.) I nodded. Sonya went on, "If you need to cry, come into my office and close the door. But if someone asks you how you are, you say you're having a great day because nobody wants to hear you're having a bad day." I said I understood and thanked her, and then she said, "Now go!" and pushed me out of her office and slammed the door. And all I wanted to do was cry!

I was so mortified. Sonya had caught me doing something she did not approve of, and this was not a great first meeting with a powerful leader whose approval I wanted. I was also mad at myself for not realizing how inappropriate it was for me to cry at the workplace and not sensing how this might land on others.

Sonya's straight talk taught me something, and it became a turning point for me. I needed to act the part of someone who was reliable and capable if I wanted to be perceived that way. I needed to create more *executive presence.* I took Sonya's advice as gospel and slowly created a positive and respected reputation. (Did I mention that Sonya became my mentor?)

Over the years, I became the person who was unflappable. I started getting jobs producing live remotes, being on-air, and working in the control room, and my power and presence became authentic. My colleagues and bosses would say, "Go to Allison; she'll get the job done." "Go to Allison; she is a problem-solver." "Go to Allison; she is easy to work with and knows what she is doing." I'm still a very sensitive person, but to be the leader I wanted to be and project executive presence, I had to *act* like the leader I wanted to be. I wanted to make sure my bosses, colleagues, and employees could trust me and find me credible. This was my first lesson in executive presence: be aware of how you carry yourself, present yourself, communicate with others, and project competence and calm. These qualities inspire others to follow you and encourage them to emulate you and exhibit what executive presence and confidence look like.

Pillar 1: Appearance

Appearance is crucial to executive presence, even in these days of casual dress. I don't mean you must look like a supermodel or wear the most expensive clothes, jewelry, and watches. It means, do you look appropriate to lead this team, deliver the news, pitch to investors, or solve a major crisis? You might be thinking, "Uh, clothes and appearance can do all that? Hmm, I don't think so." My answer is YES, it *can* do all that. Citing Sylvia Ann Hewlett again, while your appearance is not as important as gravitas and communication, you can show your presence by maintaining an attractive look. Hewlett's studies of senior leaders revealed that looking groomed and polished had a more significant impact than physical beauty, youth, height, or weight. How do men and women judge each other at work? The number one concern is: Does this person look capable and credible of doing the work? If a woman dresses in overly flashy, casual, or tight-fitting clothes with excessive jewelry, it can distract from her natural power. If it looks like she put no effort into her appearance, then someone may wonder: "Does she even care? Will she put the same minimal effort into the work I want her to do?" With women judging men, it is the same. If a man shows up with a wrinkled shirt that is partly untucked, has crazy, ungroomed eyebrows, messy hair or a beard that looks unkempt, or scuffed shoes, women will wonder whether that man is frenetic or unaware and can actually deliver on his work promise.

My rule of thumb is if a person is paying more than 10 seconds of attention to what you are wearing, you are distracting them from your message, and you are culpable of whatever assumptions they make about you. My one caveat is if what you wear is part of your personal brand. Let's say you wear a baseball cap every day — even though it is a very casual look and can sometimes be considered disrespectful. If you give context such as, "I am the biggest baseball fan. I have spent years visiting every baseball stadium and collecting baseball hats, so I wear a different hat each day." Now, all of a sudden, this accessory tells a story, becomes part of your style, and is a differentiating factor. Still, if you are at a high-stakes meeting with new people who don't see you every day, and you wear the baseball hat without giving context, it can be confusing. It's up to you to frontload any information about why you look the way you look so people don't make incorrect assumptions.

SCENARIO 1:

My dear colleague, JD Schramm, once went to an education conference with about 100 attendees. Most showed up in casual dress, and three showed up in suits. Who do you think everyone gravitated to as the leaders? Yes, the three people in suits. Of course, they were not the actual organizers of the event, but the impression they made was one of elevated executive presence.

Did those three educators dress up in suits on purpose? I don't know the answer, but it was a very telling lesson on the power of appearance. Just as you may not trust a man who says he is a doctor if he is not wearing a white surgical coat, how you show up signals something about your skills, experience, and trustworthiness. So be consistent and be recognizable.

SCENARIO 2:

I was consulting with a well-known biotech health-care company and was asked to come in and speak on the topic of "Executive Presence for Women." My point of contact was a lovely young woman I'll call Yuchen. Yuchen was pleasant, helpful, and extremely organized and handled all the logistics like a pro. I was eager to meet her at the live event. When I arrived in the lobby of the giant building, I mentioned Yuchen's name to the receptionist and was told she would come and get me. In five minutes, this young woman in yoga pants, a messy bun, and a sweatshirt approached me. "Allison?" she asked. "Yes, that's me," I answered. "Are you going to take me to Yuchen?" The woman smiled and then laughed, "Allison, I'M Yuchen!" I was startled. She looked like an intern. I did not consider this woman who greeted me as a person who was powerful and in charge.

Later, I pulled her aside and shared what I had initially thought about her when I first saw her. "Yuchen, you have never met me. You are my lead on this big event, and I truly thought you were an intern by how you dressed." She answered that everyone dresses this way in the company. I explained that my first impression of her did not align with what a person with executive presence looks like and that when meeting someone for the first time or hosting a high-stakes event like the one we worked on, it was an opportunity to show her leadership skills and executive presence in a visual and memorable way. Yuchen was grateful for my feedback and, in the future, chose to dress with strategic foresight before similar types of encounters.

Takeaway: I always say that dressing up, even half a step, is a win-win move. The worst that can happen is someone might say, "Oh, we're really casual here." And then you can answer, "I dressed up for all of you today, but duly noted for next time." The best that can happen is that you enter a new space and exude confidence and power. You show that whoever you are greeting matters to you, and you show respect by dressing for the occasion. Unless you are explicitly told to dress a certain way, dressing in an appropriate way that signals your ability to command and lead is a natural way to exude executive presence.

SCENARIO 3:

I was at *Good Morning America* and working on a Women's Health week. This meant that for a week, we would have three daily segments about women's health. I worked with a male doctor every day to plan and review segments concerning different health issues. Dr. X came into my office after each live show to discuss what went well and what the next day would involve. He was pompous and condescending and openly told me how young he thought I was to be holding this position (meaning, why was I in charge of him and all the segments?). I assumed he felt he could say this to me because I was young and a woman. As always, I was unfailingly polite and resourceful and was determined to prove I could handle everything he threw at me. I always dressed up so I wouldn't look as young as I was. Dr. X dressed like Sherlock Holmes in a three-piece suit and had greyish hair and sideburns. All he needed was the "deerstalker" hat and a pipe to complete the vision. I felt judged and nervous during these office visits. To be candid, Dr. X intimidated me and appeared so confident and experienced that I felt insecure despite knowing I was doing a great job.

Toward the end of the week, I went grocery shopping late at night (as many New Yorkers do), and whom did I see walking around the store with a cart? Dr. X himself! But this was a different Dr. X. He was wearing mismatched sweatpants and sweatshirt, socks and sandals, and his hair was mussed up. "OMG!" I thought. "This can't actually be Dr. X!" Still, I secretly followed him around the store, hiding behind aisles and peering at him whenever I could. Sure enough, it was the man, the legend, Dr. X! Then, it hit me. How Dr. X dressed during our office hours and live broadcast was his way of showing and manifesting executive presence. Maybe Dr. X was nervous about being on a number one morning show every day and wanted to prove he was the expert everyone believed him to be. Dressing the way he did was his way of putting on his armor. All I know is that I was incredibly relaxed as I joked with him the next day in the office. I had seen the emperor without his clothes, and it freed me from my insecurity. This lesson stayed with me forever. How we dress and present ourselves is a direct indication of our power and trustworthiness. I never told Dr. X that I had seen him shopping that night. The lesson he imparted to me was my reward. However, after the theme week was over and was a success, he told me that he thought I did an excellent job producing him despite my young age. "Don't worry," I joked with him, "working with you aged me 10 years!"

Pillar 2: Communication

Communicating effectively is an intrinsic part of developing executive presence. Do you look people in the eye? Is there a warmth and natural curiosity emanating from you? Are you saying things that will benefit people or inspire them? Or instead, are you looking over their shoulder to see whether there's someone "better" that you should be talking to? Are you distracted by your phone or what's happening around you? Do you speak at a pace that people can follow? Are you enunciating your words and pausing to allow your content to be absorbed successfully? As a leader with executive presence, it's more important that you say what the audience *needs* and wants to hear so they can take the action you want them to take instead of just saying what *you* want to say. As the presenter, you will always know more than your audience; however, you may be providing details and extraneous commentary that will dilute your powerful messages and make your takeaways less impactful. Communicating with executive presence shows your comfort level and ability to genuinely connect with others. Active listening, validation of another's opinions, and thoughtful responses are all part of successful communication. After you speak with a person, team, or a large group, can your audience successfully repeat what you told them? If so, you did a great job communicating with power, credibility, authority, and confidence.

Takeaway: Communication is foundational to your personal brand and executive presence. If you still feel you are not a great communicator, try these tips:
1) Know how to start and end a conversation by planning what you want to say and how you want to end your comments, so they are helpful and memorable.
2) Be an active listener. Giving someone or a group of people your undivided attention signals patience, interest, and genuine caring.
3) Be curious. Ask relevant questions so your audience senses your genuine commitment to hearing them out.

Finally, a client told me she had taken a survey about emotional intelligence and executive presence and learned what qualities she exemplified in both categories. Then she said, "Allison, do you want to know what I think your greatest gift is in terms of communication?" I was all ears. "Allison, you are SO present. Every time we talk, I see you taking in my words and concerns, and you never rush me. And when I ask you something, you take a beat and really think before answering. I feel so seen and heard by you." This is one of the most wonderful compliments I have ever received, and it makes me very conscious of always wanting to show up this way.

Pillar 3: Gravitas

The subtle but equally important third pillar in exhibiting executive presence is gravitas. Imagine a swan gliding on the water. When you think of a swan, you think of a creature that's elegant, poised, composed, and flowing smoothly on the surface. Under the water, however, there are little webbed feet paddling furiously to stay afloat. When you're in charge and in control, you're not letting anyone see those furiously paddling feet. That's what gravitas is, and a strong leader always has it. How can *we* demonstrate gravitas to those around us?

In a simple sentence, gravitas is about making everyone feel safe and that you are in charge. Even if you don't know the answer, you know how to get the answer and point someone in the correct direction. It also means that if you mess up (forget your lines, your tech doesn't work, your guest speaker doesn't show up), you can still demonstrate confidence and flexibility so that others don't think there's a problem going on. To signal gravitas is to acknowledge those around you in a manner that suggests you have elevated emotional intelligence. Some examples:

1) If you need to have a meeting on a weekend, you show genuine appreciation to everyone who has to attend, maybe serve beverages and snacks, and reassure them that you will make this meeting as efficient as possible.

2 If you have investors coming in from another country, you arrange dinner and/or entertainment that is aligned with their time zone. Or you construct an agenda that shows you are aware of their time constraints or jet lag.

3) If you fumble in a presentation, speak out of turn, or use the wrong name in an introduction, you calmly clarify and move on without drama. You can use humor in a self-deprecating manner, but not in a way that diminishes your power.

Wrong way to self-correct: "Jeez, I tested the deck this morning, and the video clip worked, I promise you. Oh well, everyone, I can't believe it's not working now! It was instrumental in explaining this concept."

Right way to self-correct: "It seems the clip isn't working, but that's okay. What the clip shows are the predictors of supply chain success using the AI algorithm. Let's move on to the next slide. . . ."

Gravitas is your ability to control your inner struggle and outwardly show calm and confidence. It takes work but can be learned.

One of my students, Rajeev, had a big fear of forgetting his lines when presenting. He was worried it would make him seem less powerful and confident. English was his second language, and I was amazed he was so fluent. I reassured Rajeev by saying if he ever forgets his words to stop, pause, breathe, look around the audience in a thoughtful way, and say the first thing that comes to his mind. He can still have executive presence despite being momentarily derailed. I suggested that he could add later, "And by the way, I want to mention one more thing . . ." and then proceed to say what he skipped. I reminded him it was more about how he handled a fumble than the fact he forgot his words. "What the audience doesn't see, it doesn't miss." Only he knew what he wanted to say. A few months later, he reached out to say his worst nightmare had come true. He was speaking to a large crowd and forgot his next thought. However, he remembered my advice and stopped, looked around, took a breath, and started again. Someone approached him afterward and said, "That was such an amazing presentation. And when you stopped speaking for a moment, it was so powerful." We had a good laugh together.

Gravitas is how you handle awkward situations. You put your audience's comfort in front of your comfort. Often, a great way to show gravitas is in the face of chaos. If you offer up your services when everyone is lagging behind, fearful of being asked to do something, you will find it is a win-win situation. First, you step up when no one else wants to and offer to lead a possible solution. This willingness to shoulder responsibility shows your confidence and leadership instincts. Second, you can ask others to assist you since you have identified yourself as the leader. You will be surprised how many people will jump at this secondary position. Third, even if you don't solve the problem, you have shown yourself to be a leader willing to take charge. You will be lauded for stepping up.

Let's face it, sh*t happens. My mantra has always been: "It's not what happens; it's how you deal with it that defines you." Sometimes, an awkward situation can shine a light on how facile, creative, or human you are. And these qualities are all indicators of executive presence.

When I was a home shopping host at a shopping network named Q2, I used to host a "picnic" show. In one hour, I would sell 20 products that all had to do with picnicking: baskets, tablecloths, folding picnic tables, thermoses, blankets, and the like. I had hosted this show many times, and one product was an extra-insulated thermos. My "sell" was that anything you put into the thermos would stay boiling hot or freezing cold. To demonstrate, my product stylists would put a ball of ice cream into the thermos. And I would turn the thermos upside down on live TV and show that the ice cream ball was still intact and frozen and did not fall out. On this particular show, when I got to the moment when I turned the thermos over, there was no ice cream in it. Instead, the stylist had mistakenly put refrigerated yogurt into it. I turned the thermos over, and strawberry yogurt poured out all over the picnic table and splashed onto my outfit. I stopped momentarily, took a breath, and then faced the camera. "It looks like they were out of ice cream today!" I said with a smile and mischievous look. Then I dipped my finger into the spilled yogurt in front of me, tasted it, and exclaimed, "However, it is still cold! That thermos really works! Now, let's go over to a product shot while I get this mess cleaned up. Live TV, folks, live TV." The director instructed the cameras to move off of me to the product shot as I quickly cleaned up the mess with assistance from the embarrassed stylist. Many colleagues asked me how I was able to keep my cool on live television. I said, "It was a human moment. And a funny one at that. But if I lost my cool and panicked it would have made the audience feel uncomfortable and I would have lost credibility as an expert and an authority figure." The audience comes first! It's one of my favorite stories, and I have learned never to show my feet paddling furiously under the water (or picnic table!).

Give Context to Strong Emotions

My final lesson in executive presence is to never let someone's bad behavior affect your behavior. Keeping your cool while others lose theirs is an excellent way to show your executive presence. A technique when I am faced with someone who is screaming at me or someone who is angry and frustrated and is ranting is to stay very calm. Then, instead of rising to their level of emotion, I quietly and calmly say, "You seem very upset. What can I do to help?" It's amazing how this can defuse a tense or emotional situation. Usually, when someone misbehaves, especially in front of others, they want attention and comfort or at least for someone to ask what's wrong. A true sign of leadership and executive presence is to keep your cool under fire. Everyone always recognizes the "problem child" in the room. As a leader with executive presence, it's more powerful to show compassion, curiosity, and to offer help. Now, there might be an instance when your power is challenged by this kind of unruly and disruptive behavior, and you don't want to seem obsequious or a pushover. Instead of empathy, you can quietly and firmly say, "I can see you are very upset right now." In these cases, it's not professional or constructive to yell back. Then continue, "Why don't you take a walk and calm down, and when you are ready to discuss this, I am happy to listen." The goal is to use professional terms and not personal terms. Never purposely diminish others, or you will look like a bully, resentful, or vindictive. What you really want to say is, "Stop acting like such a jerk. You're making a fool of yourself, and everyone is watching." However, you need to keep those thoughts in the bubble above your head. This is a personal attack, and then you are no better than the culprit causing all the chaos. Stick with calm authority and compassion and offer your help. Never go down to the other person's level, as it compromises your executive presence.

Back to my story about Sonya, the senior producer who caught me crying at work. What I didn't realize then was that if you show high emotion at work and even in your personal life, such as crying, anger, frustration, and finger-pointing, you are forcing others to deal with your feelings. And that's where the discomfort settles in. The solution is quite simple: give context to your high emotions.

1) My pet passed away last night, and I am struggling today and feel very teary.
2) My project just got canceled due to budget constraints, and I am so frustrated because I spent three straight weeks working on getting it launched.
3) I am really angry that my team was excluded from the offsite, and I want to advocate for their inclusion.

Once you let others know the "why" behind your sadness, anger, or discomfort, they will understand more clearly and not take it personally or feel put-upon by your behavior and words. Often, transparency during times of stress can help others connect to you. Showing vulnerability without making others feel uncomfortable or responsible for you is a valuable way to help them have a deeper understanding of what you are experiencing.

Quick takeaways in how executive presence can improve your personal brand:

1. **Be aware of your appearance.** Are you dressing appropriately for meetings or events when meeting someone new? If you are too casual or sloppy, people will ascribe traits to you — they may think you're lazy or not senior enough to do your job.
2. **Be aware of how you communicate and how you use your voice.** Be clear, present, and strong, and project an action-oriented aura. Rather than saying "I was wondering" or "Maybe," say "I believe" and "My plan is this."
3. **Be aware of your energy.** When you walk into a room, do you stand straight, with good energy, and are you prepared to interact? Make sure you're aware of people, and people are aware of you, because if you're not (and *they're* not), they may come away with a neutral or negative impression. Remember that eye contact, a firm handshake, a smile, and your first and last words are part of the first impression you make.
4. **Consider your differentiating factor.** What makes you special, and how do you broadcast it so that people are aware? Maybe you're a great runner, or you're good at coding. Blog about it or create a seminar to teach others. Being an expert at something teaches you how to embrace the spotlight and broadcast your talents to others because sharing with others helps you create a network, take a leadership role, and create new opportunities for yourself. This is a pragmatic way to take baby steps toward leadership and executive presence.

Conclusion: Executive presence is a skill anyone can master. It means consciously presenting yourself in a way that highlights your appropriate appearance, your communication skills, and your gravitas. Just take small steps. Imagine the first time you drove a car. You gripped the wheel tightly and pressed down on the brake with a bit too much force. Then, after driving every day, you started to feel more confident and loosen up. You are now able to change the radio station, sip some soda, or even merge and switch lanes without having an anxiety attack. Practice your executive presence every day. Act like the leader you want to be. And your personal brand will certainly benefit.

PART XI – BOOSTING YOUR WORKPLACE PRESENCE: GETTING NOTICED AND GETTING AHEAD

Wrap Up

In today's competitive job market, simply "getting by" in your current position won't cut it. If you really want to excel, stand out, and climb the career ladder, you need to do more than your basic job duties — you must flaunt your unique value and think strategically. In this final chapter, we'll cover how to do all this with "refresher" power moves. Make these moves a habit, and you'll quickly become the go-to team member everyone trusts and chooses to work with.

Develop New Skills. Continuous learning is the cornerstone of career advancement. Pursue professional development opportunities by attending workshops, taking online courses, and staying current with industry trends.

■ **Action Step:** Identify your gaps and areas for improvement. Regularly invest time in learning new skills that are relevant to your industry, making you an indispensable asset to your organization.

Network Effectively. A strong professional network is vital for career growth. Cultivate relationships inside and outside your organization to increase your visibility and open doors to new opportunities.

■ **Action Step:** Attend industry events, join professional groups, and engage with colleagues and mentors.

Take Initiative. Going beyond your job description demonstrates your leadership potential and commitment to an organization. Proactively seek out new projects and responsibilities, volunteer for leadership roles, and never say, "That's not my job."

■ **Action Step:** Look for opportunities to take on additional responsibilities and express your willingness to your managers.

Communicate Your Value. Articulating your contributions and the value you bring to the organization is essential. It's not immodest; it's necessary. Regularly update your superiors on your progress and seek feedback to continuously improve.

■ **Action Step:** Develop a habit of regularly communicating your achievements and progress to your supervisors. Don't be shy about highlighting your value and seeking constructive feedback.

Set SMART Goals. Setting and achieving goals is linked to higher performance and career success. Goals make you accountable, help you stay on track, and provide a way to measure your progress.

■ **Action Step:** Set specific, measurable, attainable, relevant, and time-bound (SMART) goals. Regularly review and adjust your goals to ensure they remain aligned with your career aspirations.

Catalog Your Success. Build a success toolkit: a well-packaged presentation of your hard work and achievements. Keep a detailed record of your wins and quantify their impact. This documentation is key evidence of your contributions during performance reviews.

■ **Action Step:** Create a portfolio or a success toolkit that includes examples of your work, such as projects, presentations, and positive feedback from colleagues and supervisors.

Heighten Your Visibility. Getting noticed involves actively promoting your contributions and maintaining a positive, can-do attitude. Be a team player and adhere to deadlines.

■ **Action Step**: Engage in high-profile assignments, volunteer for community work, and actively participate in meetings. Let your voice be heard.

You may have reached the end of this book, but your life-changing career journey is just beginning. Remember, a strong personal brand is never static. Standing out and advancing in your career requires ongoing and far-ranging work. Keep at it and you will add new chapters to your professional story — chapters that reinforce your core values and bring you joy.

By continuously seeking new knowledge and skills, you stay ahead of the curve and remain indispensable in your field. Embrace a mindset of continuous improvement and always strive to be the best version of yourself. Here's to propelling your career to new heights of success and fulfillment. You got this!

Success Stories

This chapter delves into the success stories of entrepreneurs, career transitioners, influencers, and rising stars. There are great learnings here for early-career professionals on their quest for greatness! Prepare to be inspired by nine real-life stories that provide you with practical tips for advancing your career and achieving your goals.

Entrepreneur Enthusiasts

Dan Dillon, CEO and Founder of CleanItSupply.com
From Janitor to Business Owner

CAREER JOURNEY: Dan began his journey in his father's commercial janitorial service business, scrubbing toilets and mopping floors, his fingers pruned and hair smelling of chlorine. Although he was offered a full ride to a four-year college for competitive swimming, he opted to attend a two-year college to be able to make payments on his Corvette. "College isn't the sole avenue for learning business or a profession," claims Dan. While Dan's brief college experience was beneficial for subjects like accounting and public speaking, he found learning on the job much more personally valuable. Dan's father instilled a strong work ethic in him, and he paid his dues. After the business was sold in 2005, Dan launched CleanItSupply. com, a leading online cleaning and janitorial supplies retailer. Dan leads CleanItSupply.com in day-to-day operations and distributor relations, ensuring five-star customer service. One of his biggest challenges in scaling the business is maintaining an edge in the fiercely contested realm of e-commerce. Another challenge is identifying when to hire a new team member to avoid overloading others.

STRATEGIES/TOOLS FOR SUCCESS: Employee-centric focus. Dan views employees as the foundation and most important element in any business. He prefers employees who genuinely care and exert their best effort rather than those who rely solely on talent and expect special treatment based on self-perceived value. He claims that "a customer service-driven business has to have team players — not star players — on board."

LESSONS LEARNED: Dan imparted three key lessons: 1) Always prioritize customer satisfaction; personal touch and responsiveness drive loyalty and trust. The company created over 6,000 product videos to demonstrate their products effectively, which significantly deepened connection and trust with customers; 2) Ensure equality in purchasing power by offering quality products at competitive prices and excellent service to all customers, regardless of size; and 3) Maintain strong cultural values to build a sustainable and successful business foundation.

ADVICE: "Be confident in what you do and how you do it. Don't worry about competitors; focus on your own path," advises Dan. "Stick to what you know and work hard; success will follow. Enjoy the journey, and the rewards will come, but don't expect immediate high payouts when launching a business."

FUTURE GOALS: Dan intends to keep growing CleanItSupply.com and continue to provide the very best online shopping experience and customer service on the web.

Richelle Peña, Co-Founder of RPW Consultants
From Pharmacist to Business Boss

CAREER JOURNEY: Richelle is a pharmacist, serial entrepreneur, author, and lifestyle leader. After working in the corporate world as a pharmacist, she found a different calling. She co-founded the American Pediatric Dental Group with her husband, Dr. William Peña, in 2011. They grew the business to seven locations and were acquired in 2021, exiting for eight figures. In 2022, they launched RPW Consultants to teach entrepreneurs how to build successful businesses and happy homes. Her latest project, The Lifestyle Leader, guides women to embrace their potential and create balanced, authentic lives.

STRATEGIES/TOOLS FOR SUCCESS: Building a solid team of administrators and office managers who deeply understood the dental group's purpose was essential to success. With conviction in their vision and mission, they led their team to success. Richelle says, "When people feel heard and valued, they drive growth and productivity. I embraced servant leadership and recognized everyone who contributed to the business. I was always ready to help and listen to anyone on how we could improve."

LESSONS LEARNED: The most important lesson she has learned from failure is to avoid living in misery for more than three days. Whether the setback was within one's control or not, she believes that there's always a lesson to be learned. When knocked down, the only way is up; setbacks are often blessings in disguise. Having something grounding is crucial as entrepreneurship, life, and business can be unpredictable; for Richelle, it's her faith.

Reading books and investing in personal development helps her navigate the challenges of entrepreneurship.

ADVICE: Richelle's best advice for aspiring entrepreneurs to overcome anything is to have the right mindset and support! She claims that "without it, you're more likely to fail, as you may give up when faced with obstacles. To succeed, be open to change, willing to put in the effort, and prepared to make sacrifices. A strong 'why' — a clear purpose beyond financial gain — is crucial to drive you through challenges. Start small and test your concept in the market to validate your idea and avoid costly mistakes. Remember, entrepreneurship requires resilience, adaptability, and a willingness to learn and evolve."

FUTURE GOALS: Richelle is passionate about empowering health-care professionals and entrepreneurs to master the business side of their practice. She and her husband experienced this knowledge gap, leading to stress and burnout, and are dedicated to sharing their expertise through online resources and speaking engagements. Richelle is co-author of the book *The Power Couple*, which helps entrepreneurs scale their business while balancing family. Her goal is to inspire others to see that success often comes from struggle, and she is eager to share her story to help others balance their professional and personal lives.

Abhi Madan, *Co-Founder and Creative Director of Amarra*
From Side Hustle to Style Sensation

CAREER JOURNEY: With fashion in his DNA, Abhi's once modest side hustle has blossomed into a global fashion empire, boasting an impressive network of 850 stores worldwide. Established in 2018, Amarra specializes in wholesaling high-end formal evening wear dresses under multiple labels, with headquarters in New Jersey and an additional showroom/design studio in Atlanta. Amarra remains true to Abhi's initial vision: to bring captivating designs to life for prom, formal, weddings, and quinceañera dresses. His journey wasn't without challenges, particularly navigating a fiercely competitive industry. Yet, he persevered by staying true to his commitment to sustainable fashion, incorporating luxurious and responsible materials and processes to set Amarra apart in the crowded market. From initially earning $2,000 monthly as a side hustle, the company's annual revenues now exceed $15 million, reflecting the company's remarkable growth. In recent years, the company has also taken significant steps toward its goal of becoming carbon neutral by 2025, a challenge it is meeting head-on with innovative sustainable design solutions.

STRATEGIES/TOOLS FOR SUCCESS: Abhi credits Amarra's success to the company's adept use of digital platforms, which allows their distinct designs to shine. Effective brand storytelling has greatly increased client engagement. From the outset, they recognized the vital role of technology, such as CRM and ERP systems, to streamline operations and cut costs. In addition, they have employed cutting-edge 3D design software to create lifelike models of dresses, providing clients with a virtual trying-on experience that has significantly boosted online sales.

LESSONS LEARNED: Like many e-commerce operations, Abhi has faced significant challenges in inventory management, shipping, and digital marketing. He underscores the importance of allocating resources wisely to streamline processes, reduce costs, and enhance profitability, which is critical for growth. Beyond innovative design, he stresses the significance of nurturing relationships with fashion buyers, recognizing their role in Amarra's success.

ADVICE: His advice to those considering a side hustle is to align your interests with consumer preferences, believe in your ideas, and be patient. He asserts that "persistence, market research, adapting to changing needs, and attention to detail are crucial in overcoming challenges and succeeding in a competitive market. It's also vital to be flexible and ready to embrace change, whether in fashion trends or business operations."

FUTURE GOALS: Abhi aims to inspire other young entrepreneurs to pursue their passion relentlessly, with creativity, sustainability, and a global perspective at their core. He adds, "We aim to further strengthen Amarra's position in the industry as a benchmark for sustainable luxury fashion."

Rising Stars

Ben Ettlinger, *Sales Manager at Rippling, New York (age 28)*
Sizzling Sales Success: from Dialing to Dominance

CAREER JOURNEY: His entire life, everyone told Ben, "You need to work in sales." Right out of college, he worked at Markets Group, a financial services event company, where he got his first taste of cold-calling to recruit financial industry panelists and drive event attendance. He then moved to Yext into the Software as a Service (SaaS) space, selling marketing-specific software to location-based businesses. During his two and a half years at Yext, he was promoted twice. Ben then joined Rippling as an Account Executive, where he fell in love with selling and solving complex business issues with software. He's had the opportunity to work under a senior executive who guided him in becoming a sales expert. He's been promoted twice in under two years, most recently to lead a mid-market sales team.

STRATEGIES/TOOLS FOR SUCCESS: Ben believes possessing intangibles like drive, coachability, and curiosity in his industry is essential. He says, "Success comes from being driven, coachable, and curious, and having mentors to help shape who you want to be. While your destiny is yours to create, the people you surround yourself with and confide in play a big part."

LESSONS LEARNED: Ben asserts it is crucial to allocate time effectively and focus on revenue -generating opportunities in sales. He shares, "Sales personnel often chase 'surfboards' when we should be hunting 'seals.' Always think through potential issues and de-risk outcomes to control conversations."

ADVICE: Ben believes sales are not for the faint of heart. "If you choose this career path, ensure you do everything within your control. If things don't go your way, you can still hold your head high, knowing you did your best. There are many paths in sales; discover whether you enjoy building new relationships or nurturing existing ones; there are roles for both."

FUTURE GOALS: Ben aims to continue developing professionally and eventually transition into the early-stage start-up world. He believes this goal will allow him to apply his accumulated knowledge and build a sales organization where he can impact upcoming sales professionals just as others have impacted him.

Caira Button, *Compass, Chicago (age 30)*
Real Estate Mastery: Making Every Square Foot Count

CAREER JOURNEY: Caira's career started differently from most real estate agents. In 2017, while working a 9-to-5 job, she found herself with more free time than she knew what to do with. Not one to relax for long, she turned her love for video editing into a hobby and began creating content for YouTube. Frustrated by the lack of information on studio apartments, she started her own channel, treating it like a full-time job. After moving to Chicago in 2019, people began asking her for real estate advice. This led her to get her real estate license in July 2020, launching a successful career she never anticipated. Her record-breaking achievements are noteworthy: her team achieved a sales volume of $74.5 million in 2022.

STRATEGIES/TOOLS FOR SUCCESS: Caira believes her career is more than just selling houses; she's a community builder who adds value beyond the sale. Social media has been the bread and butter of Caira's business. She says, "It's the most authentic way to help others and share tips that make a daunting move easier. It builds trust with clients, so they feel they know me before reaching out." Caira emphasizes that social media only works if you are 100 percent genuine. She recommends mastering being yourself, though challenging, as it makes all the difference.

LESSONS LEARNED: Caira shares, "Consistency is everything. Even when you don't feel like answering a client text or filming a video, you must push through and get the work done." She believes it's easier to maintain momentum than to stop and start. She also recommends answering emails within 24 hours, which she considers the "bare minimum" and believes will set you apart from most other agents.

ADVICE: Caira advises that whatever career path you choose, whether in real estate or something entirely different, two things are crucial: hard work and passion. She emphasizes that no one will do the work for you, and the most successful people are those making sacrifices because they love what they do. "Make sure you love what you do and are passionate about it," she says. Caira adds, "If you don't enjoy creating content, no one else will enjoy it either. Similarly, if you don't like working with clients, they'll sense it. Find your passion and give it 110 percent of your energy."

FUTURE GOALS: Caira runs her own real estate team, which is unusual for someone so young in their career, and she loves it. While she hopes her career continues to evolve, she's thrilled with where it is now. "I absolutely love my job and am grateful every single day. The balance between social media and real estate is fun because every day is different and never boring."

Career Switcher

Jeremy Schifeling, *Founder of The Job Insiders, and Career Development Speaker*
Rewriting the Curriculum: Kindergarten Teacher Turns Techie

CAREER JOURNEY: Jeremy started his career as a kindergarten teacher in Brooklyn and quickly realized his favorite aspect was sharing his passion for tech with students and families. He recognized his true passion for tech and education and pursued an MBA in Marketing at the University of Michigan. Since then, Jeremy has taken on esteemed roles, including interning at Apple and serving as a senior product marketing manager on LinkedIn, product marketing manager at Google, and marketing director at Khan Academy. He explains, "While I was never gifted at teaching vocabulary sitting on the rug, analyzing classroom data and composing newsletters played to my strengths. Discovering my true north and superpowers, I realized EdTech was a better fit for me." Today, Jeremy is the Founder of The Job Insiders and has published two bestselling books on LinkedIn and ChatGPT for careers.

STRATEGIES/TOOLS FOR SUCCESS: The biggest challenge was overcoming imposter syndrome to prove he belonged in tech to recruiters and himself. He translated his classroom skills into tech, focusing on audience engagement and results, which he incorporated into his résumé. He also learned what tech roles required and discovered they aligned with his existing skills: understanding and motivating others.

LESSONS LEARNED: Jeremy believes that much of human fulfillment comes from doing things you're good at that drive meaningful value for others. "Through trial and error, I found a career path that allows me to do what I love for others' benefit, which brings me great meaning. The best resource for my development has been actually doing the work, as humans learn best by getting hands-on experience. My advice is to start exploring the work you're excited about, whether through a volunteer project or building something on your own. Empathy is the number one skill; understanding your audience's needs is crucial in both teaching and tech. Recognizing this superpower's versatility was a breakthrough for me."

ADVICE: Jeremy shares, "While so many people want to learn through courses and YouTube videos, the reality is that we humans learn best by getting our hands dirty. So, my best advice to others is to just start doing the work you're excited to explore. Whether that means doing a volunteer project for a nonprofit through a site like Catchafire.org or just building something on your own that tests your new skills, don't be afraid to go back to your kindergarten self and dive in!"

FUTURE GOALS: Continue to grow his career and those served in EdTech.

Influencers

Allegra Shaw, *Co-Founder of Uncle Studios and Influencer*
A Stylish Journey from YouTube to Lifestyle Icon

CAREER JOURNEY: Allegra Shaw is the Co-Founder of Uncle Studios and a digital content creator, who made a name for herself as a lifestyle and fashion entrepreneur with the launch of her YouTube channel in 2011, which boasts nearly 1 million subscribers. Known for her effortlessly casual style and authentic lifestyle content, Allegra has built a community passionate about travel, personal growth, and emotional well-being. She is recognized as a transparent voice in her industry and has been featured in *Vogue*, *Cosmopolitan*, and other fashion and lifestyle publications.

In 2019, Allegra co-founded Uncle Studios with Shirin Soltani, focusing on creating elevated, eco-conscious fashion pieces that resonate with modern individuals. Uncle Studios prioritizes transparency, community engagement, and fostering a familial atmosphere both online and offline. Uncle Studios recently expanded in 2023 with the addition of Uncle Jeans.

STRATEGIES/TOOLS FOR SUCCESS: Allegra's strategy has always centered on authenticity and consistency. Especially in the early days, it was important for her to focus on what she wanted to create, how she wanted to represent herself, and how she would engage with the growing community.

LESSONS LEARNED: Allegra embraces "weathering the ebbs and flows of life." She claims, "When I feel confident and positive about my journey, this supports me during the tough times that inevitably come. Failures are a part of growth and help build resilience." She learned to change her mindset about failure, viewing it as part of the dance that is life and entrepreneurship. Allegra has also learned to "fail fast" — face it, learn from it, fix it, and don't do it again.

ADVICE: Her best advice would be to ask yourself, "Why?" She claims, "When I started, I saw myself as a content creator. The term *influencer* hadn't been coined yet, and there was no way to monetize content — it was a new territory." Because of this, she built her platform with the mindset of connecting and sharing rather than influencing. Allegra believes that it's important to develop yourself as a person of interest who has a specific point of view so that influencing becomes a by-product instead of the goal. She adds, "Having a 'why' that lives outside of free products and lavish trips is really important if you want to stick around this industry for a long time."

FUTURE GOALS: Allegra is most excited about the future of Uncle Studios, the brand she co-founded with Shirin Soltani. She shares, "I see it as an extension of everything I love — fashion, storytelling, creativity, and community. I am so appreciative of my online community, who have been with me since the beginning, witnessing both my failures and accomplishments as I've grown, and many of whom have supported me throughout the journey of Uncle Studios."

Morgan Lerner, *Co-Founder of GoNanas*
Dorm Room Dream to $6M Banana Empire

CAREER JOURNEY: After expressing frustration over the lack of healthy baked goods on their college campus, Morgan and her best friend Annie founded GoNanas in their dorm room while attending the University of Michigan in 2017. Using old family recipes and a shared love for banana bread, the pair set out to create a delicious treat made from real, simple ingredients. Since then, GoNanas has modernized banana bread and launched over 45 flavors of vegan, gluten-free mixes. Their mixes require customers to add their own bananas and a few other simple and wholesome ingredients like milk, oil, or honey. What once began as a direct-to-consumer brand, GoNanas is now available in over 4,000 retail locations globally, including Whole Foods, Wegmans, and Target. This year, the duo projects to do $6 million in revenue and has been recognized in the 2024 *Forbes* 30 Under 30: Food and Drink category.

STRATEGIES/TOOLS FOR SUCCESS: Building a team of advisors and mentors she trusts, can learn from, and can talk through important decisions, strategies, and challenges with has been essential. This also applies to her employees and team members. Morgan claims that "finding work-life balance and strategies for maintaining my mental health have also been vital, as the pressure and challenges we face as entrepreneurs can be hard to manage without the tools in place!"

LESSONS LEARNED: Morgan believes, "It all works out in the end. Sometimes, when we're at the beginning of the setback in failure, trying to problem-solve and figure it all out, it's hard to see the end in sight. But when you've gone through enough of those setbacks and failures and come out on the other end stronger and better for it, you learn that things always work out — a freeing lesson and an important one that applies well beyond the entrepreneurial sphere."

ADVICE: Morgan recommends that you start slow, taking it day by day. She says, "I think it's easy to get caught up in the glitzy picture of entrepreneurship that social media paints, but a successful entrepreneur knows it happens over time, not overnight." Morgan believes in getting as much feedback on your offering as possible, especially at the beginning and consistently throughout your venture, as your customers will tell you more than you know. She adds, "Be humbled by their feedback while also trusting your gut and any data you have. Also, know that you're much more capable than you think; trust your abilities. And keep going."

FUTURE GOALS: Morgan and her team have dreams of making GoNanas a household name and truly changing the baking space with their innovative mixes. She shares, "As for my role within that, I want to build an inspired and self-sufficient team so that our success truly becomes the success of our combined efforts and unique contributions." They aim to be in every single grocery store in the country and reduce banana waste because people use their spotty bananas to make their banana bread. Ultimately, Morgan will be happy to continue growing their impact and inspiring others along the way!

Noelle Downing, *Founder of Noelle's Favorite Things, Lifestyle Blogger*
Keeping It Real to Win Hearts and Brands

CAREER JOURNEY: Noelle Downing began her blog in 2013 to inspire women to embrace their bodies and celebrate life's joyful moments. Emphasizing body positivity, she encourages followers to wear what they love, regardless of body type, and strikes a chord with many. Noelle shares vibrant, relatable content from her Brooklyn home about fashion, travel, home decor, and her life with her husband, daughter, and pets. Her Instagram, with 750K followers, showcases her engaging storytelling skills, authenticity, and ability to adapt to new trends. Collaborations with brands like Google, Dove, H&M, and *Vogue* have fueled her growth as a lifestyle influencer.

STRATEGIES/TOOLS FOR SUCCESS: Noelle believes true passion resonates and builds an engaged audience who wants to learn more. While her passion is connecting with her audience about body positivity and self-love, it could be anything from activism to gaming for others. She recommends creating a weekly content schedule and claims consistency and use of video has been key to her growth. And she doesn't do it alone. Noelle shares, "I have an amazing assistant who helps manage my schedule and filming, making sharing a lot of content possible. For years, this was a part-time fun side hustle I managed solo, often late into the night, and now I'm fortunate to have help to handle the workload."

LESSONS LEARNED: As an influencer posting online for over a decade, Noelle has witnessed many changes, including the rise of TikTok and Instagram reels. "Initially, I wasn't excited about video since I had been focused on static photos for so long," says Noelle. It wasn't until last year that Noelle really "got" creating video content. She wishes she could go back and tell herself, "Wake up! This is the future!" She admits, "My video-averse mindset limited me, preventing platform growth and caused me to miss out on the fun challenge of making video content." A significant lesson learned was the importance of growing with the apps and not sticking to the same sharing format used since the start of her career.

ADVICE: "There was a time when breaking into this industry felt tricky, but now I believe that with consistency and showing up, success can come quickly!" claims Noelle. "I recommend finding the platforms that resonate with you — whether it's YouTube, TikTok, Instagram, or just one of them." Noelle believes it's best to focus on one or two platforms initially and build from there. She contends that while the first video may not be a masterpiece, it will be a valuable learning experience. "Improvement comes with time, so start now and look for ways to get better each day. The key is to begin and continuously seek opportunities for growth," says Noelle.

FUTURE GOALS: Noelle's future is as bright as her past. She aims to hit 1 million followers in the next few months and is excited about expanding to new audiences. Her journey is a testament to the power of passion and perseverance, and her future goals are a source of inspiration for all aspiring influencers.

These success stories demonstrate that with grit and authenticity, you can turn your dreams into reality. Let these real-life examples fuel your determination and guide you on your path to success.

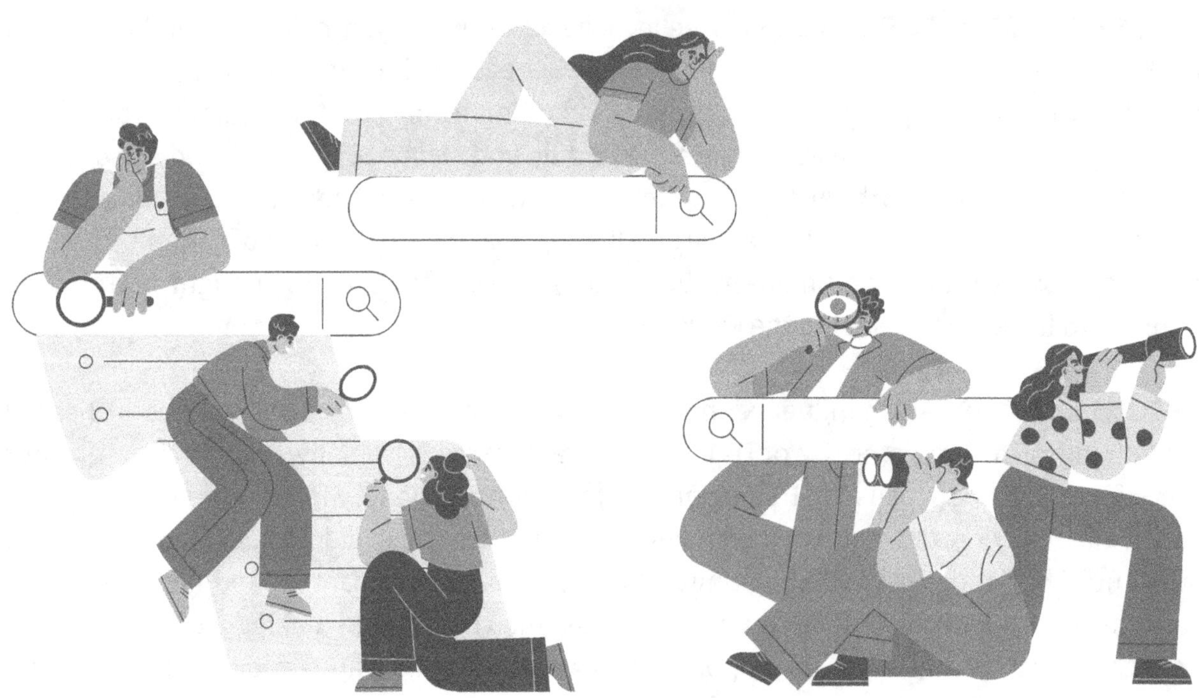

RESOURCE LIST

Job Search Tools

When it comes to the basics — finding job openings and getting your résumé in front of the right people — these should be your go-to platforms:

ZipRecruiter: **https://www.ziprecruiter.com/**
ZipRecruiter's AI career advisor "Phil" helps locate your dream job by seeking opportunities and pitching your profile to prospective employers. The platform also has a career advice blog and a "one-click apply" feature. Notifications are sent to candidates once employers view their applications, keeping you informed about the recruitment process.

Indeed: **https://www.indeed.com/**
Indeed allows users to filter millions of job listings by salary, location, and type (e.g., full-time, part-time, remote, contract). The site's "Indeed Apply" feature allows you to upload your résumé and easily apply for positions.

LinkedIn: **https://www.linkedin.com/feed/**
Beyond networking, LinkedIn is also a great job board. You can filter opportunities by experience or by companies where you have LinkedIn connections. You can also save jobs, set up alerts, and take assessments. LinkedIn Premium, which costs $29.99/month or $239 annually, allows you to contact recruiters directly.

Glassdoor: **https://www.glassdoor.com/index.htm**
Glassdoor provides anonymous employee reviews about salary, culture, benefits, the interview process, and more. It's important to note that the information is self-reported and may not always be accurate — so combining Glassdoor with other sources like company websites and industry publications gives the best perspective.

Idealist: https://www.idealist.org/en

Idealist specializes in job listings for nonprofits, social-impact businesses, and corporate social responsibility initiatives. It offers job openings, organization directories, events, career development resources, and pay and benefits information.

Wellfound: https://wellfound.com/

Previously known as AngelList, Wellfound is a job search website for those in the technology industry, working remotely, or interested in start-ups. Its detailed job descriptions allow you to see salary ranges, benefits, equity options, and information about company leadership. The website has a one-click application tool.

CareerBuilder: https://www.careerbuilder.com/

CareerBuilder's easy-to-use search engine allows you to find jobs, see salary information, and read career advice blogs. The site includes proactive notifications and career assessment tests.

Snagajob: https://www.snagajob.com/

Snagajob caters to hourly job seekers in the restaurant, retail, and hospitality industries for companies like Dunkin' Donuts and Uber. You can create a free profile and browse career advice and interview tips.

LinkUp: https://www.linkup.com/

LinkUp aggregates job listings directly from companies' career pages, pulling from over 50,000 websites to source current, high-quality, legitimate job opportunities.

SimplyHired: https://www.simplyhired.com/

SimplyHired aggregates listings from various sources and redirects you to the original opportunity. The site provides résumé templates, one-click applications, and email alerts.

USAJOBS: https://www.usajobs.gov/

USAJOBS is the official platform for federal government job postings, essential for those seeking public sector employment. You can save jobs, create alerts for specific opportunities, and track your application.

Niche job search sites include:

- Dice for technical jobs: **https://www.dice.com/**
- HRCrossing for human resource jobs: **https://www.hrcrossing.com/**
- Swipe Files for marketing jobs: **https://www.swipefiles.com/**
- ProBlogger for writing jobs: **https://problogger.com/**
- eFinancialCareers for finance jobs: **https://www.efinancialcareers.com/**
- HigherEdJobs for jobs from colleges and universities: **https://www.higheredjobs.com/**
- Ladders for executive-level positions: **https://www.theladders.com/**
- Health eCareers for health-care and medical jobs: **https://www.healthecareers.com/**

Networking Tools

Your network is among your most valuable resources. Use these tools to grow and nurture it.

LinkedIn: **https://www.linkedin.com/feed/**
With over 1 billion users globally, LinkedIn is *the* networking platform for professionals of all ages and experience levels. Users can connect with contacts, receive suggested connections, and join LinkedIn groups and events. For further details, refer to LinkedIn, Part IV (page 108).

Eventbrite: **https://www.eventbrite.com/**
Eventbrite, known for event management and ticketing, also specializes in local networking events and career fairs — including remote happenings. You can filter networking events by date, price, category, format, and language.

Meetup: **https://www.meetup.com/**
Meetup is a platform for connecting like-minded people. Its professional networking component boasts over 60 million members and 10,000 groups, some with over 20,000 members.

Fishbowl: **https://www.fishbowlapp.com/**
Fishbowl is a professional networking app with over 1 million active users and 11,000 communities. The app allows you to join different "Bowls," or groups, and have candid career discussions anonymously within your industry.

Jobcase is part job marketplace, part social media platform for workers worldwide. It's affiliated with MIT's Computer Science and Artificial Intelligence Lab.

Résumé Development and Optimization Tools

Everything about your résumé requires careful attention, from the font to the formatting. These tools can help you get everything just right.

Novorésumé: https://novoresume.com/

Novorésumé streamlines the résumé creation process. It offers customizable templates, a cover letter creator, an error-checking tool, and compatibility with applicant tracking systems (ATS).

Canva: https://www.canva.com/

Canva is a graphic design platform for creating a wide range of visual content, including résumés, presentations, and social media graphics. It's known for its customizable templates and intuitive design tools, which allow users to create professional-quality résumés in minutes.

Zety: https://zety.com/

This résumé and cover letter builder features templates tailored for various job types. It also entails a résumé score checker, career blog, and multiple download formats, including PDF, Word, and TXT.

Resume.io: https://resume.io/

Resume.io assists with résumés and cover letters, featuring AI-powered writing support, a cover letter generator, and *The Elevator* — a blog with advice for job seekers.

Jobscan: **https://www.jobscan.co/**

Jobscan can create and optimize résumés for specific job types. It uses AI to compare résumés against specific job descriptions and offer actionable suggestions.

Grammarly: **https://app.grammarly.com/**

Grammarly is an AI-powered writing assistant that assists with grammar, punctuation, style, and tone.

QuillBot: **https://quillbot.com/**

QuillBot is an AI-powered paraphrasing tool. It helps users reword text by suggesting alternative phrasing and synonyms and can be calibrated to various writing styles and needs.

Harvard Action Verbs:
https://www.alumni.hbs.edu/Documents/careers/ActionVerbsList.pdf

This Harvard Business School resource suggests powerful verbs, parsed by industry, to sprinkle across your résumé.

Skill Development Tools

Whether you just graduated or are nearing retirement, you should never stop learning. Here are the best tools to indulge your curiosity.

Coursera: **https://www.coursera.org/**

Coursera is one of the largest online learning platforms in the world. It partners with over 325 universities and industry partners to offer accredited courses, specializations, professional certificates, guided projects, and bachelor's and master's degrees. Coursera is especially useful for those who are changing career paths.

Skillshare: **https://www.skillshare.com/en/**

Skillshare is an online learning community focused on creative industries and the arts. You can access over 25,000 educational videos and classes taught by creative experts. While a subscription is required, new users can obtain a one-month free trial.

Udemy: https://www.udemy.com/

Udemy is an online learning and teaching platform with an extensive range of IT-based courses. The platform offers critical skills on technical topics like AI and coding.

LinkedIn Learning: https://www.linkedin.com/learning/

LinkedIn Learning offers thousands of courses taught by industry experts on business, technology, design, professional development, and more. It provides personalized recommendations, flexible learning schedules, and certifications.

Career Assessment Tools

The following career assessment tests can evaluate your skills, interests, and personality type, ultimately helping you choose the right career path.

Myers-Briggs Type Indicator (MBTI):
https://www.themyersbriggs.com/en-US/Products-and-Services/Myers-Briggs

The Myers-Briggs Type Indicator is a popular and robust personality tool. It details personality traits, preferences, and learning strengths and styles. By understanding your MBTI type, you can identify career paths that align with your tendencies and interests.

StrengthsFinder: https://www.gallup.com/cliftonstrengths/en/252137/home.aspx

This hour-long assessment uncovers the unique ways you think, feel, and behave. After completing the assessment, you can purchase a full report that ranks dozens of traits, such as strategic thinking, relationship building, influencing, and executing.

CareerExplorer: https://www.careerexplorer.com/

Career Explorer's assessment poses questions that correspond to 150-plus personality traits. The platform has a database of more than 1,500 career profiles and uses advanced machine learning, psych cosmetics, and career satisfaction data to ensure accurate and up-to-date results.

Holland Code (RIASEC)   Test: https://openpsychometrics.org/tests/RIASEC/

This free test features 48 questions and matches users against six types of career interest categories.

The MAPP (Motivational Appraisal Personal Potential) Assessment:
https://www.assessment.com/

The MAPP™ career assessment has been taken by over 9 million people worldwide since 1995. This 15-minute test features 71 different questions regarding likes and dislikes.

Princeton Review Career Quiz: https://www.princetonreview.com/quiz/career-quiz

This free, 24-question quiz by test-prep company The Princeton Review is on the shorter side, but still gives detailed results and helpful job advice.

CareerOneStop Interest Assessment:
https://www.careeronestop.org/ExploreCareers/Assessments/interests.aspx

This career quiz from the US Department of Labor matches individuals' interests to careers after asking 30 short questions. These responses generate a list of careers tailored to your unique preferences and average pay and education requirements.

Truity: https: //www.truity.com/view/tests/personality-career

The Career Personality Profiler™ test combines interest and personality assessments to identify the most suitable career paths. Results detail preferred tasks, work approaches, and areas for improvement.

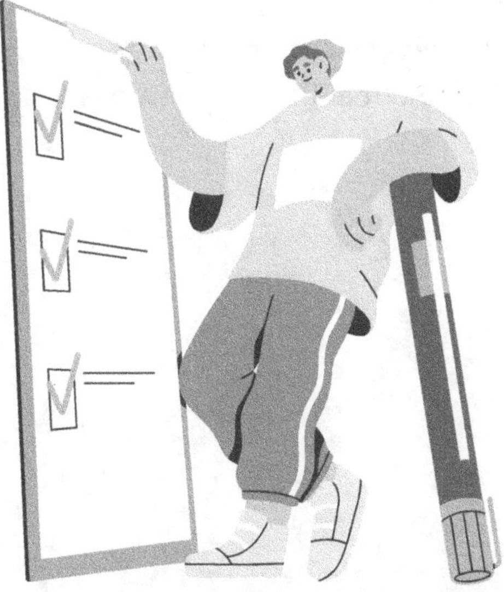

Interview Preparation Tools

Just like any other performance, job interviews require rehearsals. Let these tools be your coach.

HireVue: **https://practice.hirevue.com/signup/3m4pjuhLArd6v5kvbT6BHv/**
HireVue is a prominent global leader in HR management. The platform lets you conduct free practice interviews. It's an excellent opportunity to become familiar with virtual interviewing in a secure environment without sharing data or interview content.

InterviewBit: **https://www.interviewbit.com/**
InterviewBit is an interview preparation platform for coders. It features practice problems, interview prep, and coaching courses for languages like Python, Java, C++, and JavaScript.

Big Interview: **https://www.biginterview.com/**
Big Interview is a subscription-based job training platform that enhances interview skills and boosts confidence. It features mock interviews, résumé courses, and a vast database of interview questions. Complementing these features is a comprehensive video training curriculum that covers all facets of the job hunt.

Interviewing.io: **https://interviewing.io/**
Interviewing.io offers anonymous mock interviews tailored for ambitious engineers. Users can also access Interviewing.io's coach package and be matched to a mentor who will customize a curriculum.

Glassdoor: **https://www.glassdoor.com/interview/index.htm**
Glassdoor's interview index features interview tips and real-life interview questions that others were asked.

Website and Personal Portfolio Tools

Creating a personal website or portfolio gives you a significant edge, showcasing skills and achievements beyond just a résumé. Here's how to get started:

■ **First, purchase a domain name.** Your domain name (yoursitename.extension) is your web address — your URL. While purchasing a name is straightforward, finding an available one can be challenging. Opt for a name that aligns with your personal brand and is easy to spell and pronounce. Domain registrars like Domain.com, Namecheap, Network Solutions, and GoDaddy offer domain registration services with annual fees typically ranging from $10 to $20.

■ **Then, start building your website:**

☐ **Squarespace: https://www.squarespace.com/** Squarespace is an easy-to-use website builder for users of all technical abilities. Users can create a custom site or choose from pre-designed templates. The platform offers seamless content organization, built-in analytics and SEO tools, and user-friendly social media integration and blogging functions.

☐ **WordPress: https://wordpress.com/** WordPress is a top choice for creating websites, ranging from simple blogs to complex e-commerce platforms. It offers a wide selection of customizable themes and plugins, plus advanced design, security, and marketing tools.

☐ **Wix: https://www.wix.com/** Wix uses AI to create websites, helping develop text, logos, video, design, and more. It also provides a user-friendly data dashboard for monitoring website performance and a step-by-step guide for SEO.

☐ **GoDaddy: https://www.godaddy.com/** GoDaddy's Website Builder enables you to craft responsive websites without technical expertise via a drag-and-drop editor. You can also add features like an online store and shopping functionality.

☐ **Medium: https://medium.com/** Medium is a platform dedicated to publishing and sharing writing. Writers can earn money through the Medium Partner Program based on their reader engagement and subscriptions.

Social Media Management Tools

Sometimes, you need a little help handling your social media platforms. That's where these tools come in.

Buffer: **https://buffer.com/**

Buffer streamlines the scheduling, publishing, and analyzing of content across social media channels. Its AI assistant allows you to generate ideas, repurpose content, run experiments, and stay consistent through all platforms and posts.

Hootsuite: **https://www.hootsuite.com/**

Hootsuite supports planning, scheduling, and syndicating social media content. Its most popular feature allows you to manage messages across multiple accounts simultaneously. Other benefits include social media listening and an AI social media writer for generating ideas, captions, and hashtags.

Iconosquare: **https://www.iconosquare.com/**

Iconosquare lets you schedule, publish, and analyze content with a focus on the visual, making it ideal for Instagram and TikTok. It also supports Facebook Pages and LinkedIn and offers AI features for generating captions and hashtags.

Salary Research and Negotiation Tools

Determining how much you're worth and then ensuring you earn that is a key part of any job hunt. These tools help make that hard job more manageable.

Glassdoor: **https://www.glassdoor.com/**

One of Glassdoor's standout features is its extensive salary database, which is informed by millions of salaries. You can input your desired job, location, and employer to gauge compensation fairness and competitiveness.

Payscale: **https://www.payscale.com/**

Payscale provides salary and compensation data to help individuals and businesses make informed decisions. You can research salaries across industries, access blogs on fair compensation and negotiation practices, and receive a personalized "salary report" based on your experience and location.

Salary.com: **https://www.salary.com/**

Salary.com provides insights into compensation trends, salary benchmarks, and personalized salary reports. Its most unique feature is its "Cost of living wizard," which allows you to input your current location and desired destination to see how expenses like housing, groceries, transportation, and health care may vary — helping inform decisions about relocating.

Levels.fyi: **levels.fyi**

Levels.fyi is a compensation data resource with salary breakdowns by company, level, location, and skill. Its motto is "Get Paid, Not Played." You can explore job roles, salaries, and benefits and leverage features like the meeting cost calculator and community connections.

Remote Work Platforms

For those seeking the flexibility of a WFH job, take advantage of these tools:

FlexJobs: **https://www.flexjobs.com/**

FlexJobs is a subscription-based platform with over 40,000 online jobs from 5,000-plus companies. Its listings span more than 50 career categories, including full-time, part-time, freelance, and temporary roles. Subscribers can take unlimited skills tests, and if they score higher than 70 percent, it will be visible on their profile. Nonsubscribers can also take these skill tests, but for a fee.

Remote.co: **https://remote.co/**

Remote.co is a resource hub for all remote work tailored to your desired title, company, or position. The platform's resource section provides articles to help you navigate the challenges and opportunities associated with remote work.

We Work Remotely: **https://weworkremotely.com/**

We Work Remotely is one of the largest remote communities, with over 4.5 million visitors. Job seekers can find a variety of full-time, part-time, freelance, and contract positions across categories like programming, design, management, finance, customer support, sales, and marketing.

Remote OK: **https://remoteok.com/**

Use tags and filters to easily navigate Remote OK's 60,000-plus remote jobs. You can search by recruiters, experience level, and job type. Subscribers receive daily email newsletters featuring the latest job listings, and the platform's community page offers forums, discussions, and networking events.

Working Nomads: **https://www.workingnomads.com/jobs**

Working Nomads is a job board for those seeking remote work with additional flexibility in location and schedule. Typical job descriptions on the platform include "About the Role," "Responsibilities," "Requirements," and "Why Work with Us" sections.

Company Research Tools

Knowledge is power. It's always wise to do your homework on companies and cross-reference information from multiple sources to ensure accuracy.

Crunchbase: **https://www.crunchbase.com/**

Crunchbase provides extensive data on private and public companies and start-ups, serving as an essential resource for job seekers, professionals, entrepreneurs, and investors. It features company profiles, funding details, key personnel, and industry analysis.

Owler: **https://corp.owler.com/**

Owler provides information on companies, competitors, and industry trends. It aggregates data from various sources, including public filings, news articles, social media, and user contributions to create profiles for millions of companies worldwide.

Glassdoor: **https://www.glassdoor.com/**

Each company featured on Glassdoor has its own profile page, offering key details such as an overview, mission statement, locations, industry, and size. Additionally, you can gain insights into the company's background by exploring CEO approval ratings and previous employer feedback.

BuiltWith: **https://builtwith.com/**

BuiltWith helps identify technology trends and website technology profiles such as hosting providers, analytic tools, and content management systems. It's commonly used for market analysis, competitive intelligence, and sales lead generation. BuiltWith covers over 85,000 web technologies across over 673 million websites.

Google News: **https://news.google.com/**

Google News is a valuable tool for company research. It allows you to track and search a company's activities, culture, industry position, and reputation. Google News also offers a platform to understand a company's public perception and reputation.

Start-up Opportunities and Insights

For those seeking the thrill of a start-up environment, there's no shortage of tools to connect you with the right opportunity.

Y Combinator: **https://www.ycombinator.com/**

Y Combinator is a leading start-up accelerator and venture capital firm that provides seed funding, mentorship, and connections to early-stage start-ups in exchange for equity. Y Combinator features a Job Guide and one-on-one career coaching for those seeking start-up job opportunities as well as personalized career guidance.

GitHub: **https://github.com/**

GitHub is the world's leading developer platform, boasting over 100 million developers. It enables software developers to create, store, manage, and share their code, and the platform's job board is essential for those seeking programming opportunities.

Stack Overflow: https://stackoverflow.com/

Stack Overflow is a community for developers to learn, share their programming knowledge, and build their careers. It allows users to ask questions, provide answers, and collaborate on a wide range of programming topics. Users can leverage its robust job board to explore career opportunities and connect with hiring managers.

Entreprenista: http://entreprenista.com/

Entreprenista is a membership community for current and aspiring women entrepreneurs and founders to connect, get educated, find vetted business solutions, and access expertise to power their businesses. The community platform provides over 10 virtual and in-person monthly events, hundreds of hours of educational videos, and dozens of member perks.

Freelance and Gig Platforms

Whether you're a one-person agency or moonlighting after your day job, these tools can kick-start your freelance career.

Upwork: www.upwork.com

Upwork offers access to over 850,000 active clients and tools for project management, communication, and payment processing. You can find work opportunities through the talent marketplace by creating a profile, searching for jobs, submitting proposals, or via the project catalog, where clients can place orders directly.

Freelancer: https://www.freelancer.com/

Freelancer is one of the world's largest freelance marketplaces, boasting over 72 million registered users and 23 million projects and contests. You can search for job listings based on skills, location, and language.

TaskRabbit: https://www.taskrabbit.com/

TaskRabbit allows freelancers to find local projects spanning over 50 categories, including painting, yard work, plumbing, and delivery. Users pay a one-time registration fee and keep 100 percent of their job earnings. TaskRabbit operates globally in eight countries and has a unique partnership with IKEA.

Fiverr: **https://www.fiverr.com/**

Fiverr is an online marketplace for creatives across hundreds of categories, including website design, 3D design, content creation, video animation, and architecture.

Toptal: **https://www.toptal.com/**

Toptal, a premier freelancer platform with a remote workforce, helps companies scale teams on demand. Prospective candidates undergo a 2–5-week comprehensive screening, including technical assessments, live interviews, and mock projects mirroring real-world scenarios. Only 3 percent of applicants pass Toptal's screening.

Crowdspring: **https://www.crowdspring.com/**

Crowdspring connects businesses with freelance designers for creative projects like logo, graphic, and web design. Clients can collaborate directly with a designer of their choice, enabling a more personalized and tailored workspace.

Tongal: **https://tongal.com/**

Tongal is a global hub for content creation catering to studios, brands, and talent worldwide. Its community numbers over 160,000 independent creators, and projects range from video advertisements to product design.

99designs: **https://99designs.com/**

99designs links businesses with a worldwide network of freelance designers. Clients post design briefs to outline their needs and preferences, and designers then submit their concepts and proposals.

Internship Tools

Internships are often the first step in a career but an important one, nonetheless. These tools can help start you on your professional journey.

Handshake: **https://joinhandshake.com/**

Handshake is a top career hub for college students, providing access to job and internship postings, career fairs, and employer events. The platform boasts 18 million students and alumni, 550,000 employers, and 1,200 universities, community colleges, and boot camps.

WayUp: **https://www.wayup.com/**

WayUp is a job search platform for college students and recent graduates. Users create profiles that match them with internships or entry-level positions based on their interests, experience, and skills. The platform's matchmakers assist in finding suitable opportunities, while users can also independently search and filter jobs by company, industry, or location.

College Career Centers

Take advantage of your college career center to significantly boost your prospects for landing internships and employment postgraduation. Career centers host events like career fairs and industry-specific gatherings, providing prime opportunities to network with potential employers and learn about job openings. They offer tailored support through career counseling, alumni connections, workshops on career development, résumé writing, professional etiquette, interview preparation, and more.

Productivity/Organization Tools

One of the most essential parts of the job search process and your work life is staying organized — you don't want to miss that interview, application, or project deadline. Creating order can supercharge productivity by ensuring that nothing falls through the cracks.

Google Calendar: **https://calendar.google.com/calendar/u/0/r**

Google Calendar is a time-management tool for tracking schedules, setting reminders, and creating events. Its features, such as event notifications, color-coding, and seamless integration with other Google services like Gmail, allow efficient management of appointments and deadlines. You can access your schedules in different formats and sync them across multiple devices.

Google Drive: **https://drive.google.com**

Google Drive is a cloud storage and synchronization service that enables you to store, access, and share files from any device. Its seamless integration with Google's collaboration tools, such as Docs, Slides, and Sheets, allows easy project sharing.

Evernote: **https://evernote.com/**

Evernote is a leading note-taking platform for creating, editing, and collaborating on notes. It allows for seamless note-taking and sharing among colleagues or teams. Its web clipper tool enhances productivity by allowing you to easily store images and articles.

Slack: **https://slack.com/**

Slack is a workplace communication platform that streamlines communication and reduces reliance on emails and meetings. It simplifies team interactions through group chats, one-on-one messaging, and specialized channels for specific topics. Additionally, its video call feature facilitates efficient collaboration across departments, offices, and external partners.

ClickUp: **https://clickup.com/**

ClickUp is a productivity platform for team collaboration. It provides a centralized workspace for brainstorming, product design, task management, planning, and more. ClickUp integrates with popular tools like Google Drive and Slack, streamlining workflows and enhancing productivity. It can also serve as a notepad, board, mind map, and recording tool.

Asana: **https://asana.com/**

Asana is a web and mobile platform that helps teams manage projects, organize tasks, and set deadlines in one place. It lets team members assign projects and easily check tasks, responsibilities, and deadlines.

1Password: **http://1password.com** *(Note: this is "one" not "I")*

1Password is a password management website and app that securely stores sensitive data like passwords, banking details, and medical records. It offers the industry's largest bug bounty and undergoes regular third-party audits, enabling users to generate, store, and autofill passwords. A key feature, "Travel Mode," lets users remove specific information before traveling to reduce risks from potential threats such as border checks or theft.

Trello: https://trello.com/

Trello is a versatile project management tool that organizes tasks, projects, and deadlines with an intuitive board layout. It supports collaboration with assignable, trackable tasks and allows prioritizing tasks from 1 (highest) to 5 (lowest) in its customizable interface.

Entrepreneurship Programs

If you're looking to launch your own company rather than join an existing one, these programs are for you. While some programs listed are free, many require a fee.

Wharton's Entrepreneurship Acceleration Program:
https://online-execed.wharton.upenn.edu/entrepreneurship
This program helps entrepreneurs plan for future success through live and recorded sessions, assignments, quizzes, and interactive discussions.
Length: Three months
Time: Three to four hours per week
Level: Medium

Becoming an Entrepreneur from MIT Launch:
https://www.edx.org/learn/entrepreneurship/massachusetts-institute-of-technology-becoming-an-entrepreneur
This program covers various aspects of entrepreneurship, from ideation to market research, product design, testing, and pitching.
Length: Six weeks
Time: One to three hours per week
Level: Medium

E-Commerce Essentials: How to Start a Successful Online Business by Skillshare:
https://www.skillshare.com/en/classes/e-commerce-essentials-how-to-start-a-successful-online-business/121692420
This class, led by Tracey Wallace, the Director of Content at Klaviyo, answers the fundamental question "Where do I begin?" about starting an e-commerce business.
Length: One hour
Level: Easy

Startup School by Y Combinator: https://www.startupschool.org/

Y Combinator is one of the most elite online education platforms. Its course provides guidance from the world's leading start-up accelerators.

Length: About 7–10 weeks (self-paced)
Time: One to two hours per week
Level: Hard

Sara Blakely Teaches Self-Made Entrepreneurship by MasterClass: https://www.masterclass.com/classes/sara-blakely-teaches-self-made-entrepreneurship

Sara Blakey, the Founder of Spanx, teaches aspiring entrepreneurs how to turn their ideas into viable, profitable businesses.

Length: Approximately three hours
Level: Easy

BerkleeX: Creativity & Entrepreneurship: https://www.edx.org/learn/entrepreneurship/berklee-college-of-music-creativity-entrepreneurship

This course, led by Berklee Institute for Creative Entrepreneurship Founder Panos Panay, will unlock your creativity and show you how to use it for career development or business innovation.

Length: Four weeks
Time: Three to five hours per week
Level: Medium

The Essential Guide to Entrepreneurship by Guy Kawasaki: https://www.udemy.com/course/entrepreneurship-course-by-guy-kawasaki/?couponCode=LETSLEARNNOWPP

Guy Kawasaki tackles the process of starting a business, from launching and team building to marketing and product evangelizing.

Length: Self-paced
Time: Four hours
Level: Easy

Corporate Entrepreneurship: Innovating within Corporations Specialization from the University of Maryland:
https://www.coursera.org/specializations/corporate-entrepreneurship
This course explores how to create new business opportunities within existing corporations.
Length: Two months
Time: 10 hours per week
Level: Medium

ABOUT THE AUTHORS

Stacey Ross Cohen: Few marketing experts possess the savvy and instinct of Stacey Ross Cohen. An award-winning brand professional who earned her stripes on Madison Avenue and at major television networks before launching her own agency, Stacey specializes in finding, cultivating, and perfecting brands. She is the CEO and Founder of Co-Communications, a public relations, marketing, and design agency with offices in New York and Connecticut. Since 1998, Stacey has coached individuals and businesses across various industries — from real estate  to health care to education — and expertly positions their narratives in fiercely competitive markets. She is particularly passionate about helping college-bound students and early-career professionals activate their personal brands and become tomorrow's leaders.

A staple at industry conferences, Stacey recently made her debut on the TEDx stage. She is a contributor at *Entrepreneur*, *Huffington Post*, and *Thrive Global* and has been featured in *Forbes*, *Crain's*, *Newsweek*, *USA Today*, and a suite of other national media. She holds a BS from Syracuse University, an MBA from Fordham University, and a certificate from NYU Leonard Stern School of Business in Media, Technology, and Entertainment.

Stacey is an entrepreneur at heart. She started her first business when she was just 14 years old and is now a member of a prominent angel investor group. Standing out has always been a matter of course for Stacey. As a twin, the struggle to cultivate her own identity made her more sensitive to the need to be bold and unique.

Allison Kluger: Allison Kluger is a four-time Emmy-nominated producer with over 25 years of experience in broadcast media and entertainment, from network television (*Good Morning America*, *The View*) to new media platforms, including electronic retail, interactive television, and digital media. She is also a freelance writer and media consultant. Her superpowers are innovative content creation, expert messaging, and media coaching.

Since 2013, Allison is a Lecturer of Organizational Behavior at Stanford's Graduate School of Business (GSB). She teaches four courses, three of which she created: Reputation Management, Strategic Communication, Personal Branding (which she teaches with Tyra Banks), and Strategic Pivoting for Your Next Chapter (which features guest speaker Alex "ARod" Rodriguez). Allison has also created seminars and workshops on "Executive Presence for Women," "Storytelling as Strategy," "Personal and Business Branding," and "Media Training."

Allison is the recipient of the Dorothy J. King Lecturer in Leadership for 2017–2018 and the MSx Teaching Excellence Award from Stanford GSB, 2024. She is an advisor for many of her graduate students' new ventures. She also mentors young women and men in leadership and personal branding and gives lectures and keynote speeches worldwide. She is a voracious reader and is currently writing a book. She also officiates weddings and raises her two boys and Australian shepherd with her husband. For more details, testimonials, videos, and photos, visit www.allisonkluger.com.

Kudzi Chikumbu: Kudzi Chikumbu, a lifestyle influencer and marketing authority, expertly connects and builds community through creator marketing, partnerships, and education. He works at the intersection of digital content, community, and communications to discover and amplify diverse trailblazing talent. Kudzi is a sought-after speaker who firmly believes that "authority is your cheat code to success."

He was born in Zimbabwe and grew up in South Africa as an accountant and management consultant, shaping his views on race relations and diversity. Kudzi began his career at Deloitte in South Africa. He went on to complete his MBA at Stanford Graduate School of Business.

Kudzi is the creator of the social media phenomenon Sir Candle Man, which brings a new, relatable, and inclusive voice to the fragrance industry. Sir Candle Man has been featured in *The Hollywood Reporter*, *WWD*, *NY Mag*, and *The Rachael Ray Show*. Kudzi also authored the book *Let It Burn: Illuminate Your Life with Candles & Fragrance*.

Kudzi has been listed in *Fortune Magazine's* 40 Under 40 list and *The Hollywood Reporter's* Next Gen: Hollywood's 35 Rising Executives 35 and Under. He received ADCOLOR's Innovator Award and was recognized as *AdWeek's* Experiential Executive of the Year, the Culture Creators' Tech Honoree, and Variety's Hollywood's New Leaders. A torchbearer for authenticity, Kudzi lives in Los Angeles.